POLICE AND THE MEDIA

POLICE AND THE MEDIA

—Bridging Troubled Waters—

Edited by

PATRICIA A. KELLY, PH.D.

Associate Professor, Journalism
Northeastern University
Boston, Massachusetts

CHARLES C THOMAS • PUBLISHER
Springfield • Illinois • U.S.A.

Published and Distributed Throughout the World by
CHARLES C THOMAS • PUBLISHER
2600 South First Street
Springfield, Illinois 62794-9265

This book is protected by copyright. No part of
it may be reproduced in any manner without
written permission from the publisher.

© *1987 by* CHARLES C THOMAS • PUBLISHER
ISBN 0-398-05352-9
Library of Congress Catalog Card Number: 87-6502

With THOMAS BOOKS *careful attention is given to all details of manufacturing and design. It is the Publisher's desire to present books that are satisfactory as to their physical qualities and artistic possibilities and appropriate for their particular use.* THOMAS BOOKS *will be true to those laws of quality that assure a good name and good will.*

Printed in the United States of America
Q-R-3

Library of Congress Cataloging in Publication Data
Police and the media.

   1. Public relations--United States--Police.
2. Police and the press--United States. 3. Police
and mass media--United States. I. Kelly, Patricia A.
HV7936.P8P556   1987   659.2'93632'0973   87-6502
ISBN 0-398-05352-9

To Aunt Marge,
With Love,
For Her Love, Support and Belief in My Work

FOREWORD

POLICE AND journalists will welcome this book by Patricia Kelly, for it fills an important civic need. The book's lucid analysis of persistent tensions between news media and law enforcement agencies is long overdue.

It is probably safe to assert that there are few, if any, American communities where misunderstanding between police and media has not occurred repeatedly, curtailing effectiveness of both.

A former police reporter, I have observed the frictions described in this book in every city and town where I've lived or worked. From Boston to Honolulu, from Columbia, Missouri, to Sparks, Nevada, the same issues turn up. Police say newspapers, television and radio news departments make too many errors. Reporters say accuracy is difficult whenever police refuse to cooperate. Police complain that reporters frequently demand information which would tip off criminal suspects to sensitive investigatory details. Reporters respond that police violate the First Amendment by denying access to information the public has a right to know. Law enforcement agencies say journalists often ignore the Sixth Amendment by disseminating information which could jeopardize a defendant's right to a fair trial. Journalists argue that a free flow of news is essential for an informed citizenry to discuss and scrutinize affairs of government, including the criminal justice system.

An irony in the debate, often heated, is that the best journalists and the best police officers have so much in common. Both chose their careers expecting limited material rewards and abundant public service opportunities.

This book will contribute to understanding on both sides. As understanding grows, police and media obviously will benefit. Also standing to gain will be the public. In fact, the public, which must rely so critically on police for protection and news media for information, may benefit most of all.

LaRue W. Gilleland,
Director, School of Journalism
Northeastern University
Boston, Massachusetts

PREFACE

IN THE EARLY 1970's in Marblehead, Massachusetts, a town renown for its spectacular scenery of seascapes and reverence for its American Revolutionary forefighters, I first covered police as a daily beat.

Dawn would break as I drove up to the station, and the smalltalk-swap and the sharing of a cup of coffee provided a welcome lull before the pressured grind of my 10 A.M. copy deadline. I stayed longer than usual one morning to gather the details on a fatal motorcycle accident, and one of the police officers who had been on that call returned. His face was ashen, his expression a mixture of frustration, hopelessness and a kind of abiding sadness.

Amid the confusion of a shift change, he began to talk — not really to anyone — but I heard him. He rolled up his uniform sleeve to reveal bruises on his forearm made by the imprint of a hand. "She kept clinging to me," he said. "She kept clinging to me and begging me not to let her die, and I told her I wouldn't, but she did, and there was nothing I could do about it." He was referring to the 19-year-old woman who had been a passenger when the operator lost control of the cycle at high speed on a curve. She died en route to the hospital, holding on to that cop as her final life's gesture.

Despite the scores of motor vehicle accident stories I have written since that day, I have never forgotten that victim's name, nor the what, why, when, where, how of that event. That is so because I was unable to forget that officer's seeming soliloquy. He had confounded my stereotypes. He had sent into tailspin my smug expectation that police officers were aloof automatons who were able to perform grisly duties with dispatch because they weren't really human like the rest of us.

In the years of reporting that were to follow, I remained grateful for that glimpse of that patrolman's suffering, for it helped me shed a mind set which could have crippled intentions not only to present news objectively, but especially to do so with some measure of humanity.

I would never meet that mythic police officer framed in superhuman proportions by the distorting sources of my own preconceptions and inexperience. He or she did not exist, does not exist, and, I pray, never will.

This book is, in part, about such false expectations which contribute to making adversaries out of journalists and law enforcement officials. It is also about the real ones that keep both sides in defensive posture and, I think, legitimately so: those areas which have already been subjected to complex adjudication. These are the thorny informational access issues that have reporters pushing in the interests of the public's right to know and police officers pulling back in the interests of a victim's right to peace and privacy, or the informant's need for protection, or the defendant's right to a fair trial. There will probably never be winners in those tugs of war, but a precarious balancing act may be achieved.

And, centrally, this collection is about expectations that police and press can and should work to communicate with one another more clearly, with more consistency. We are far more alike than different in our motivations, our job environments, our work procedures and our career missions. The common ground is there. We can meet more easily and more often in cooperative ventures that better serve our common public.

Patricia A. (Babcock) Kelly

ACKNOWLEDGMENTS

MY GRATITUDE to my husband, Dick, for his inspiration — and for sharing with me and my students the knowledge, sensitivity and experience he has also shared with fellow police officers during his ten years of service with the Massachusetts State Police Psychological Services Division (Stress Unit). He understands and cares in ways that reinforce the special bond which marks the brotherhood.

I am most grateful to Janet M. Ford for her invaluable assistance in preparing the manuscript — for her skilled fingers at the computer keyboard, her organizational abilities and her sharp copyediting eye. I thank, too, Joan K., C. Robert and Scott K. Risney of The Office Extension, Plymouth, Massachusetts for their fine clerical support services, their indefatigable good cheer and helpful spirits. With Janet, they aided in pulling into sharpened shape the once formless parade of pages.

I also wish to express my thanks to graphic artist William A. Liberti for his assistance in materials preparation and for his advice; to Sharon Wilmore for her bibliographical and transcription work and her patience in proofreading; to Annell E. Stewart and Amy B. Cohen for their help at the proposal stage.

I am indebted to LaRue W. Gilleland for the overview provided in his foreword.

And, of course, I am beholden to my contributors — the men and women from the fields of law enforcement, journalism, education, law, photography; and my former students who are just launching their careers — for the talents and diversity of insights and perspectives that are represented in this work.

P. A. K.

INTRODUCTION

A CRITICISM frequently levelled by police at the media and vice-versa is that each group knows not nearly enough about the working world of the other.

In "Police Work, 1983," Associated Press writer John Barbour presents a view of contemporary policing that dispels any Dark Ages distortions we might have of the men in blue and how they are protecting and serving. There are now women in blue and minorities, and they are far better-educated than their counterparts of yesteryear, and their jobs are far more complex. Barbour shows how the new American city — the urban product of social and judicial revolutions — is being policed by the new American cop.

In "Stress: the Cop-Killer," I consider how that new American cop is coping with the emotional fallout of his or her day-to-day job performances: the stressors posed by unrealistic public and self expectations, frequently unresponsive administrations and legal systems, and often times hostile interactions with the media.

The novice-eye's view is often insightful because it is fresh and unfettered by preconceptions. That perspective is presented in "Student Press Meet Real Police; Student Police Meet Real Press." College journalism majors assigned to spend a shift with police officers and criminal justice majors likewise instructed to do the same with journalists discover that reality is more riveting than fiction. One aspiring journalist recounts the terror and other lessons of a high-speed chase; while would-be cops are astounded by the ethical deliberations of a radio reporter. In "Whom Do I Alienate — the Cops or My Editor?", a reporter-in-training explains to her criminal justice studies classmates the workings of a newsroom and the uncompromising pressures of deadlines.

In "Police vs. Press: There's Always Tension," former *Washington Star* reporter Michael Kiernan points up an irony in the conflicts that often occur when the worlds of police and press intersect. Those worlds have much in common, he says; they are both powerful visible institutions which put a high premium on ingenuity, investigative aptitude and individual contribution. Yet, they both persist in viewing one another in "simplified, stereotyped terms." Police administrators interviewed criticized media coverage of their departments as scatter-shot and inconsistent, and Kiernan advises that increased journalistic effort be extended to generate in-depth coverage to police as an institution, that reporters pay closer attention to day-to-day police life.

Kiernan also interviews veteran police reporters who reminisce on the then and the now of their police beats.

Los Angeles Times staff writer David Johnston expands on Kiernan's theme in "The Cop Watch." He urges reporters to increase the sophistication of their police coverage, to release the rich, important stories that lurk beneath the surface of routine police news.

Staff Sgt. James C. Sartori, a public information specialist for the Massachusetts State Police, asks that police reporters play it fair with cops by arming themselves with knowledge—by learning police procedures. In an article derived from a transcript of remarks he made to an audience of college journalism majors, he maintains that if police beat reporters know how police officers do things—effect arrests, evaluate probability for a drunken driving charge, decide when force or their firearm must be used—then those reporters will be better able to judge when law enforcement officials are doing their jobs properly and when they are not. The result, says Sartori, will be a more balanced accounting.

How balanced an accounting do reporters receive, however, from those persons who disseminate the "news" from within a police agency? Sociologist Mark Fishman, in "Police News, Constructing an Image of Crime," hypothesizes how police decisions on the "newsworthiness" of incidents affect what journalists have access to as the raw materials of news. He also explores how police concerns for managing public order and managing image can have an impact on selection.

Other kinds of image projection can promote distorted views of professional policing which do nothing to increase public understanding of the police function. In "Shooting Down T.V.'s Cop Shows," David Johnston again writes with critical insight about police and the media. This time he contends that prime-time police dramas do their subjects a disservice by inaccurate and sloppy portrayal of police procedures, creating misconceptions many times for the sake of dramatic effect. The television medium should, he concludes, present police operations more responsibly, with verisimilitude.

Perhaps if journalists and cops in training could experience, even briefly, the task demands and pressures of one another's worlds, such fictions could be replaced by reality. My husband, Richard Kelly, a Massachusetts state trooper, and I decided to test that theory in an educational experiment. In "Police and the Media," I tell what happened to puncture the stereotypical expectations of criminal justice and journalism majors who shared a class called "Police and the Media," taught by a journalist and a police officer. Key to that experiment was the assignment of journalism majors to play cops and criminal justice majors to play reporters in a mock hostage-taking incident videotaped and then critiqued by the participants.

In our classroom, the police and press "actors" locked horns when each attempted to perform what he or she perceived as his or her mission. David M. Mozee Sr., former director of news affairs for the Chicago Police Department, suggests practical ways to prevent such clashes at incident scenes in real life. In "Police/Media Conflict," he urges police administrators and press liaison officers to have valid reasons for their news dissemination decisions and to eliminate any arbitrary treatment of media personnel. Mozee stresses the importance of meetings between both groups to discuss policy, procedures and mutual or disparate needs in a spirit of cooperation.

On-the-scene antagonisms can and have escalated into embittered stand-offs, and *Los Angeles Times* media critic David Shaw examines hostile police/press encounters at breaking-news sites. His article entitled "Police-Media Relations: A New Low" includes a post-mortem dissection of police and media performance at a 1979 demonstration by Iranians in Beverly Hills, Calif. Push literally came to shove there, and Shaw tries to reconstruct the pieces to ascertain what went wrong with a heretofore fairly civilized relationship.

Lt. Ronald B. Jones, former supervisor of the public affairs unit, Louisiana State Police, offers some answers for the 1980's to head-off the kinds of confrontations delineated by Shaw. Jones poses what he terms remedial strategies. He differentiates between "hot" and "cold" crisis scenes, emphasizes the negative results of allowing media to become part of the unfolding dramas and underlines the necessity of police to preserve the integrity of the police function, while providing the press with the data they have the right and the obligation to make public.

It is not always, however, the crisis incident of widespread impact that intensifies the reverberation of those discordant chords. *Boston Globe* police reporter Kevin Cullen takes a critical in-house look at how media coverage, including that of his own newspaper, may have prejudiced the case against a Boston police detective suspended on charges he assaulted an illiterate restaurant worker during a prostitution arrest. In "Boston: No Winners in Chinatown Case," Cullen discusses that officer's perceptions that undue and distorted focus was played upon his story.

And it is not always, also, that either the physical scene or a specific personality serves as catalyst for confrontation. Police and press remain substantively divided on philosophical issues which underpin many decisions by law enforcement officials to withhold information. In "Nagle's Gag Order Manipulates News," we see an apparent arbitrary and capricious news blackout policy being implemented by one police chief.

But in the series, "Naming Names . . . "we see a more balanced and reasoned approach to news dissemination. The police administrators and editors alike whom I interviewed are grappling with the gray areas of decision, hoping to encourage police accountability to the public, while not hamstringing law enforcement in its designated functions to protect and serve that same public.

Donald M. Gillmor, professor of journalism at the University of Minnesota, shows us why police may be, at times, almost paranoid about providing details of cases yet-to-be tried or in the process of adjudication. In "Crime Reporting, From Delirium to Dialogue," he provides valuable historical perspective, tracing the development of crime reporting from the days of "jazz journalism," which may have been "fun" for a reporter, but "horror" for a defendant, to a period of "introspection and dialogue" with the courts. Gillmor concludes his 1971 article with a prediction of pervasive use of cameras in the courtroom.

Gillmor's closing was informed and prophetic; for in "Reporting Rape: Live T.V. Coverage Generates Debate," we have the lead in to a case study of the so-termed Big Dan's rape trial. Identification of a crime victim—especially a victim of that crime—has traditionally been an issue between media and law enforcement officials. The introduction of videotape into the courtroom has itself introduced ethical nuances never before considered, but debated hotly when the specifics of the March, 1983 rape in a New Bedford, Massachusetts poolroom galvanized nationwide attention. One editor tells us why his newspaper refused to identify the victim; another explains why his newspaper did the opposite. A rape victim not associated with that case (as a speaker at a seminar held by the media to examine implications of Big Dan's coverage), recounts her mental anguish at the way her local newspapers handled her story. And an attorney explores the legal and humane ramifications of how the media, in general, covers the crime of rape.

Big Dan's promoted among sensitive and conscientious journalists a soul-searching which sharpened their perception that the weight of the First Amendment only increases the press' responsibility to be vigilant about maintaining high ethical standards. In "Ragsdale: On the Police/Press Connection," James Ragsdale, editor of *The Standard-Times,* New Bedford, Massachusetts, makes an ironic observation. He notes the importance of codes of "clean" conduct among prosecutors, press and police, but rather rues the fact that these same rules and regulations have made journalists and police officers somewhat distrustful and polite strangers.

What are these rules and regulations? Included is a representative sample: a reprint of the Sigma Delta Chi Code of Ethics for journalists and the Delaware State Police police/media guidelines, governing interactions between that agency and the press.

Phil J. Record, associate executive editor of the *Fort Worth Star-Telegram,* and past president of Society of Professional Journalists, Sigma Delta Chi, underscores the importance of journalists balancing commitment to the First Amendment with a renewed reverence for responsibility. In "Journalists Reach for Credibility," he affirms the role of a free press as a watchdog for society, but urges individual reporters to "get better," to cease ignoring the rights of others, invading the privacy of others, and arrogantly undertaking every assignment by assuming the worst of the situation or the interviewee.

If individual reporters can work to get better in these ways, what can individual police officers do from their vantage point to take the chilling edge off police/press interaction? Lt. Michael T. Wright, who is in charge of public information for the New York State Police, talks about just that topic in "Confessions of a Pragmatist." He relates how his agency has come, through painful and graphically instructional experiences, to recognize that it is very important for police to "exist in the media" and to recognize that the police/media relationship is "a two-way street."

Atty. Joseph E. Scuro Jr., a San Antonio, Texas lawyer who specializes in representing police clients and who has had extensive press coverage as a result, has some pointers for police chiefs designing public relations policies. In "Police Administrators Should Face Press with Facts, Not Fear," he asserts that the best way to defuse potential police/press clashes is to give the media what it deserves—accurate and complete information within reasonable deadlines.

The final article is another one by Dave Mozee, who, since leaving the Chicago police, has served as a police management training specialist with Institute of Police Technology and Management, University of North Florida.

Mozee leaves us in an optimistic frame of mind, for he sees a mutually productive period ahead for police and the media. At IPTM he is centrally involved in educating public information officers from all sections of the country, both sworn and civilian, to perform that function for their agencies, both large and small. In "What's Ahead for Police and Press: The P.I.O. Paves the Ways," he outlines specifically, in great detail, what the optimum education should entail. It should, be believes, certainly include instruction on why good media relations are important for citizen support and cooperation, why free media process is necessary to democracy, and why the public does have a right to know what public employees are doing, and how they are doing it.

Patricia A. (Babcock) Kelly

CONTENTS

                                                                Page

Foreword—LaRue W. Gilleland vii
Preface ix
Acknowledgments xi
Introduction xiii

**SECTION I. THE WORKING WORLDS OF POLICE
AND PRESS AND WHAT HAPPENS WHEN THEY MEET** 3

POLICE WORK, 1983
John Barbour 5
   Hints of a Partnership 5
   The Key—Police Presence 12
   Let the Punishment Fit the Crime 18

STRESS: THE COP KILLER
Patricia A. Kelly 24
   For Female Officers, Problems Are Double 31
   Living Up to An Image, Or Putting On a Front? 32
   Prevention, the Best Medicine 41

**STUDENT PRESS MEET REAL POLICE; STUDENT POLICE
MEET REAL PRESS** 48
   Policing in the Real World: A Tale of Squirrels, Chipmunks
   and a Scary Ride
   Mark F. Slattery 48
   On the Road and on the Beat
   Stephen W. Bishé and Robert A. Costa 55
   Whom Do I Alienate—the Cops or My Editor?
   Lisa M. Pane 62

POLICE VS. THE PRESS: THERE'S ALWAYS TENSION
Michael Kiernan 65
COVERING THE POLICE BEAT
Michael Kiernan 74
THE COP WATCH
David Johnston 78
IF YOU COVER POLICE, LEARN OUR PROCEDURES
James C. Sartori 85
POLICE NEWS: CONSTRUCTING AN IMAGE OF CRIME
Mark Fishman 98
    Appendix A 112
    Appendix B 113
    Endnotes 113
    References 116

SECTION II. THE ISSUES WHICH DEFINITELY DIVIDE AND SOME TENTATIVE SOLUTIONS 119

SHOOTING DOWN TV'S COP SHOWS
David Johnston 121
POLICE AND THE MEDIA: DEBUNKING THE MYTHS
Patricia A. Kelly 127
    Endnotes 140
POLICE/MEDIA CONFLICT
David M. Mozee 141
BOTH BLAMED: POLICE, MEDIA RELATIONS—A NEW LOW
David Shaw 146
THE PRESS AT THE EMERGENCY SCENE: ISSUES AND ANSWERS
Ronald B. Jones 159
BOSTON: NO WINNERS IN CHINATOWN CASE
Kevin Cullen 168
THE POLICE/PRESS PUBLISH OR NOT TO PUBLISH, BROADCAST, OR NOT TO BROADCAST ISSUES 173
    Nagle's Gag Order Manipulates News 173
    Naming Names: Identifying Perpetrators and Victims— the Police and Press Perspectives
    Patricia A. Kelly 175

WHAT WAS A CUSTOM IS NOW LAW
Patricia A. Kelly 180
NEWSPAPERS FOUGHT FOR LEGISLATION 185
"I'M VERY AFRAID OF A POLICE STATE"
Samuel Rotondi 188
CRIME REPORTING: FROM DELIRIUM TO DIALOGUE
Donald M. Gillmor 191
      Endnotes 203
REPORTING RAPE: LIVE TV COVERAGE GENERATES
A DEBATE
Bill Seymour 205
THE LESSONS OF BIG DAN'S
James M. Ragsdale 209
WHY WE USED HER NAME
Charles M. Hauser 213
A RAPE VICTIM TO THE MEDIA: "DON'T YOU KNOW
YOU'RE DEALING WITH PEOPLE AND PEOPLE'S LIVES?" 216
A LAWYER'S ARGUMENT: SPECIAL VICTIMS NEED
SPECIAL REMEDIES
S. W. Sweetser 221
      Endnotes 226
ON THE POLICE/PRESS CONNECTION
James M. Ragsdale 228

SECTION III. ETHICS, RULES AND REGULATIONS 231

CODE OF ETHICS OF THE SOCIETY
OF PROFESSIONAL JOURNALISTS, SIGMA DELTA CHI 233
NEWS MEDIA RELATIONS AND PUBLIC INFORMATION
POLICY OF THE DELAWARE STATE POLICE 236
      Appendix A 252
CREDIBILITY AND ETHICS AND THEIR IMPACT
ON OUR PROFESSION
Phil J. Record 255

SECTION IV. SUMMATION 267

CONFESSIONS OF A PRAGMATIST: THE P.I.O.
AS TRUTH SAYER
Patricia A. Kelly 269

POLICE ADMINISTRATORS SHOULD FACE PRESS
WITH FACTS, NOT FEAR
Joseph E. Scuro, Jr. 276

WHAT'S AHEAD FOR POLICE/PRESS RELATIONS? P.I.O.s
PAVE THE WAYS
David M. Mozee 280

POLICE AND THE MEDIA

SECTION I

THE WORKING WORLDS OF POLICE AND PRESS AND WHAT HAPPENS WHEN THEY MEET

POLICE WORK, 1983

JOHN BARBOUR

HINTS OF A PARTNERSHIP

AMERICA'S POLICE in 1983 are vastly different from the men in blue who faced an America in turmoil some 15 years ago. It was a time of temper that terrified the nation and rattled its faith in law and order.

Today's police are better educated on the average, less experienced perhaps, and definitely shorter than the 6-footers who rode the riot-ravaged streets of the '60s.

But those changes are superficial compared to the revolution in the jobs they do. Police Work 1983 is tougher than it was a decade or two ago.

Today the courts frequently redefine police power and officers have to relearn the law. Cities have cut police budgets and departments are leaner. The courts have ordered police to redress their ranks to mirror the minority mix of the communities they serve and some white officers have quit rather than face the dilution of ordinarily meager chances for promotion.

---

*John A. Barbour, who joined The Associated Press in 1953, is considered one of the most versatile writers in AP Newsfeatures, covering subjects from politics to consumer affairs, profiles to issue stories. As special writer in science he covered the space program from Sputnik, 1957, through 1972. His publications include *In the Wake of the Whale* and *Footprints on the Moon*.

†[ORIGINAL EDITOR'S NOTE: The urban unrest of the 1960s carried a bitter message: America's cities had changed; their power structure had not. The American cop, an instrument of society, was caught in the middle. After years of judicial and social revolution, there are hints that a partnership between people and police works, that order precedes law. In a three-part series titled Police Work, 1983, *Sunday Morning* magazine explored how the new American cop copes with the new American city.]

‡The series is reprinted with permission of The Associated Press. The original editor's notes and the headlines are reprinted with permission of the Worcester (Massachusetts) Telegram and Gazette, Inc.

Today, to equalize standards, police have to teach English to Hispanics, teach ghetto-raised black youths how to swim, city-bred whites how to drive and women how to increase their hand and wrist strength so they can squeeze a trigger.

At the same time, to combat community fears of police violence, they have had to teach veteran officers not to pull a trigger, or even draw a gun as freely as they might have two decades ago.

Still, some cities, notably New Orleans, Chicago and St. Louis, have undergone more than 30 federal investigations each last year on charges that their police violated the civil rights of citizens, usually by excessive use of force.

How society polices itself, how it insures the domestic tranquility, how it guards its property and yet refrains from encroaching on the rights of any citizen has always been an uneasy balance.

Today's police are asked to do all of that, and in addition to nabbing burglars, chasing down robbers, freeing hostages and catching killers, they are asked to pacify the community to give each citizen the perception of security. All of this in the face of a crime rate that rose monotonously over the last 20 years, of persistent street crime in big cities especially, and of a pervasive drug market that reached into suburbs and small towns as well.

There was some encouraging news in early September, however. The Justice Department Bureau of Justice Statistics disclosed that the number of victims of crime dropped 4 percent in a year, one of the most dramatic declines in a decade.

Too many variables are involved to allow pinpointing any one cause, but Dr. Steven Schlesinger, bureau director on leave from Catholic University, says two salient reasons were police-organized neighborhood watches and targeted action to land career criminals in jail for a long time. So it appears that the criminal justice system — which begins with the cop — is beginning to work better.

There are some 17,000 police departments out there from Los Angeles' Parker Center to New York's No. 1 Police Plaza. No two are alike. There are scores of philosophies on how police officers should function, how much discretionary power they should have, even different notions on what weapons they should carry, what bullets they should fire, and whether they may lock an arm hold around a violent person's neck.

There is no national standard, no norm, even precious few reliable national statistics to measure one department against another. Policing perhaps because it affects each locality so deeply, has always been locally designed, responding to the political structure of the community. That alone has made the police slow to respond to minority perceptions, to serve the ghetto.

Citizen Involvement Starts to Pay Off

Patrick Murphy, once New York police commissioner and now head of the Police Foundation, remembers, "Our police until 30 or 40 years ago were in fact enforcing segregation in some states and de facto segregation in others."

James Q. Wilson, Harvard professor of government, vice chairman of the Police Foundation, and once chairman of a White House task force on crime, points out that until a reform movement of the 1930s, the police had fallen into sad ways, corruption was rife, and they "often used excessive force, especially on newer immigrants." A look backward only makes the changes in police work more graphic.

The nation's first city police, dating from 1844, became known as the "finest" New York could field. The finest have endured many changes in the political weather, not always with good grace.

The infant New York was a manufacturing city with a large Irish immigrant work force. When the Irish struck for higher pay, the manufacturers brought up blacks from the South to take their jobs. The Irish unleashed their temper, reportedly killing many of them over a single weekend.

Alarmed, the city fathers created a police force, something Detroit's black police chief, Bill Hart, finds grimly amusing: "It is ironic that the first police agency in America was formed to protect black folks."

The Irish were persecuted by the new police until, gradually, they acquired political power and status and, with it, a place in police ranks. The same pattern was followed by subsequent waves of immigrants, Italian, Jews, Germans. The in-place segregation of blacks and Hispanics, broken by political power resulting from demonstration and riot, has led finally to the police department, aided and abetted by court orders, and sometimes by newly elected black mayors.

Most American police two decades ago were white and male. The first blacks were hardly welcomed. In Detroit, one white officer assigned a black partner rode with his window down as if there were a bad smell in the car. The black officer rolled his window down too, and the pair rode that way through Detroit's daunting weather until they made their peace.

Minorities, Wilson says, hardly knew who the police were in the 1960s. The police were more part of the ghetto fence than a peace-keeping force in the ghetto itself. Detroit's Hart says minority-police encounters were often demeaning, sometimes terrifying: "It wasn't so much the physical abuse as it was the verbal abuse. The foul language. Instead of asking you in a quiet mannerly way, they yelled and called you a lot of off-color names, embarrassing you in front of your friends, wives, children."

On the heels of the riots, a presidential commission in 1967 urged police integration for these reasons: Minority officers would reduce white police prejudices; they would aid in understanding the language and subcultures of minorities; they would reduce the possibility of unnecessary conflict; and in time, they would become privy to community information that might warn of coming trouble and help solve crime.

In short, they could help crack the ghettos. Integration came slowly, but surely.

Detroit, under a new charter and a black mayor, Coleman Young, began hiring more blacks and promoting one black or female, for every white male promoted. Today, Detroit, a city which is two-thirds black, has a force which is one-third black. It was a more equal proportion than that, but budget cuts forced the layoff of some 700 low-seniority officers, 85 percent of them either black or female.

Miami, today has a force about 17 percent black in a population 20 percent black, and 39 percent Hispanic in a population 60 percent Hispanic. Eight out of every 10 new officers hired are either female or from minorities.

In Washington, D.C., a city 70 percent black, 68 percent of the police force is black and 52 percent of the patrolmen are black. Elsewhere, in the South, developments are less dramatic. Macon, Ga., 44 percent black has a police force about 28 percent black, and Birmingham, Ala., 54 percent black, has a force 20 percent black, up 4 percent in two years under a court consent decree and a black mayor.

Nationally, an independent study shows a longer road to parity. Based on some 1,200 cities down to the 10,000 population level, the study shows that about 7.6 percent of sworn officers are from minorities against a minority population at large of 21 percent. Only 3.6 percent of sworn officers nationally are women.

The progress in large cities has been costly. Many veteran whites, who saw their career opportunities narrowed by arbitrary minority promotions, fled the forces. Some bitterness lingers in cities like Miami and Detroit.

The loss of such officers and others who didn't return after layoffs, along with the natural attrition in aging ranks allowed cities to hire younger replacements. One result was that in many departments the educational level rose. In four years in New York City, the percentage of officers with some college education has more than doubled, to over 30 percent.

Some departments, such as San Diego, now require two years of college for employment. Elsewhere, too, the percentage of police officers with some college training is impressive — Kansas City, Mo., 57 percent; Allentown, Pa., 37 percent; Aurora, Ill., 39 percent; Colorado Springs, Colo., 40 percent; Des Moines, Iowa, 44 percent; Lansing, Mich., 44 percent.

Generally, the growing departments have higher educational levels. Seventy-five percent of the San Antonio, Texas, force of about 1,200 has some college, for example.

But a better educated, more ethnically tuned force hasn't solved every problem in human relations. The police in the 1980s are still seeking ways to get close to the communities they serve.

They were closer to them yesteryear. In the long march from unarmed nightwatchman to armed cop on the beat, the officer became a neighborhood fixture. But as cities grew and changed, neighborhoods became less distinct.

Wilson says the police changed too, yielding too often to the temptations for corruption and abuse of power in densely populated, increasingly anonymous cities.

A reform movement in the 1920s and 1930s was aimed both at stifling corruption and bringing police under tighter control. Officers were put in squad cars in constant touch with headquarters by radio. They were quickly dispatched, but still at the end of the radio leash.

It worked well enough for a while. But by the end of the '60s, many experts contend, the squad car had become a cocoon, insulating cops from the people.

Some departments encouraged aloofness, both in the name of efficiency and as a check on corruption. In New York City, for a time, no officer could be assigned to the neighborhood where he lived.

"Now," says Dr. Larry Sherman of the Police Foundation, "it's dawning on us that passing the time of day may be a good way of getting information on who's committing crimes, or at least build a relationship so you can ask someone."

The most effective crime prevention technique has been citizen involvement. Neighborhood and block watches now carpet the nation's big cities, and some of the smaller ones.

Add the use of citizen volunteers to do various jobs for the police department, citizen mobile patrols with CB radioes in Detroit, reserve officers sans guns walking beats with sworn officers in Los Angeles.

Sir Robert Peel, who started the first police department in the Western world in London, 1828, decided his personnel should be drawn from the community itself, tempering coercion with understanding and respect. In short, "friendly" policing, as opposed to "stranger" policing. The Constable on Patrol (COP) led to the English Bobby.

Oddly, today the British visit American cities like Detroit to see how police have adapted the technique to today's fragmented cities.

The organized neighborhood watch, as America employs it, began with Elie Wegener, the wife of a Lutheran minister in Philadelphia. One night she looked out her window and saw one of her elderly neighbors mugged. She ran to the rescue and with help subdued the mugger. That night she and a police sergeant sat down and worked out a plan whereby neighbors watch out for each other. That was some 15 years ago.

Today Detroit has 4,000 of some 12,000 residential blocks organized and the crime rate is 65 percent less than in unwatched neighborhoods.

In San Diego, Chief William Kollander claims the largest crime prevention program in America, some 3,870 neighborhood alert groups totalling some 400,000 people in a population of 900,000. Active crime is down 30 percent.

Police are striving in other ways to draw closer to communities.

In Los Angeles, where a thin force of 6,900 patrols 465 square miles, the city is subdivided into the equivalent of smaller cities up to 200,000 population. Each has a deputy chief who spends half his time dealing with local leaders, their problems and fears.

In Miami's Dade County, 2,300 sworn officers cover some 2,000 square miles around the clock. Sheriff and director of Metro-Dade Police Bobby Jones is proud of team policing.

After the riots of 1980, he faced a Liberty City black ghetto where everything was bad: "When a police car goes in, the first thing people do is throw rocks and bottles at them. You've got a hostile crowd of 200 people. It's impossible to police in that kind of atmosphere."

Jones put black and white teams into the ghetto on foot. "We told them very simply, this is your beat. You're on foot. You're to get to know the people, their problems, and you're going to enforce the law. You're going to pacify this project and you're going to do it with an awareness of the human side. There are people there who want to live safely and securely."

"We asked for volunteers," Jones says, "and we got plenty, veteran officers. We reduced crime by half in four to six months. It was amazing. I can't remember the last time we had an assault on a police officer there."

Jones even tried his team concept in affluent areas. In Key Biscayne, residents liked it so much, they squawk when he reassigns officers. The people even bought three-wheel motorcycles for beach patrol.

In Detroit, Hart has a system of 50 ministations, manned by volunteers and a sworn officer who is free to roam the neighborhood, make house calls.

In Miami, a 32-square-mile city with some 1,000 officers, Chief Ken Harms is studying the ministation idea for areas like black Overtown and Hispanic Little Havana.

Boston recently put 40 percent of its force on foot patrol, more than any other American city. Flint, Mich., although hit hard by the auto slump, passed a tax increase to finance more foot patrol officers.

Some departments that are too strapped for manpower to field officers on foot have tried variations. Ft. Lauderdale, Fla., claims success with a three-wheel motorcycle. Other cities use scooter and mounted cops. New York City has always used foot patrols, especially in Manhattan, where cars can be an encumbrance.

Ken Harms, while he is experimenting with foot patrols, notes that a man on foot can cover an area of only one block by six. "If you took that area and overlaid it in Miami, we'd need five times the number of officers we have. It's easy to say a vehicle operates as a barrier to communication, but it is still the most efficient way to deliver police services."

Efficiency, hard to define. Patrolman Herb Rodriguez, one of Harms' squad car officers, cruises a precinct that reaches from ghetto to a slipping downtown. Routine. Keeping things neat. Fluent in Spanish, he stops once in a while to chat with residents, doesn't carry a nightstick because it looks offensive.

He's a cop because his father, shot by a robber, is paralyzed for life. The radio barks out a stabbing report. Rodriguez is first on the scene, bouncing the curb into a vacant lot. Witnesses are afraid. The victim won't talk. As usual, Rodriguez says, the object is to get patched up, get back, get even.

The area is flooded with green and white squad cars in search of someone named Jackie. Nothing.

Less than two years on the street, as are 65 percent of Miami's cops, Rodriguez is learning how to cope with frustration. After intense academy training, on the job training.

Education, youth, dedication are welcomed in the new breed of cops, but street experience makes a difference. In Dade County, Sgt. Bill Press is one of the veteran officers who closely supervises the less experienced.

One of his cars is answering a call and Press speeds to the scene. A young black, whose car was overheating, made an illegal left turn to get it off the road. Nevertheless he's ticketed. Press thinks a more seasoned officer would have let him off with a warning.

Later, two of Press' men stop another driver. According to the police computer, the car is stolen. The driver has a record for car theft. He insists he's only taken the car to a paint shop for his employer.

Press orders one young officer to check the owner and the employer—before making the arrest on what seemed like an open and shut case. The computer was wrong.

The driver was only inches away from another entanglement with a system that doesn't let go easily. Experience spared him that and the police an embarrassment of the kind that tarnishes their reputation.

Such confrontations, by the thousands, go into the making of the police image. And while cops are hardly regarded with affection everywhere, a beginning has been made in a number of communities to change the anonymous enforcers of the '60s into officers with a growing rapport with the citizenry.

In contrast to a decade or two ago, says Detroit's Hart, his men now can go into any community and the people "know every crook in the area. They'd point them out to us and we'd look them up. They'd point out the dope pads and we'd close them down. After two or three years, they discovered we were sincere. We began to get a measure of respect from the community that we never had before.

"It was nice to come to work in the morning."

THE KEY—POLICE PRESENCE

If one tactic of today's American policeman is to show the flag of law and order on the streets, another is to lurk in the shadows. Criminals are discovering that cops are those things that go bump in the night. This, report on Police Work 1983, explores ways that police target their action so that few can have the impact of many.

Sgt. Tom Burke's cops are nearly invisible. They fade into the white stucco background of West Los Angeles. In T-shirts, dungarees or worse, they look like the felons they are out to catch.

But in reality they are a highly efficient task force, ready to hit the streets at any hour, turned out of bed by a hot lead and the adrenalized drive of cool pursuit.

Their bottom line is stopping crime in progress.

"Nabbing them red-handed," the cops of yesteryear might have said. But actually the latest evolution, as police everywhere reach into their bag of tricks to keep up with the latest trend in crime and find some tactic to deal with it.

The task force approach, a theme with dozens of variations, is an example of targeting police effort, hitting where it counts, getting the most out of the police dollar. Part of a necessary shift in police strategy.

There are fewer cops today than there were a decade ago. New York's once robust force of some 30,000 is now some 23,000. Proposition 13 pruned the Los Angeles P.D. While major crimes rose 46 percent in five years to 1982, the police had to trim more than 500 officers from already thin ranks.

At the same time, total arrests declined 22 percent and the city had to abandon a team-policing concept that showed promise of quieting difficult neighborhoods. It didn't have the officers.

With few exceptions, police dollars have been cut across the country. The police can do less today than they could 20 years ago. They have a mandate to do it better.

There are some indications they are. In a September report, the Division of Justice Research of the Justice Department said the number of crime victims nationally has dropped 4 percent in 1982, the first dramatic decline in 10 years. One reason: targeted police efforts against career criminals, a new cost-effective tactic against an old enemy, and a step away from being trapped in the day-to-day routine.

While they struggle to gain rapport with the communities they serve, while they hire to mirror the racial mix of those communities more realistically, they have to deal with the infuriating, imperious telephone: Everyone wants a cop on the scene two minutes after they have dialed for help.

So they have to resort to innovation, the retailoring old techniques to fit modern priorities, designing frugal tactics to replace omnipresence and sheer force.

"There are big things going on in policing," says Prof. James Q. Wilson of Harvard, vice chairman of the Police Foundation and once chairman of a White House task force on crime.

"But police are a scarce, increasingly costly resource that must be used with great precision. If there was a name for what they are being asked to do today, I'd call it targeted neighborhood-oriented patrol. . . . Figure out how they can have the greatest impact."

Targeting means more than the random patrol of streets, more than answering the homeowner's call for help, calls which usually come after the thief has fled.

In Minneapolis, Washington and more than 90 other cities, police home in on felons, either newly released from prison or with convincing records which suggest old habits are hard to break.

In New York, Connecticut and elsewhere, they set up roadblocks to snare drunk drivers and catch others in their bag as well. New York, Los Angeles and other major cities have resorted to sweeps of chronically troubled areas. In Newark, N.J., they've put patrolmen back on the streets to reclaim them from loitering predators. In San Diego, plainclothesmen haunt the youth gangs.

Effective as these techniques are, they inevitably bring the cop and culprit into a potentially hot confrontation. And that inevitably comes as a shock to the culprit.

In New York's Manhattan, a lone pedestrian on the way home late at night becomes aware of two youths following for a dozen blocks on nearly deserted Manhattan Avenue. He is slugged as he tries to leap to the safety of a bus — and then finds himself in the arms of a plainclothes police sergeant.

The sergeant apologizes; cops had been shadowing the muggers but had to wait for the strike. The two assailants are spread-eagled on the street, each with a police gun in his face. It was all over in a minute.

Robbery is the terror of urban crime. One study shows that the six largest cities, with only 8 percent of the nation's population, have a third of the nation's robberies. Eighteen percent are committed in New York City. But not this one.

So, target the robbers, target the burglars. Target the rapists. Wilson explains:

"If you have a problem with kids hanging around on street corners, you have the police go back on foot and work the streets. If you have a problem with high-rate burglars, you set up a sting operation. If you have a problem with armed robbers, you stake out the liquor stores."

Or you stake out the criminals themselves.

Sergeant Burke's task force is drawn from L.A.P.D., the sheriff, and communities such as Beverly Hills, Culver City, Santa Monica. It can cross from jurisdiction to jurisdiction, something that never hampered thieves.

The task force's intelligence also crosses jurisdictional lines. Detectives in the various forces that cover Western Los Angeles are swamped. Many handle 200 cases a month. They lack time to concentrate on individual cases with all of the costly legwork and gathering of evidence. But they know their customers.

From fragments, witnesses, field reports, parole and probation records, individual criminal habits, they can make a pretty accurate guess of who is likely to do what to whom. But you can't take a guess to court.

Police became alarmed when serious crimes began to develop in West Los Angeles. A group of detectives sat down and worked out the task force concept. They know that less than 20 percent of cops make 70 percent of the arrests, and it was from the 20 percent they chose task force members.

In one recent case, the task force's eyes fell on three men, two brothers and a cousin, in trouble since their mid-teens. One had just served three years for killing his 15-month-old son.

The plainclothes cops began a close surveillance, eventually tailed the trio to West Hollywood where they hit a supermarket. The task force deployed outside while the bandits ordered the 10 people within to lie down on the floor.

"We watched it go down," says Burke. Because of the danger to the victims, the officers planned to corner the bandits at their getaway car nearby.

But as the robbers emerged, a woman ran from the market shouting robbery. An officer grabbed her out of the way. As one bandit turned, gun in hand, the task force opened fire, killing the two brothers. The cousin was caught at the car.

The task force is close-mouthed about its techniques, even its numbers. As one police official explains, some hostage-takers have become expert in police special weapons (SWAT) team methods from watching television and reading newspapers. They prefer to keep crooks in the dark about task force methods.

But basically it boils down to knowing a crook's method of operating and keeping an eye on him.

It was through such piecework that the task force zeroed in on a gang of youths marauding in West Angeles, robbing and mugging targets of opportunity—people at a bus stop, entering cars, otherwise unsuspecting and vulnerable.

But through its intelligence lines and eyewitness reports, the task force narrowed the suspects down to nine, discovered them congregating one night at a house, followed them and caught them cold as they pounced on a party of five leaving a restaurant. They guess the nine were responsible for up to 100 previous muggings.

By nature, chronic criminals are the most dangerous. One Monday last August, the team, using aircraft, a van and a taxi, trailed a quintet of robbers, probably part of a Cuban gang of 10 responsible, among other things, for a $19,000 holdup of a homosexual bar the week before.

This time the robbers' target was a liquor store. On the way out, two of the bandits, police say, flashed guns. They were shot dead on the spot. Two others fled in a stolen car, were trapped in the garage of a luxury apartment house and killed. The fifth was captured alive. The case came under investigation, however, because the last pair apparently was not armed.

Commander William Burke, the staff officer who heads task force operations, says the officers are trained to avoid the use of deadly force at almost any cost. "We keep tight control, so we do not have the administration of street justice. But ultimately, the criminal makes the final choice."

In the course of 917 arrests in 22 months, task force guns were fired only three times. Six people were killed.

There is always the potential, says Burke, "that we will confront somebody who says you're going to have to take me."

Task force duty is certainly more hazardous, he says, but the control of police firepower is much firmer than it would be if a squad car happened on an armed robbery in progress.

As an instance of both hazard and control, he cites the pursuit of a group of Russian-born extortionists that had been preying on Russian immigrants. Confronted by the team, they drove their car at the officers, injuring several. No shots were fired then or later when the task force caught them at their home base.

Task force operations produce the kinds of arrests that prosecutors love. Conviction rates are high because robbers are caught in the act and burglars have hot merchandise in their hands. Ninety percent of task force arrests are for felonies, and the cases are solid.

That means a lot of felons are put away for a long time. So, Burke estimates, the fewer than 1,000 felons that the task force took off the streets means up to 10,000 fewer felonies a year while those felons serve their time.

There are dozens of variations to the theme of "active" targeting of known felons. In Minneapolis, police keep tabs on the eight ex-convicts they think are most likely to repeat. The Target 8 offenders, as they are called, are given more than the usual parole or probation surveillance. The mere fact that police know them by sight becomes a deterrent. Washington, D.C., has a similar program in which the targets are changed periodically.

Says Larry Sherman of the Police Foundation: "They'll follow them around for 48 hours or even a week under constant surveillance, trying to catch them committing a crime. They don't tell them they are targets. In Minneapolis, the word gets out who the targets are."

The overt Minneapolis approach does not sit well with the targets, one of whom complained that he feels intimidated and stays home a lot. Public defenders see it as an abridgement of civil rights and an invasion of the privacy of people who have already paid their debt to society. The police, they say, are overstepping their authority by arbitrarily singling out the eight targets. So far the constitutional questions have not been tested.

From Colorado Springs, Colorado, to New York City, career criminals are getting special attention since police believe that 10 percent of the nation's criminals produce half of its crime.

Focusing police efforts, however, can produce problems down the road to criminal justice. Some police complain that no one is looking at the system as a system. If the police produce more good arrests, and the prosecutors march into court loaded for bear, and the judges sentence, it inevitably squeezes the prison system already short of space.

Deputy Chief Ron Frankle of West Los Angeles is proud of the targeting activities of his task force, but he worries for the rest of the system. He sees a need to coordinate prison space, police manpower and court space, and right now the problem is prison space.

"Lack of it makes policing harder, when criminals are released back into society," he says. "Otherwise all this talk about deterrent is rhetoric. A person who has been through the system a few times understands it. What does he care if he gets another line on his rap sheet?"

LET THE PUNISHMENT FIT THE CRIME

[From the staccato shorthand of the police radio, it would seem the world has gone berserk. Part of it has. In today's complicated cities, the police must sort out crime, target their efforts, rather than just run the lot off the streets. Here are some of their successes, in the final story on Police Work, 1983.]

The American police officer presides over some 17,000 disparate cities and towns, each with its own psyche, its own welter of priorities, its own social and economic blend.

He is expected to skim off the crime while the kettle boils. As many officers will tell you, it's often a frustrating, aggravating job, haunted by inescapable realities:

- The public expects a crime-free environment, which it will never get. Yet the public pays little attention to its criminal justice system. It demands the police get the scavengers off the streets, but scrimps on judges and jail cells.
- The city has changed. It is not a homogenous unit. Miami's streets, for instance, are a tangle of ethnic interests and minorities.
- Justice, as it is meted out, has changed. It may take 60 seconds to make an arrest and months to make a case. After two decades of defending defendants' rights against inequitable police methods, the courts are listening to arguments that the victims of crime have been ignored. Yet, bogged-down courts have had to compromise to move cases out with the net result that the police have become more efficient than the system they serve.
- The face of crime has changed. The citizen's fear of predatory crime and noxious nuisance are No. 1 priority. There is less time to deal with underlying causes, whether drug traffic or ghetto that has become a school for thieves.
- Punishment is not always appropriate to the crime, especially in matters involving youths. In that area, criminal sanctions may be outmoded. The police and the courts are experimenting with ways of intervening in a budding criminal life.
- The faces of the criminals are too often the same, prison-pallor fresh, back again ravaging the streets, sometimes even while under indictment or parole.

Suspicion of police methods persists in varying degrees, fed by incidents like the conviction last month in Miami of a police officer for shooting a black. Two other officers were acquitted earlier, while a fourth awaits trial in other shooting incidents. At a congressional hearing in New York, complaints by blacks of police brutality were aired in September. The mayor, the police commissioner, and other city officials boycotted the hearing as a "political circus."

Harvard's Prof. James Q. Wilson, an expert in police matters, says today's citizen sees crime in three predominant forms:

"There is the fear of being victimized by a stranger, mugged on the streets, your liquor store held up, a stranger breaking into your house while you're away, or worse, while you're there. Predatory crime.

"Second, people are concerned about their neighborhoods. They're worried about kids on street corners, junkies, derelicts, alcoholics, panhandlers, a whole collection of things that make people extremely apprehensive about being on the streets.

"The third thing is spouses and lovers who can't control their temper, and cut and kill and shoot."

The last category seems to be the least amenable to police action. Well over half the murders occur in the home or between people who know each other, and most arise from arguments involving drink, sex, money or property.

Wilson says that police intervention in non-lethal domestic violence seems to work; arresting a violent partner is a useful dampener even if the victim won't press charges. But these are tough problems because the quarrels are played out in the privacy of the home. They nevertheless affect a community's sense of security.

The other kinds of crime that offend that sense of safety fall clearly in the police domain, and many large city departments today do what Wilson would have them do.

To combat predatory crime, police concentrate on the high-rate offenders. They stake out the places criminals hit. They use sting and undercover operations to penetrate the outlaw mechanism.

"For keeping neighborhoods clean and peaceful," Wilson says, "you'll have to use police foot patrol working in close cooperation with neighborhood organizations. All police chiefs say they do this. Some in fact do."

Much of predatory crime comes from the repeat or career criminal and something like 90 police forces make some effort to track these individuals.

In Los Angeles, Minneapolis, Washington, D.C., and other communities, it is done prospectively, tailing people waiting for them to get into trouble. In New York City that didn't work. Big Apple suspects became suspicious themselves and lay low. It may be more difficult to tail someone in a dense vertical city than in a dispersed horizontal one.

Yet New York Police Commissioner Robert J. McGuire and his deputies have brought dramatic drops in burglarly and robbery, which were rapidly increasing until two years ago.

They decided that police work only begins with the arrest. They established a computerized Career Criminal File. When a member of the 25,000-name club is arrested, he gets special treatment.

Supposing, McGuire says, a suspect has already served twice for robbery and is caught in a stolen car.

"Normally, he would go through the criminal justice system and quite frankly fall through the cracks. He'd take a misdemeanor plea to a stolen car or joy-riding, and he'd get credit for time served, and he'd be out.

"Now, his name pops up in the computerized central billing facility: John Doe, career criminal."

Even though car theft is not classic robbery, detectives take a hard look at Doe. They augment the case with whatever additional evidence and eyewitness reports they can glean. They spend a lot of time on John Doe. Their findings are then presented to the district attorney who demands a plea to the top court, who will not plea bargain. He is prepared to go to trial.

"We're given him a solid evidentiary case," McGuire says. "They can stand tall in court. If a guy pleads guilty, as many do, we can then present the whole package to the judge who more often than not will be persuaded that this is a bad guy and should go away. We're getting very good prison sentences."

As with many career-felon convictions, they cut twice, if current theory is correct. One career felon in jail for a year is not just punishment; it could mean five crimes uncommitted on the street while he is away.

In adjusting to its own crime sprawl, New York City has found a number of ways of targeting its efforts. There are monthly meetings around the city of borough and precinct commanders who pore over the output of 125 studious detectives. Those detectives go over piece by piece the robbery picture for the entire city, constructing patterns from the raw figures.

They develop target zones, where police power should be focused. Central Robbery has the authority to move in foot cops, scooter cops, mounted patrols and plainclothesmen as needed.

"We've had a dramatic reduction of robberies in this city over the last 24 months," says McGuire.

A rather simple innovation helped. Police call it the Robbery Identification Program, or RIP.

A group of detectives in Central Robbery took to analyzing cases. They found most culprits not only had prior arrest records, but usually like to work close to home.

RIP was launched in the 90th Precinct, an area in Brooklyn including large enclaves of blacks, Hispanics, and Hasidic Jews. Robbery was commonplace. Police developed a mugshot file of everyone with an arrest record.

Normally, mugshots are kept at central headquarters, and there is a delay in getting victims there. But with a select book of mugshots at the precinct house, victims could be brought in quickly while memory was fresh and before fear set in. More often than not they spotted their assailant.

RIP was so successful that it was expanded first to six precincts, now to 23 of the 75 in the city.

Sometimes the arrests are chain-reactive. Two youngsters delivering Sunday papers in the Bronx were robbed of $11 in collection money. At the precinct they picked out the picture of the robber and he was quickly arrested. Faced with the certainty of jail, he identified another suspect, wanted for shooting a police officer. Before the investigation was wrapped up, a gang of nearly 20 had been exposed.

In the last six months of 1982, says Sgt. Jack Hughes, busily setting up new RIP's, the original six precincts producted 176 percent more arrests than in all the previous year. Those six precincts had 9 percent of all robbery arrests in the city. They did it with 1 percent of the personnel.

Effective police work, however, can produce a paradox. One effect is adding to the overload of courts and prisons. New York's criminal court, for example, handled 204,617 misdemeanor and felony cases in 1982; the figure may be 50 percent higher this year.

The backlog in Manhattan and Brooklyn alone was 11,000 in September, and the crowding of the criminal calendar is not confined to New York. One consequence, much deplored by police, is the kind of plea bargaining that buys time for a sentence out of proportion to the nature of the crime.

In Miami, says Police Chief Ken Harms, caseloads are "impossible." A judge who might be able to handle up to eight jury trials a month has to find a way to dispose of 150 cases, most of which go to plea bargaining or other disposition. The result, says Harms, is that slightly more than 2 percent of the total felony cases are tried.

The American Bar Association's experts say that a court should try at least 5 to 10 percent of the cases that come before it. When the courts are forced to compromise on too many cases, the real deterrent vanishes.

Says Harms, "The community is going to get what they want ultimately. They are going to have to make some informed commitment to the quality of life."

The community, and its quality of life might be better served by a separation of courts into those handling serious crime and public nuisance, Wilson suggests.

"What do you do with alcoholics, junkies, derelicts, panhandlers and rowdy kids?" he asks. "They make life miserable for people, but do you send them to prison?"

His public nuisance court would put people under peace bonds, ordering them to stay away from certain neighborhoods, putting them into detoxification programs for drugs and alcohol abuse. Violators of such terms would be put into community service programs "where they clean up the vacant lots they've littered with all those empty bottles of Thunderbird wine." If that fails, then a week in jail.

Juveniles need special attention, too. Some are certainly tomorrow's felons in training. Yet juvenile courts have tended to protect their special status, says Wilson, "a status that was defined in the early part of the century when few people under 18 did much seriously wrong anyway.

"They may have gotten drunk or run away from home, but they didn't have guns and they didn't have heroin and they didn't have cars."

But it is still not necessary, he says, to bring juveniles into adult courts. Juvenile courts should take juvenile crime more seriously and provide appropriate facilities to handle serious offenders without sending them to a prison jammed with recalcitrant and brutal adults.

Florida has taken a step in that direction. It has sent some two dozen young criminals to an insect-ridden, sweltering 15-acre camp in the swamps northwest of Lake Okeechobee, where they work to clear land.

Inmates live in a communal tent, earn points to move to an air-conditioned trailer and more points toward eventual release. Succeed or fail, it is an attempt to give youths a last chance to get back into society.

In various cities, police themselves seek to intervene in young lives at a time when intervention can still be useful. San Diego, for example, has plainclothesmen assigned to wean away kids from the hard core of youth gangs — and get the hardened ones off the street.

When first-offense youngsters are brought in, says San Diego Chief of Police Bill Kollander, "we try to find out what the problem is" through interviews with parents and biographical essay written by the youngster. Youthful offenders are put to work on odd jobs, such as waxing police cars. They are counseled by officers.

"It works," Kollander says. "What amazes us is that these youngsters will work three Saturdays cleaning police cars and come back the fourth on their own, primarily because they want someone to want them, to care, to help them be useful."

STRESS: THE COP KILLER

PATRICIA A. KELLY

A YOUNG Marblehead police officer begins to weep softly, uncontrollably at the scene of a double motor vehicle fatality.

A mid-career state trooper, his nervous system "totally fragmented," feels he is somehow tarnishing his badge when "I just started to cry, I was crying, I was doing something a man does not do, especially when that man is a state trooper."

And a veteran Lynn patrolman responds to a complaint on the graveyard shift, swallowing a "fear" regenerated by the Russian roulette odds "that you never know whether this will be the same old kind of call or whether there will be someone there with a gun or a knife. And then that terrible panic feeling sets in, and I try to hide it because I do not want my partner to know, I cannot let him down."

These are admissions by ordinary men who face extraordinary expectations from the public they "protect and serve," from the administrations to which they answer, from the legal systems that often mock their efforts, and from their most unrelenting critics—themselves. There are times they feel they're swimming in a sewer; as caretakers of humanity seen at its unrelieved worst, they have been called society's garbagemen.

---

*Patricia A. Kelly, an associate professor of journalism at Northeastern University, Boston, Massachusetts, was a staff reporter and assistant editor with the *Daily Evening Item*, Lynn, Massachusetts. For her police beat reporting and feature writing, she has received first-place awards in regional and state-wide contests sponsored by United Press International, New England Press Association and the Massachusetts Press Association.

†(ORIGINAL EDITOR'S NOTE: Because of the sensitive and personal nature of their stories, many police officers consented to an interview only if their identities would be protected. When an officer is referred to by department, that department affiliation is an accurate one. When the speaker is referred to by a "North Shore" designation, that label was chosen because he or she felt the content of what was said could reflect adversely on the specific department.)

‡The series, including updates by the author, is reprinted with permission of the *Daily Evening Item* (Lynn, Massachusetts). The series appeared in that newspaper in March, 1983.

They are imaged as super-human, one-person composites of lawyer, marriage counselor, judge, doctor, and forensic expert.

They are susceptible to occupational hazards that, according to one stress counselor, ironically, seldom seriously compromise their professional performance, but more often leave them standing one unsuspecting day waist-deep in the piles of shards that were their personal lives.

"You look at the high rate of alcoholism among police officers, and you look at the divorce rate, and then you look at the quality of policing despite those factors," says Trooper Richard E. Kelly, co-director and psychological counselor for the Massachusetts State Police Stress Unit. "And then you say, God bless them, there is very little that seems to make a real severe dent in the performance of their duties; all goes to pot in their lives and they still perform at least minimally and usually optimally."

A Moral Consideration

A trooper who sought Kelly's help when he "hit bottom," supports the observation, saying, "I was having a bad time at home, I had family problems, I had been through a divorce, but I did not feel I was having job problems. In retrospect, maybe my efficiency was hurt. It was evident to other people at work my problem was too much booze, but I was never drunk on a duty. In other ways it might have shown. Cops cover for each other, you know. I was operating on less than eight cylinders, but I was operating."

The adverse effects of professional pressures upon the police officer-as-human-being are now being addressed as a moral consideration inextricably related to the quality of law enforcement.

The psychological and physical damage that can result from the mismanagement of career-related stress may be more than debilitating for police officers. It can be terminal.

Kenneth T. Lyons, national president of the International Brotherhood of Police Officers says "Stress problems among their men are driving our police chiefs up the wall, and it's not just the alcohol problem, but the suicide problem as well that really concerns me." Only two other occupations have higher suicide rates, said Kelly, and divorce rates run nearly twice as high as other professions.

A national Police Foundation study says 30 percent of those divorces can be directly attributed to the job.

A sample compiled for the National Institute of Occupational Safety and Health, based on interviews with 2,300 police officers in 29 departments, showed 23 percent were having serious problems with alcohol, 20 percent were having difficulties with their children, and 10 percent were doing battle with drugs.

Police work also has a high rate of heart attacks, premature death, and what police psychiatrists term "psychophysiological disturbances leading to organic diseases," such as backaches, tension headaches, ulcers, skin disorders, hyperventilation and bronchial asthma.

Preliminary studies conducted by the Massachusetts State Police peg the premature death rate at eight to 12 years after retirement for its population with an average retirement age of 48.6 years. Thirty-five percent retire with disabilities, the divorce rate is estimated at between 50 and 75 percent, and the alcoholism rate is "consistent with national figures for police at 15 percent."

Measuring the Cost

The visible costs of unrelieved and chronic job stress for police officers are high and measurable in absenteeism and disability statistics. The toll subject neither to public comprehension nor sympathy is the personal price—the disillusionments that develop into depression and despair, the burnout which seeks a cure in the bottle, pills, or both.

Edward C. Donovan, a 25-year veteran of the Boston force who once aspired to be a professional comedian but went into police work because he wanted to help people, recalls the times when, strung out on "booze and pills, paranoid and cynical," he contemplated putting his gun to his head, or aiming his police cruiser at a tree.

He had to reach rock-bottom before he could begin his recovery and the conversion to what is nearly a religion to him—preaching that negative stress can slowly debilitate the bodies of police officers and insidiously murder their souls unless those stressors are confronted, coped with, or prevented.

Donovan, director of the Boston Police Stress Unit, has counseled many officers from the North Shore either troubled or in trouble—or both—since the inception of that program amid a sea of administrative skepticism in the early 1970's. In days when, according to Donovan's definitions, "no one knew what the hell stress was," the unit launched by him and fellow officer Joe Ravino was the only and last outpost for "cops who had to face the fact that your mind can make you sick, as well as your body."

Through the gospel spread by Donovan, (looked upon by his peers as a guru of sorts because he doesn't hesitate to say, "I am an alcoholic and I almost took my life, and anything I talk about, I have been through,") traditional barriers between police personnel and mental health services began to be bridged.

The same study which sampled 2,300 police officers nationwide also concluded this group was below average in taking advantage of mental health services.

"I Go to Them...."

"I never tell one of our officers when he needs help to come to me, and I will sit behind a desk and I will straighten you out," maintains Richard Walsh, stress officer for the Metropolitan District Commission police. "I go to them. If they want to meet me at a Dunkin' Donuts or in their home, I will go there. It works better that way."

"Police are notoriously skeptical about mental health personnel, and in some cases, understandably so," says psychologist Dr. John J. Barry of Stoneham, the majority of whose clients are police officers or their family members. Barry provided the psychological resources for the fledgling Boston Police Stress Unit, has consulted with the state and MDC stress units, and has counseled many a cop from Greater Lynn and elsewhere since he opened his doors to private practice 11 years ago.

Barry, an ex-marine, comes from "a police family."

"My father was a policeman for thirty-five years. Two years after his retirement, he was dead, which is pretty standard," he says. "Two of my brothers are policemen. One, Charlie, was secretary of public safety for (Gov.) Mike Dukakis and is director of the Law Enforcement Management Institute at Babson College, and my youngest brother is a sergeant at Station One, Boston. So you could say I have a personal as well as a professional interest in the subject of police and stress."

Barry, Kelly, Donovan, and Walsh share the ability to allay the distrust police habitually harbor toward psychological help, because they themselves have membership in the brotherhood, either honorary or real. And their credentials, earned at institutions of higher learning, in service, or both, are respected.

"There is no mystique about who we are or what we do. This is no cloak and dagger operation, and we do not move about under cover of darkness performing lobotomies," laughs Kelly, who with Corporal Philip A. Trapasso splits the duties of counseling state troopers and officers, handling 400 cases out of a population that remains slightly more than 1,000 since the unit's inception in 1977. (That figure includes some relapses.)

Gaining Credibility

Kelly, who has a bachelor of science degree in psychology and a master's in counselor education, says the success of the Boston unit and its credibility helped launch the state unit in an "atmosphere of very little resistance." Endorsement by the superintendent and the president of the association made it clear the unit would not be "management-oriented," but a real "fence-walker," being outside and above-and-beyond any union-management issues. Introducing the stress unit "in the antiseptic atmosphere" of the training academy, and holding family seminars helped thaw officers who might have had difficulty warming to the concept, he says.

Since its inception, approximately half the unit's caseload involves troopers; 13 percent are of the ranks of corporals and above; 17 percent are family members of officers; and 19 percent are civilian members of the force or officers from other police departments who either do not have help immediately available or "just don't want to go to anyone locally."

According to Kelly's and Trapasso's statistics, eight percent are referred to hospitals, 23 percent to psychologists, three percent to psychiatrists, and two percent to other agencies. "The rest we deal with ourselves, and we co-work many of the cases we refer out," Kelly said.

Most who take advantage of the support services do so because they recognize a need.

"Seventy-one percent of those who come, come voluntarily," says Kelly. "About 14 percent are what I call forced voluntary—their superiors have given them the ultimatum, either you get help or you go up on charges—and another 15 percent are already in the glue, and this is part of their punishment, so to speak."

But an officer, if not directed by a superior, must voluntarily submit. "We will not take information and go up to him and say, 'We hear you're having trouble,'" continues Kelly. "Sometimes someone might say to an officer he should come to see us, and the officer will then say, 'yeah,' and nod his head in appropriate response. We consider that a volunteering."

At the MDC, which covers portions of Lynn, Nahant, and Revere, the hierarchy needed some strong proof of the need for a formal stress unit.

"There were some hard nuts to crack," admits Walsh, who holds a bachelor's and a master's degree in psychology. "MDC officer Jack Mahoney tried to convince the administration several years ago that there was a place for such services. But the prevailing sentiment then was, "everyone has problems and everyone, including officers, should cope with them."

"There were budget restraints, so there was no green light until an incident in which an officer had a run-in with a citizen off the job. "When that came to the superintendent's attention it sort of woke him up, and he said, 'my God, I guess there is a need.' "

Problems "Run the Gamut"

In that one-man program, Walsh grapples with "problems that run the gamut."

"I deal with alcohol and marital difficulties, and sometimes I get a question that has nothing to do with the overall stress topic, like I have a social disease, and how do I get rid of it without telling my wife," recounts Walsh. "I get disciplinary cases when a guy screws up, and he is told the ramifications of what he has done could be delayed if he seeks help."

Walsh adds that the "alcohol problem with our officers is minimal; we do not have half the problems the Boston police have, but we do have problems, and some of them are bizarre. We do not know how to handle complex phobias, but we know where to send them, and we also use for referrals the standard alcohol and drug treatment facilities."

Swampscott Police Chief Peter J. Cassidy candidly concedes the experience of his department proves that officers most affected by job related stress are not always employed in big cities, fighting so-called big-city crime.

"Eight men here of a force of 33 have during the past five or six years had problems with alcohol, and have done something about it through the only avenue we have traditionally had, the program at Mt. Pleasant Hospital, Lynn," says Cassidy. "Only one of those men was ordered to do so. The rest agreed on their own to straighten out their acts, and that they did."

The alcoholic treatment facility's services, range from a two-week in-hospital detoxification to out-patient counseling and what Cassidy labels the "God-sent" spinoff of Alcoholic Anonymous. "A tremendous brotherhood draws those guys together in AA. Some had serious problems with the bottle, some not so serious. The latter decided to straighten themselves out before they did become serious and faced a crisis.

"There's no question in my mind as to what was a major factor in their problems," he continues. "It is the stress of the job."

Cassidy says it's not difficult to pinpoint on-duty the men whose worlds are beginning to disintegrate off-duty. "When you're close to it, you see it, you hear things, you can see it in the general conduct, and often you almost know it before they do themselves."

"My Family Life Was Gone. . . . "

One of Cassidy's officers who found his salvation at Mt. Pleasant said he finally admitted that job pressures he had masked fed his drinking, and because of that drinking, "I was a social outcast and my personal and family life was gone."

"Peter Cassidy is an innovative chief," this officer says, gratefully. "He's out of the new school, he's using the resources available to him, he believes in interceding, and he watches the pattern of his employees on the job."

The pattern Cassidy and other administrators watch for is the one that reflects the telltale presence of burnout, the condition of cops who have overdosed on mismanaged or unmanaged stress.

In discussing burnout as it relates specifically to police work, Dr. Jack Seitzinger, director of the greater St. Louis (Mo.) police academy, labelled the burned-out cop "a crispy critter."

These "crispy critters," says Seitzinger, account for 70-80 percent of all complaints against their departments.

Lethargy, cynicism, and the general loss of physical and mental energy, the manifestations of burnout, are among its less lethal effects. Physical and verbal abuse, the misuse of firearms, recklessness, hostility, and over-aggression can trigger incidents that serve neither the safety nor the interest of the public or the officer himself.

"Look, in thinking back, I could see some signs in myself," says the Swampscott patrolman. And now I can see it when it happens to others. There is the 'who-cares attitude,' there is the going to work every day and just not caring. Then, of course, there is the absenteeism."

Bending the Rules

Chief Cassidy has seen a dramatic reversal of his department's absentee figures since his officers' "personal problems" have been confronted as conditions related to job performance on a practical level, and to the man's general well-being on a moral level. He sees his officers as investments, representing countless dollars in training and compensation. And he sees them as human beings, whose mental and physical health affect the lives of other human beings.

"If you have to bend the rules to save the man, then you bend the rules. He has got to have help. If he has to have time off to get that help, that is what happens. And other smaller things can help, like making households happy by keeping a guy on a shift that makes him happy," says Cassidy.

A North Shore police officer tells the story of an "old-timer" who used to put out "in the boonies" whenever possible because he was often drunk on the job. In fact, when he would make a radio transmission, his peers would often tell him to repeat his words "because you're coming in drunk."

The anecdote shows how law enforcement hierarchies often treated "crispy critters"—by transferring them or putting them in low-profile situations, and if that didn't work, by retiring them on disability or firing them. All are examples of what Cassidy rues as "waste of investment."

FOR FEMALE OFFICERS, PROBLEMS ARE DOUBLE

Separate but equal attention is just beginning to be focused upon those the experts feel are doubly-jeopardized candidates for job-generated stress problems—female police officers.

"We have pressures the men never thought of," says a North Shore woman who has been a member of a municipal department for several years.

"There was the expectation by the men, as soon as I came on the job, that I would automatically screw up. And then there's also the other problem, the expectation because you wear the uniform you are somehow no longer a woman. You cannot win. I keep telling people that by putting on the uniform, I didn't have a sex change operation. But few seem to believe you."

"There have been more difficulty with the assimilation of female police officers than other groups," says Trooper Richard Kelly, co-director of the Massachusetts State Police Stress Unit. He thinks some of the problem has been due to the perception that they receive preferred treatment, that their attributes of courage and strength are not the same as male officers, or that they might not be able to physically perform comparable to a male standard.

"When a woman takes on a male macho job, she takes on the male macho diseases," says Boston Stress Unit Director Edward Donovan. "Also she feels she has to prove herself even better than the men, many of whom feel castrated by a woman on the job. And a woman has been raised to show her emotions, been taught that it is okay to cry, and now she comes on the job and feels she has to start covering up those feelings."

"We are just beginning to learn about the female role and we have much to learn," says psychologist Dr. John Barry of Stoneham, who has counseled female police officers in his capacities as a consultant with the area stress units and in his private practice.

LIVING UP TO AN IMAGE, OR PUTTING ON A FRONT?

A Swampscott patrolman stands mutely in the courtroom, attempting to swallow his rage and mask his mortification.

A youth he describes as "a virtual one-person crime wave," has just had his case dismissed by the judge. He was caught in mid-act breaking into a home. The homeowner as witness came repeatedly to testify, but the hearing was delayed and delayed, and on this day, she risked losing her job by staying beyond the morning session.

The judge heard the case at 4 P.M., chewed the officer out for letting the witness leave, and dismissed the charges. "I'll never forget how that kid and his mother stood there and laughed, laughed at me," recalls the officer.

The jeering by the accused, the verbal humiliation by the judge, the release of a budding criminal, guilty in fact and exonerated by the system, certainly were stressful experiences for that law enforcement official. It was one more occasion when he did not feel good about himself and what he was doing. He was once again like the proverbial Sisyphus, forever rolling that stone uphill, only to have it forever roll backward.

He cites the experience as one of a kind that "I stored somewhat somewhere inside me," even though he thought its effects were over once the courtroom's doors closed. It was the layered effect of such storings, he says, that contributed to and perhaps maybe even caused "drinking to become the biggest thing in my life." Only after two weeks of treatment at Mt. Pleasant Hospital, Lynn, and recovery bolstered by the support system of Alcoholics Anonymous and a sympathetic chief did he begin to understand the personal toll of frustrations turned inward.

Pressure From the Courts

The courts are, say stress experts and the police themselves, one of the major sources of pressure and disillusionment.

"Sometimes you just feel judges have their heads in a bag," says former Lynn resident and State Trooper Dean Bennett, based at the Peabody barracks. Plea bargaining is often one of the frustrations."

Bennett recalls a recent case in which a 19-year-old was arrested on a drug-related charge after he was found "stoned" in his vehicle. He was treated leniently by the courts, and from the perspective of the police, the painting of the accused by his attorney as a guileless first-offender put the teenager back in operation.

Within weeks the young man was found dead of an overdose.

Bennett does not feel the courts did the kid a favor.

"Sometimes a cop becomes the easy fall guy for the system," he says. "Maybe in a rape case, the d.a. does not believe the victim's story or doesn't want to prosecute for some reason, so it's easy to point the finger at the cop and say he messed up the case by doing something wrong on the report."

"The courts are too lenient and as a police officer you're in the middle," says a young Marblehead patrolman who does not wish to be identified.

Research on the topic of police and courts label this being "in-the-middle" as a straddling of two models of justice. One is the due process in which the rights of the accused are of tantamount importance. The other is the model in which crime must be controlled.

And as the most visible symbol of our criminal justice system, the cop is also the one most easily held responsible for any of its negatives.

"Sometimes I feel like a frontline soldier," complains the same patrolman. "I was walking down the street in Marblehead one day with my baby on my back, off-duty, and a woman comes up to me and says, 'You killed him, you killed him.' She was blaming me for the death in a car accident of a local teenager. She said we as the police should have done something on occasions that we supposedly saw him drinking. Can you imagine how I felt?"

Ironically, this same patrolman concedes he had broken down at that accident scene and started to cry, overwhelmed by his helplessness and by the waste of young life. "My lieutenant had to snap me out of it. He put his arm around my shoulder and told me to perform as an EMT just as we do in training sessions, and I did. But the scene really got to me."

Living Up to the Image

That human suffering does "get to" police officers who more often mop up the blood than prevent its spilling has also been focused on as one of the worst stressors. The pressure comes from denying or burying those feelings. Why? Because society has traditionally held a machismo view of the police officer as, says Patrolman Edward Donovan of the Boston Stress Unit, a cross between "Hoot Gibson and John Wayne." Unfortunately, the man or woman tries to live up to the image.

"People expect cops to be gods, peacemakers, to take on half a dozen guys without mussing up a uniform, to settle an argument so both sides win," says Dr. John Barry, a psychologist who counsels police officers, "People expect too much of a human being."

"I was in court once when a defendant complained to the judge that I was too abrupt," recalls Trooper Bennett. "Thank goodness the judge pointed out a police officer making an arrest is not required to be friendly."

The Herculean image becomes destructive when it promotes an officer to be so concerned about maintaining self-control that he refuses to express any emotional turmoil.

Incidents tend to affect the first responders differently, although police agree that certain kinds of calls tend to be mutually traumatic.

"Children calls, they are terrible," says Trooper Bennett. "I recall in the early morning hours dreading calls to a home because they often involved babies and the sudden infant death syndrome. I remember once a mother in panic threw a baby who had stopped breathing 60 feet across the lawn to us." The officer caught and revived the infant.

The witnessing of another officer "in a state of collapse" over a child he could not revive haunts a Swampscott police officer and helps him discuss his own vulnerability: "I was in an emergency room and I saw this other cop come rushing in, giving a baby mouth-to-mouth resuscitation. He was still trying to breathe life into the child who was dead, and this big cop just fell to his knees and started to cry, right there. I never, never forgot that."

"One of the incidents I had trouble coping with was finding a young kid hanging," recalls Marblehead Patrolman Kenneth L. Nickerson. "I was sick about it, but I knew I had to get over it, and if I didn't I wouldn't be able to do my job."

Seeing young people die and having to break it to parents deeply bothers Trooper Bennett.

"I investigated a double fatal recently in Peabody," he says. "What a tough, tough thing, seeing needless death caused by speeding. And how do you tell a mother and father the pride of their life, their beautiful 16-year-old daughter, is dead? You might just as well be going to their home to cut their legs out from under them."

The Real World

Then there is the aspect of police work that is repulsive and revulsive, realities known to police officers and romanticized by the public.

"The real stressors are the ones caused by unreal perceptions, and the public holds unreal expectations about police," maintains Trooper Richard E. Kelly, a director of the State Police Stress Unit. "We are not Barney Miller or Adam 12; we generally do not do CPR on young, beautiful women, but the victims are usually old, and there is vomit, and it smells, and it is dirty."

A North Shore female police officer remembers somehow working through and performing well at a fire scene using "mind control," which was effective until she began to reflect on the experience.

"I have a horrible fear of fire, and yet I managed to work on a victim, to no avail. I calmly went home to take a shower and I looked down and saw bits of burnt human flesh on my body, and I started to gag and vomit."

"Maybe we are animals of habit, and maybe police officers especially get accustomed to acting like machines," remarks a Swampscott officer who thought he was assimilating his negative experiences well, until the alcohol he sought relief in became the monkey that clung tenaciously to his back.

"My wife would ask me, 'What did you do at work today?' and I would say, oh nothing, when in reality I had to stand guard of a decomposing body, and it wiped me out. So every day I would go home and say the same thing, but something would be stored deep inside me, and the bad stuff would linger and linger."

Sometimes even routine duty can cause stress.

"The worst thing in the world for me is to make an arrest," confides Marblehead Patrolman Nickerson. "You're depriving someone of just about everything he has. When I arrest someone, I'm so nervous, my heart is pumping away, and frankly, I hope he gets bailed as quickly as he can."

"Some Kind of Hero"

Complexities of the law and the attendant paper work, non-supportive administrations, biased treatment by the media, and the hostility of the community are complaints common among officers.

"It's getting so officers have to carry a computer to check on the contingencies under which they can make an arrest," complains Dr. Barry.

"The organization you work for gives you no backing, no support," claims Donovan. "A police officer is constantly called on to make split decisions, and if you are wrong, you have to eat it. The department works to protect its own rear end, like any quasi-military organization."

"Sometimes you're very afraid of making the wrong decision. I've been sued twice, both times on thoroughly ridiculous grounds, but sued, nevertheless," says a Swampscott officer.

"You have, on one hand, people looking up to you like some kind of hero in their time of need," he says, "and on the other, you stand there in a parking lot having to take some real guff from a person who has illegally parked in a handicapped parking space and taunts you about why you're not out getting the real criminals."

Psychologist Barry believes that reporters who substitute subjective questioning for objective probing in their crime coverage do a dire disservice to police officers, and needlessly increase their stress level. Dr. Barry admits he is "biased and coming from the cop's vantage point," but maintains that his jaundiced view of the media is an inescapable conclusion of his many years of treating cops in crisis.

"I don't want to give the impression that I think all media people are monsters, they are not," he says, after recounting a list of incidents he feels shows journalists in a negative light. "But I do think reporters on the street ask pretty damn stupid questions. Instead of fact-gathering, they ask 'How do you feel?' questions."

It is interviewing of that design which Barry feels betrays "lack of sensitivity, lack of training and lack of awareness" about the physiology and psychology of human reactions under stress—as well as an obsession with summarizing complex emotional issues which do not lend themselves to truth in abridgement.

"Journalists need to know more about the psychology of confrontation," he says. "They are looking for the quick headline. They ask a cop how did you feel when you did thus and so? Or they ask a woman whose daughter has just been mutilated and is totally distraught, how do you feel? It is unbelievable, some of the stuff they ask. In those situations, one doesn't feel, one reacts."

Press clippings he reviews of incidents involving his clients, the anger toward and distress about that coverage he has seen displayed by these men and women in the privileged privacy of his practice have made him increasingly protective of his police officers:

"My general instinct is to veer away from the media if at all possible, because I perceive it as the kind of thing that can only do damage, so my feeling is, stay the hell away from the media."

He does, however, fall short of sharing that cautionary sentiment with officers involved in "traumatic" and publicized on-duty incidents, officers who have been referred to him for psychological support services, or who have sought such on their own.

"I don't advise them not to talk with the media, that is not my job," he says. "If they ask me, I refer them to their own administrations for guidance. What I am concerned about is what ramifications the coverage might have for the individual and his family."

Barry tempers his criticism of the press with the observation that many times a lopsided story emerges because gag orders have been issued from the police administration, preventing the officer from presenting his version in a public statement.

He recalls a group counseling session during which a police officer who had shot a crime suspect vented his frustrations about conclusions drawn from his silence and the impact that news slant had on his personal life.

"His administration told him not to say anything, so he could not explain why that suspect had been shot in the back," says Barry. "The television news played the brutal policeman angle; his father was watching that coverage and had a cardiac seizure. That cop tied the comments by the media to the seizure, and he was raging, really raging. We had to work to calm him down. He had felt comfortable about what he had had to do, and he was very, very angry."

What can be done to free the flow of information to assure that the integrity of an on-going investigation is not compromised, while insuring that a balanced story is compiled and circulated?

Realistically, says Barry, nothing, unless you want to espouse what he concedes is an extremist view and one which journalists would certainly see as having more than just a chilling effect on First Amendment rights and privileges.

"When police can't give their version, when they cannot talk until a case comes to court, it seems to me it would be fair to hold the write-up in abeyance until both sides have had their fair day," he says. "I don't even know really how adequately a so-termed police spokesman can represent the officer's story, since he is x number of steps removed from the incident."

But he also notes he would settle for a kind of middle ground, where journalists would report the facts they are able to gather and confirm, and refrain from what he calls distortions based on stereotypes and geared to unjustly stir sympathy for the perpetrator of crime.

"I counseled a cop not long ago who had been in an incident very traumatic to him," he relates. "He had fired on a kid throwing bricks from the roof of a house after his partner had been downed. He hit the kid, a 14-year-old, in the jaw. According to the interview in the press with his mother, this kid belonged with the angels. The cop was first cleared by his administration and told his performance was understandable. The media showed clips of the mother at the hospital and so forth, building up an implication in the interviews that he had been shot because he was a Puerto Rican. This happens many times—you see portrayals of crime suspects shot by police, and they are shown in their Confirmation suits, and they have records in some cases as long as your arm."

This kind of media coverage, Barry insists, is just one more stressor that a police officer faces in a series of stress-inducing, job-related pressures that promote a sense of cynicism and diminished self-worth.

More distressing to Donovan than these "cumulative stressors," is what he calls "the big one, the killer."

"What you see most often on a police officer's face is fear, and fear kills," he says. "Fear will bring on guilt, and guilt will bring on addiction to alcohol or pills or both."

"Even an apparently routine call makes you fearful," admits a Marblehead patrolman. "You get a report there might be someone in a house and you get there and you think you have to go in there and that person might have a gun, and you are scared."

Gun Calls the Worst

"The gun calls are the worst," agrees Bennett. "You never know when they'll happen. I remember we started to chase someone on a stop sign violation and the incident ended up in a real gun fight."

But the idea that he should not feel fear, that he should not, in fact, he buffeted by any of the emotions, often secretly tortures the truly stressed officer and retards any overtures for help.

Not being able to separate the professional from the personal identity often results in one of the most commonly-shared and most critical stress-inducing syndromes — the figurative inability of the officer to shed his uniform.

"Cops would like to be one of the guys, but they can't," said Richard Walsh, MDC stress unit officer. "They go to a party, and if they're introduced as a cop, the joint which would have normally got passed around does not, the talk about the 'good buy' on a cb radio that normally would have happened does not, and the cop is not able to surrender his job."

"I get paranoid about it sometimes," says a North Shore officer. "I went into a bar to have a drink off-duty, and I saw someone there I had arrested for drunk driving. So I left, being afraid to let him see me drink. Look, I also smoke pot sometimes, and maybe that is bad, but I do it. I feel bad because I'm supposed to set an example and I feel there's a terrible double standard when I arrest someone on a pot charge."

"Did you ever notice that whenever a policeman goes somewhere, even socially, he sits with his back to the wall — casing the joint, so to speak?" asks Donovan. "His juices never stop flowing."

"I've ruined quite a few parties by my presence," laughs Nickerson. "Most often, people wander away from us into other rooms to do what they're going to do, to dabble in what they are going to dabble in, and I find myself alone with my wife and maybe a close friend, usually another officer."

What happens? Often, officers begin to either isolate themselves and become loners or, what some feel is worse, socialize exclusively with other officers.

Other Officers Understand

Such a pattern is almost inevitable, says Dr. Barry. "He gets off at two in the morning, comes home to a mausoleum — everyone is asleep — watches the boob tube for a bit, then decides to go out with the boys and swap sea stories. Soon, often, a booze problem begins."

"I do find comfort in another officers understanding," says Nickerson. "If there's a bad night, another cop will come over and we'll talk it out. And as I talk I have one fear. I keep asking myself, 'What could I have done better in that incident?' and try to look at it as a learning experience."

But often, the blurring of job and home life results in some turning their homes into mini-police states, unable to stop "playing cop" with their children.

Metropolitan Officer Walsh and State Trooper Kelly also counsel families of police officers and sometimes deal with inordinate pressures placed, particularly, on children.

"A cop often expects his kids to be perfect," says Walsh. "He would never expect him to hang around a corner, light up a joint, or drive like a maniac, or drink. But the kid sees himself as a typical adolescent, and those are things a typical adolescent often does."

Self-isolation can have a disastrous effect on an officer's marriage. "Swimming in a sea of negativity" (Dr. Barry's phrase), they tend to begin to believe the bad is all-encompassing. "Remember, police officers are the only employees I know who are paid to go out and look for trouble," says Donovan. Drug addicts, prostitutes, sexual offenders, deaths in all shapes and forms, and husbands and wives cheating on each other are part of the daily parade of their work life. They can become suspicious, cynical and very uncommunicative.

"I stopped talking, and she stopped listening, or maybe it was the other way around," says a trooper whose marriage ended in divorce and who was in a second "messed up family situation," when he habitually drank "to get drunk."

"The job wears and tears on a marriage," Dr. Barry sadly states. "And by the time some of these marriages come before me for help, my help is like trying to put a bandaid on the Hoover Dam."

Brian Alley, alcoholism counselor at Mt. Pleasant Hospital, Lynn, has taken the penchant of officers to isolate themselves and turned it into a positive channel for communication.

"There was a real strong resistance by officers with drinking problems to seek help at AA," says Alley. "They would say to me, 'How can I arrest a guy for driving under when I might be sitting next to him in an AA meeting the next day?'"

Alley's answer was to form a weekly group therapy session for North Shore police officers billed as stress counseling therapy, with the prevailing motivation for attendance being past or present bouts with the bottle.

"The brotherhood concept works wonderfully here," says Alley. "During the week, they check up on each other, particularly if they think someone is ready to break out again."

Says one Lynn officer, a member of the group, "My job made me a loner, but here I found out there are other people who think like me, police officers who have never been able to speak out, who are doing so for the first time. I find out the job is hard emotionally for them too."

PREVENTION, THE BEST MEDICINE

In writing a proposal to convince the State Police hierarchy of the need for a full-time stress unit, its co-director, Trooper Richard E. Kelly, termed the stressors on police "astronomical."

He saw the formalization and acceptance of the unit as the creation of mechanism "to treat, train against, or prevent the disease of pressure that will eventually destroy the first and only line of defense society has against itself," — its police force. And he pleaded that such steps be taken to "insure that the police profession does not become a self-destructive exercise in futility."

The societal changes that have made these "astronomical" demands are a given.

The line officer by himself can do little to reverse what Kelly defines as "loosening of nationwide moral inhibitions, inconsistency in the court system, injustice in the penal system, increasing deliquency of youth, increasing rates of divorce, incidents of civil disobedience, spiraling inflation, increased public tendency to initiate grievance procedures, high rates of unemployment, and the increased sophistication of the criminal."

But, maintains Kelly and other police stress experts, measures can be taken to make officers far less vulnerable to the debilitating effects of mismanaged stress.

The Buzzword: Prevention

The police stress buzzword of the 80's is prevention.

Within the past several months, a pilot program likely to become a national model was launched in Massachusetts to make diagnostic and treatment facilities available to many suburban departments, some on the North Shore.

Last fall, Kenneth T. Lyons, national president of the International Brotherhood of Police Officers, told members that in an effort to be as interested in the "health and well-being" of officers as in "their union rights," an employee assistance program was being established. The purpose was to "confidentially assist IBPO members and their families with stress/alcohol problems."

The National Institute of Alcohol Abuse and Alcoholism through its state bloc grant program, channeled funds to the Commonwealth of Massachusetts Division of Alcoholism. The division then awarded $200,000 to finance the IBPO proposal through August, 1983.

Saugus, Marblehead, and Swampscott police are eligible to tie into both the treatment and training aspects of the program.

"I think we have a unique thing going here," says Anna Laszlo, executive director of the IBPO Employee Assistance Program. "We have public sector labor unions working with management on police stress and alcohol problems, and by its very nature the IBPO involves representation in many smaller departments where these kinds of services have not been traditionally available."

Two full time clinicians are available for assessments, counseling, and referrals. The training part makes use of working officers to give peer assistance to other men and women and their families.

Swampscott Police Officer Terry Lee is on the panel forming the curriculum for a two-day training session of those from member departments who have volunteered to serve as "assistance officers."

"We will be trained to spot trouble and trained in what to do about it, and where to make referrals, if necessary," explains Lee. "And that does not just apply to the officer; it applies to members of his family, including children."

Marblehead Police Officers Glover Preble, Kenneth King, and David Bouchard have been attending IBPO planning sessions, and Saugus police union members are reviewing material on the problem.

National President Lyons emphasizes no police officer would be turned away, even if employed by a department that does not have IBPO membership.

Chiefs' Opinions Differ

Saugus Police Chief Donald Peters, however, refused to say whether his men might need to avail themselves of stress management or alcohol counseling.

"I would rather not say. I handle a problem between the man and myself if there is one. I might have used the Boston stress unit in the past, and I might not have. If they need help, help is there."

Chief Thomas Fay of Lynn doesn't see stress as a "problem" in his department. "If my men had problems, I would make referrals, but they don't. One or two maybe had some alcohol problems in the past few years, and they went to Mt. Pleasant, low-key, no publicity. Maybe stress has caused some retirements, but that is hypertension, that is not stress."

However, Edward Donovan, director of Boston's Police Stress Unit, says through years he has counseled officers from North Shore departments, including Lynn. Among the more unique of the Boston unit's programs are sessions held exclusively for police women, and post-shooting trauma counseling sessions for officers who have "shot or been shot at."

Lynnfield Police Chief Paul Romano has made referrals to the Boston unit "if there is a specific problem, especially if a man has trouble dealing with a specific incident."

"There is help out there now, and the men know it. Years ago, a problem might have gotten out of hand and a guy might have turned to booze. But today he is more likely to seek help before something happens."

Romano also makes referrals to Dr. John Barry of Stoneham, psychologist in private practice and a consultant to area stress units.

Marblehead Police Chief John Palmer also has Dr. Barry as a support source and says if a problem with one of his officers comes to his attention, he moves to make an appropriate referral.

Nahant Police Chief Joseph P. Manley confirmed officers in small departments also suffer from stress, and has taken advantage of the Boston unit's services.

"I have the advantage of a small department and therefore an intimate relationship with the men. I can see the indicators early. But I would like to see some on-going requirements, such as regular physicals. There are no requirements to be met after entry, and it is not good for men under extreme stress to be carrying guns. I believe one hundred percent in these stress programs."

Some say better screening of candidates could prevent having the wrong man in the wrong job, defining before it's too late the personality more apt to crumble under the pressures of what Marblehead Chief Palmer calls "the rules you knew about when you signed on." Palmer and Chief Peter J. Cassidy of Swampscott have been particularly enthusiastic about the concept of psychological screening.

"With good selection devices you can eliminate the chance of getting the guy who will lose his cool seriously, who comes home one day and fires five rounds into the washing machine or the side of the house," contends Dr. Barry, who has done extensive screening tests and interviews for departments across the state.

Assessing Vulnerability

"What we can assess is a vulnerability to stress," he explains. "We try to aim for the individual with a low anxiety level who is least likely to respond to stress by developing physical symptoms, who knows how to handle pressures. We do it in tests, through interviews, video-taping. What I would like to eliminate is the feeling that because someone does not 'pass' this, then that should be construed as derogatory. We look for a particular set of characteristics suitable for a particular job. If you go to medical school, you are expected to have certain qualifications."

Ongoing education ranks high on the state police stress unit's list as a major preventive measure. All recruit classes at the academy receive instruction in ways to reduce the likelihood of being debilitated by pressure, how to manage it, and where to go if the approaches fail.

For troops already on line, Dr. Barry would like to see the physical fatigue syndrome combated.

One North Shore police officer, tells the chilling anecdote. "One time, I was talking to my partner for a couple of blocks. He was driving the car, not answering, and I discovered that he was asleep."

"Shorter tours of duty should be considered," according to Dr. Barry. "Double shifts should not be worked, and maybe there should be a limit on overtime. When you are that tired, your judgment goes and you are talking about people who have to make a judgment in a matter of milliseconds. Of course, when I talk to chiefs about the problem of fatigue they start bitching at me for trying to screw up their manning charts. And then the union, on the other side, says I am advocating taking money of their pockets.

"Officers do not have to try and grab every bit of overtime. And we need to train our sergeants to spot early any of the troops acting out of line, even if arms have to be twisted, to see behavior changes, to see officers acting impulsively, or coming in with an odor of alcohol, or coming in stoned. And they need to let us help them without being a pipeline back to the administration."

Save Men, Save Money

Barry cites as "unbelievable" the amount of money that can be saved by such applications. Through a tedious job of hand collating records, Barry found between 1973 and 1977, the early years of the Boston Police Stress Unit, there was a 12 percent reduction in absenteeism.

Swampscott Chief Cassidy has instituted a new policy which may seem like a minor measure, but has helped lower the anxiety of his officers.

"Our men have been responding to an astronomical number of burglar alarms, most of them false. The call would come, the adrenalin would pump, the tension is tremendous. Our policy of charging for false alarms has reduced the incidence 120 percent. All kinds of calls have increased dramatically. We are doing with the same manpower an incredibly increased work load. A typical figure in the early '50's would be 32 motor vehicle accidents a year. In 1981, there were 371.

"It's hard enough a man has to go to an accident scene and pick up the dead and broken and try to go home and forget it," Cassidy adds. "Maybe we can do something about stress that is needless."

Ironically, what perhaps is most self-defeating about combating stress is the type of person who is most attracted to police work and who, typically, makes the finest contributions. Trooper Kelly says it is the "type-A" personality: Hard-driving, hard-working, a person who likes a fast pace and perfection.

A state trooper, recovered with the aid of stress counseling, therapy with Dr. Barry, Mt. Pleasant Hospital, Lynn's alcohol program, and the AA, sees himself as this kind of "perfectionist."

"I like doing things well," he confides. "I was most critical of myself, and I sought relief through alcohol from my self-torture that I was not quite perfect enough."

"It is very hard for cops to admit they have problems. The more publicity that can be given that fact, the more you can make people aware of that, the better. People put trust in you."

Simple Guidelines for Relieving Stress

The experts themselves would be the last to claim there's an easy or imminent solution to the complex problems of job-related stressors.

But experience and research have resulted in some preventive guidelines:

"Develop your own internal thank-you mechanism, and tell yourself you have done a good job when you know you have," advises Dr. Barry. "If you wait for a citizen to tell you, you'll never hear it."

"For God's sake, do not just socialize with police officers, do not just talk with cops about police work and end up feeling more negative," says Donovan. "Get with positive people in other professions. And if someone comes up to you at a party and starts in on you on a job matter because you're a police officer, find out what that person does. If he's a plumber, ask him to come up and fix your toilet. That ought to end it.

Escape from your job, give variety to your life, and maybe your wife will stop complaining, "For Christ's sake, aren't you ever off duty?"

Sufficient relaxation, good nutrition, and regular physical exercise are advocated by Trooper Kelly and Philip Trapasso of the State Police Stress Unit. (A Marblehead police officer who works the midnight shift says he sometimes eats six meals a day, does not sleep well, and is convinced he is "destroying" his body).

The State Police Research and Development Unit is currently forming a rigorous, ongoing physical fitness regimen for its officers.

Better relationships, according to Kelly, should be established between police units and the community and press.

"It works both ways. We need to stop seeing ourselves as Fort Apache," he argues. "We need to make ourselves more a part of communities. Also, both police and press would do well if they get along well. We need accurate flows of information."

Dr. Barry advocates "more cooperation between the administration and patrolman, a level of understanding" that does not result in subtle punishments against officers who seek mental health services.

"Don't stick the report in the personnel file and point it out to him when he comes up for promotion six or eight years later," he admonishes.

Perhaps most important of all, for personal emotional health and general well-being of marriage and family, share your feelings and share yourself.

"Vent. Communicate," they exhort. "Talk to, not at, each other."

"If you have to do what a police officer has to do, then you better be willing to share it with someone with whom you have a loving relationship," agrees Marblehead Patrolman Kenneth Nickerson. "My wife is my listening ear for both the good and the bad."

State Trooper Dean Bennett of the Peabody Barracks echoes this sentiment.

"My wife is very aware of what my job life is like, many a night she has sat up listening to me ramble and wind down. I do not deceive my family. If I am in a rotten mood, I tell them why, I tell them it's because of my day or something that happened, that it has nothing to do with them."

Bennett also says his days off are clearly "family days."

"I'm lucky. My pay differential with the master's means I don't have to do special details, and my kids look forward to my day off so we can do something together."

"Law enforcement marriages are hard, but there are successful ones, and they can be worked at," asserts Dr. Barry. "Spend time with the wife, communicate, even if just for a cup of coffee or an afternoon of window shopping."

The officers interviewed who experienced the most severe problems with stress were unanimous in defining an attitude change (both self-induced and from the public) they believed would have helped reduce the personal price they have already paid.

"Please do not look down on a cop because he has a problem," begs a Swampscott patrolman. "We are human, please see that we are human."

STUDENT PRESS MEET REAL POLICE; STUDENT POLICE MEET REAL PRESS

POLICING IN THE REAL WORLD: A TALE OF SQUIRRELS, CHIPMUNKS AND A SCARY RIDE

Mark F. Slattery

IT WAS approximately 10 A.M. on Friday, April 26, when officer Joe Ferguson drove up to the side entrance of the Framingham Police Station.

Most of my nervousness disappeared when he strode into the lobby and announced, with a wide grin on his face, "Okay kid, any bank holdup calls today and I'm sending you in first."

With that, we were off. I was still very unsure about how all of this would go. What would we be doing? Would I be able to question Ferguson? I wasn't even sure whether I should get in the front seat or the back (I sat in front). My biggest worry was that I would spend four hours driving around and not see any action. My worries were needless.

The "Chipmunk" Patrol

As Ferguson steered patrol car 959 out of the parking lot, he told me that for the next four hours, we would be patrolling Section 2, which is

---

(EDITOR'S NOTE: The following articles were originally papers submitted by Northeastern University students Mark F. Slattery, Stephen W. Bishe, Robert A. Costa and Lisa M. Pane as part of a project in the "Police and the Media" course taught in 1985 by myself and my husband Trooper Richard E. Kelly, Massachusetts State Police. Steve and Bob, as criminal justice majors, were assigned to spend a shift watching a reporter at work. Mark, as a journalism major, was asked to do the same with a police officer. Lisa, a journalism major, volunteered her brief overview of the process of newsgathering at the newspaper where she performed her cooperative employment assignment for the university. She did so in response to questions posed in class by her criminal justice studies classmates. All four graduated that year. Mark is with the Peace Corps in Guatemala. Steve is working in a law office and attending Suffolk University Law School, Boston, Massachusetts. Bob is employed in hotel security in Boston. Lisa is a reporter with the *Brattleboro Reformer* in Brattleboro, Vermont.)

made up of businesses and low-income housing on the south side of Framingham. Section 2 is one of the busiest of the eight sections Framingham is divided into, Ferguson explained. He likes working the south side, he said, because he stays busier, and thus the time goes by faster. He calls the middle and upperclass residential sections on the north side the "squirrels and chipmunks patrol."

At 42 years of age, Ferguson is a 20 year veteran who, at this point, likes what he is doing and is in no hurry to leave the force. Divorced, he has three children, one of whom recently joined the Framingham Police Department, despite his father's urging to get into another field of work.

While his divorce was not a direct result of his being a cop, it did contribute, he says, to a breakdown in communications. He talked about the night, a few years ago when he was still married, when he came home from a shift at 3 A.M. and immediately went into the bathroom for a long, hot shower. He had discovered a corpse in a junkyard "with maggots crawling all over it." Said Ferguson, "I just wanted to get under a shower and wash the stink off. I didn't tell her about it because I don't believe in bringing the job home with me. I didn't want to think about it anymore."

Some Disillusion

Ferguson said that he joined the police force for two reasons: job security, and because he wanted to be in public service. He said that while the job security has always been there, he quickly became disenchanted with reason number two, largely due to the drug scene he had underestimated and the domestic problems he encountered.

Asked to compare being a cop today to being a cop twenty years ago, Ferguson cited better work conditions, better cars and new modern equipment obtained by taking advantage of federal grant money. He talked about the gym that is just about completed.

Located in back of the police station, it has a basketball court, weight room, raquetball courts, sauna and shower facilities. It was built with money from the Framingham Police Union, on property donated by the town. Ferguson has also noticed an improved public perception of cops. "It's not great," he said, "but at least the pig business has gone by the boards."

Ferguson does not believe he is being chauvinistic when he says that while there is a place and a need for women on the force, they have "no business out there" on the streets. Besides the physical problems presented by a "120 pound female trying to subdue a 200 pound male," said Ferguson, "People just come down harder on women."

Visibility Important

As we slowly cruised the streets, Ferguson explained that his main purpose is to be seen. "It puts people at ease when they see the 'bluebird of happiness' rolling through," he said. "Except the housebreakers," he quickly added.

Ferguson has been on the day shift for about a year. He said that while the crimes are the same, there are much more of them during the night. He immediately noticed a big difference in the attitudes of people. "When I first got on the day shift, I couldn't believe it when people would wave to me and say 'hi!' " Already today, he has exchanged waves or hellos with a half dozen people.

Of course, he said, it doesn't matter what time of the day it is if you stop them for a violation. Most of them, he said, will become nasty, defensive, or both. "The biggest thief in the world will arch his back and say, 'Why are you picking on me?' Cops can do 50 good things for you. They remember the one bad thing."

Civility a Goal

Ferguson said he always tries to treat people in a civil manner. "But I've been on the force 20 years. I don't have to take shit." He is a firm believer in mind over matter—"I don't mind and you don't matter." "It's not nice to fool with Mother Nature, and it's not nice to—with Mr. Policeman," is another Fergusonian principle.

After driving through the streets of Section 2, we pulled into the parking lot of St. Stephen's Church to look for inspection sticker violations. Ferguson said he doesn't believe in speeding tickets, and only writes them because he has to. He gives a 15 mile radius, but believes it is unfair to give someone a $50 ticket for going 15 m.p.h. over the speed limit, when a person going 30 m.p.h. over the limit can only get the same $50 fine. "There should be a point system like they have in other states," Ferguson claims. "Like a buck for every mile over the limit."

Only a few minutes passed before a car without a sticker passed. Ferguson quickly pulled the car over, talked to the driver, and came back to the car seeming both irritated and amused. The driver had given him a registration with a local address, and a California license. "Claimed he didn't think he needed a sticker because he had a California license. Guy must think I'm an idiot." The driver got a ticket for his efforts.

At 12:15 P.M., after another drive through Section 2 and a quick stop at a convenient store for a lunch of soda and crackers, we parked once again in the parking lot of St. Stephen's.

We had been there about five minutes when a black Buick Skylark travelling westbound plowed into a yellow pickup truck about to exit a parking lot directly in front of us. Nobody was injured and damage was minimal. Ferguson drove across the road and began filling out the accident report. Two minutes later, before he even had a chance to finish, a beige van also travelling westbound rammed a beige and brown BMW from behind. A two-year-old child in the back seat became hysterical as the mother quickly unbuckled his car seat and took him out.

A Calming Influence

In what could have been a chaotic scene with six upset adults and one screaming child, Ferguson swiftly handled the situation by calming down all parties and then finishing the paperwork on the first accident before attending to the second one.

He finished with the second set of reports, and after advising the mother to take the child down the road to the Framingham Union Hospital for a precautionary checkup, we went back out on the streets. I was pretty excited about having witnessed two accidents. In fact, I figured if nothing happened the rest of the shift, I'd have still made out all right. But as things turned out, I hadn't seen nuthin' yet.

As we drove, Ferguson talked about the criminal justice system, especially pertaining to juveniles. "The system pampers and covers kids way too much. It's way too easy on them. Take stolen cars. If you catch him twice, throw his ass in the slammer. I'm not saying for a whole year, but for 30 days. If it was harder on juvies in the beginning, they wouldn't get into the big things later." Ferguson said he believes in programs like Scared Straight, in which juvenile offenders are brought into a prison to see what it's really like.

Neither Ferguson nor I realized how ironic his words would become in the next half hour.

It was about 1:15 P.M. when Ferguson got a radio call to report to the station, which is located in Section 2. Ferguson was given a complaint phoned in by a resident of the Muster Fields, a low income housing complex made up primarily of minorities. The complainant claimed that a car was speeding in and out of the complex, loudly peeling out the driveway each time it exited. The check of the car and license plate number showed that it had been stolen the previous week.

Ferguson and I drove down to the Muster Fields, and slowly cruised around the complex, looking for the car, a red 1974 Capri. We had just about completed a full circuit of the complex when Ferguson alertly spotted the Capri just as it turned a corner and disappeared from view. Had we arrived at our spot five seconds later, or had the Capri turned the corner five seconds sooner, the driver would have been home free. Talking, an hour earlier, about what makes a good cop, Ferguson had included in his list, "You gotta be lucky—be in the right place at the right time." He was.

The Chase Begins

Ferguson sped up to the Capri, which was going about 40 m.p.h. in a 25 m.p.h. zone. The driver did not realize we were behind him for several seconds. When he finally looked out the rear view mirror and saw us, he took a sharp left onto another road and accelerated to 50-55 m.p.h. Ferguson followed on his heels. The Capri soon came to a pronounced curve in the road, and the driver lost control trying to negotiate it. The Capri turned sideways, tires skipping and screeching over the surface of the road, and barely missed a row of parked cars. The driver, in trying to straighten the car out, compensated way too much and the Capri slammed headfirst into an empty school bus parked on the side of the road, pushing it over the curb and five feet onto someone's front lawn.

The driver and the passenger in the front seat were driven through the windshield, and ended up with their heads on the dashboards and their arms outstretched over the hood of the car. The girl in the rear was sprawled over the back of the front seat. It was completely silent. I was sure they were dead.

"I'm Hurt"

Five seconds passed (it seemed like 30 or 35 seconds, but I know it could only have been five) when the passenger in the front seat began screaming, "I'm hurt. Help me. Help me." Ferguson radioed for assistance and then walked over to the Capri and opened the front door to check out the situation. The driver pulled himself free of the windshield, struggled to his feet, took a step, and flopped to the ground, confirming the fact that it is very difficult to walk on a broken leg. The girl managed to get out the back door. With blood dripping from the three-inch gash across her forehead that would leave a permanent scar to remind her of this day, she quietly sat down on the grass and waited for help. Only the passenger in the front seat couldn't get out. He was trapped.

A firetruck and more cruisers arrived within minutes, and two ambulances pulled up several minutes later. Lt. Brent Larabee, who serves as police spokesman and was the person who handled my request, also arrived quickly on the scene. I got the impression he was more than a little alarmed when he heard over the radio that the patrol car in which I was riding was involved in a chase.

The emergency medical team got the trapped passenger out without too much trouble, and tended to all of the injured. The driver was taken away with an air bag protecting his broken leg and his right arm in a sling to protect his broken collarbone. The trapped passenger needed a neck brace to protect against spinal injury. An officer was required to ride with the ambulances, since all three were under arrest for using a motor vehicle without authority, operating to endanger and speeding.

It was soon learned that the driver, a 14-year-old student from Farley Middle School, had already been arrested earlier in April for three stolen car charges. He apparently wasn't worried about the consequences he would face in juvenile court.

No Sympathy

The consensus of the officers on the scene seemed to be that the kids in the car got what they deserved. While I didn't expect an outpouring of sympathy for them, I was surprised at the apparent lack of concern about their condition. While nobody said anything, I sensed that several of the cops felt that this was a sort of justice. The court system would only slap them on the wrist. At least now they had paid for their crimes.

Both police and neighbors who had gathered talked of how lucky it was that no kids had been outside at the time. One mother said, "Thank God my son was inside taking his nap. He's usually out riding his Big Wheel on the sidewalk." Her comment was made more dramatic by the fact that several tricycles, Big Wheels and other toys cluttered the front yards of several nearby houses. In another hour, many students from the McCarthy Elementary School would be walking down this road on their way home.

As for my own reaction to the incident; when we first got the call, I was excited about the prospect of seeing some action. Even after Ferguson had spotted the Capri and sped up behind it, I was thinking, "Great, I'll get to see Ferguson make an arrest. This will be great for my paper."

When I realized the Capri was not going to stop voluntarily, and Ferguson hit the sirens, thoughts of seeing an arrest and of my paper vanished, and a strong fear took its place. Immediately, my left hand dug into the seat and my right hand clutched the door handle. My feet nearly put a hole in the floor as I braced myself for the worst. I thought for a second of putting on my seat belt, but I couldn't talk my hands into action.

The chase didn't last more than 10 seconds. The Capri was out of control almost from the start. I knew it was going to hit something. It was only a matter of time.

Relief Reaction

When the Capri slammed into the bus, I was filled mostly with revulsion, because I honestly thought they were dead. I was also relieved. The crash meant the chase was over and I was safe. I did feel some sympathy for the accident victims, but I also agreed with the cop who called them "stupid sons of bitches." After I got over the shock, I reverted back to my line of thinking before the chase, "This will be great for my paper." One indication of the shock I experienced is that, as I now look over my notes, I realize that most of the notations I made after the accident are illegible.

I knew that my tour of duty had ended when Lt. Larabee asked me sarcastically, "Seen enough?" I had. Ferguson dropped me off at the police station before heading to Framingham Union Hospital to check on the victims/suspects.

In four short hours, I had witnessed three accidents. I had not prepared myself for anything like what happened. I realized that it must be very difficult for police officers to ride around all day performing their usual tasks, yet still be prepared for anything to happen, like Ferguson was on April 26.

On the way to the station, I asked Ferguson about his actions and reactions to the incident. "My adrenalin was going," he said. "I wasn't scared, though, because I was in control of the situation. I wanted to get alongside the car so if the driver stopped, got out and ran, I wouldn't have to chase him on foot. You were scared because you were in the passenger seat and it's five times worse for the person in the passenger seat. You had no control over the situation."

It was a good experience for me, in that I was able to feel some of the danger and pressure that police officers must be ready to face every day. I was very fortunate to ride with a good, veteran cop who was eager to share his experiences and ideas on police work. Despite all the positive aspects, however, I was glad when it was over.

ON THE ROAD AND ON THE BEAT

Stephen W. Bishé

and

Robert A. Costa

Bishé's Report

I arrived at WEEI's newsroom at 3:50 A.M. and waited for Steve to show up. The newsroom was basically what I expected, or imagined: a large, open room with no windows, lots of desks and typewriters, scanners, a teletype machine, and lots of electronic machinery. I found it to be cluttered, yet organized. While I waited I watched three TV sets, one tuned to each of the networks; during this time there were 2 or 3 employees (all in very casual attire) pounding the keys of ancient manual typewriters. As more personnel came in, they were friendly and cooperative, yet all were busy.

Steve arrived at 4:25 A.M. and after some introductory banter, took me over to his desk, where he has a Bearcat 220, a Bearcat 300 and a Regency scanner set up. These are constantly squawking, and he follows up any interesting calls. One of the first things Steve does is go through the latest and the first editions of the *Globe* and *Herald* to see if any stories have changed; if so, he may make a copy and look into the story.

Fire Calls Come

Before we really got into anything, there were two separate fire calls from the scanners, one in Salem and one in Mattapan. The Salem fire turned out to be pretty bad, and something he spent a lot of time on during the morning. Steve called the Salem police and got enough information to do a live report from the newsroom about it. When broadcasting live from the newsroom, Steve likes to have the scanners loud and typewriters going for background noise — he says it's more authentic and sounds more like a newsroom.

In between news of the fire in Salem, Steve "made his rounds;" this entails calling police departments to see if anything is happening. He has a printed list of departments to call, starting with metropolitan Boston and going through the state police, the "major suburbs," and if it's slow, the "outlying suburbs." On this particularly slow, rainy morning, Steve called 45 departments where reportedly nothing was happening. He has what he explained as a "telephone relationship" with most of the departments—many of the phone answerers know him through his daily calls and usually, he said, let him know if anything is going on (this was a very slow morning as Steve spent 10 minutes chatting with one cop about golf and fishing!)

Independent Worker

Steve pretty much works on his own and makes his own decisions about what stories to cover, with just a little guidance from his editor. He said he basically covers whatever is "newsworthy," although he didn't elaborate as to his own definition of that term. He explained to me that they keep myriad background files of cases still open, those unsolved or where a suspect is still-at-large, etc. These files contain almost anything, from newspaper clippings to WEEI's own old scripts of a story—anything from which they can create a story with little other present information; these files are used when a suspect is arrested, or paroled, etc., in order to make a coherent story. Also a boon to a good, or a better story, is to have taped interviews, and to use about 20 seconds of tape, called a "bit," during an on-scene broadcast. Steve always asks the interviewee's permission before taping, and usually goes through a mini-rehearsal of what he wants to be on tape. He explained continuous-loop cartridges (carts) used when taking bits of a taped interview to be used during a broadcast, including how to splice the tape (to eliminate "ums" and "uhs" thereby making the interviewee sound better), how to record onto the cart, and how to use the cart in a broadcast and keep the whole thing running smoothly. Steve also told how he likes to pull more bits out a taped interview for the next broadcast so it appears the story is being worked on between broadcasts.

The Night's Stories

By 6:30 A.M. Steve got the Deputy Fire Marshal of Salem on the phone for a taped interview and we found out that it was a multiple-alarm fire which started in a residential structure and spread to a laundromat, causing $200,000-250,000 damage. Three people were injured, two with severe burns and a fireman with smoke inhalation.

The fire had suspicious origins and is under investigation by the arson squad.

In another story (brought about by a tip from a colleague) Steve found out (and I think got a scoop) about an unusual DWI arrest by the MDC in the Blue Hills.

A rookie cop, on his second week out of the academy, during a routine stop with his veteran partner, found two hand grenades on the front seat of the suspect's car; on investigation, they found four rifles, four pistols, teargas, grenade launchers, ammunition and four knives in the trunk. The Bureau of Alcohol, Tobacco and Firearms was called in. The man arrested claimed he was a "gun collector."

The final story he covered was on the road. We rode up to Peabody in Steve's company car, which is also loaded with scanners, a two-way radio, and a cellular phone. In Peabody we went to the police station where earlier they arrested a youth for making and selling bombs in the high school. By the time we arrived two bombs (of seven outstanding) had detonated and three had been turned in, leaving two more outstanding. The kid had a book on how to make explosives, had bought all the materials legally, and did it to make money.

We interviewed one of the detectives who made the arrest; he was very cooperative, answered all questions to the best of his knowledge, was not evasive on any matters, and even went off the record to explain how the arrest came to be. I noticed that when the detective asked to go off the record, Steve put his pad and pencil down on the table, and when talking to a lieutenant who didn't want to be interviewed he put down his tape recorder — on inquiry Steve said he didn't think most reporters consciously put aside their pads or recorders, and some, he said, even use off the record information. Steve also interviewed and asked questions before going on tape so the officer knew what to expect and what he would answer with.

Steve did a broadcast over his two-way radio from the car using a bit from the taped interview, and he taped two more "updates" in to the station to be used in later broadcasts, enabling him to be free to pursue other matters while seemingly still reporting on the arrest.

Steve is basically after updates and any new general information — he doesn't get super detailed or nit-picky. I asked him whether the amount of cooperation we got from the Peabody Police was usual or not and he replied that he usually doesn't have much trouble with police because he's quite honest and frank with them, but not pushy. He usually lets them more or less call the shots. He told me he often "plays dumb" and has the officer repeat information Steve already knows. If the officer is somewhat tight-lipped, he says he tries to "schmooze them up a little," or butter them up, trying to make them feel more comfortable and loosen up, and realize that he's not there to crucify them. Some police are nervous because of past bad press, so Steve tries to calm them down, and through editing, splicing, and taking bits, he tries to make the officer sound good and feel good, thereby getting whatever facts he can and presenting them, and the police, in the best possible light.

Some Surprises

Since I really didn't know what to expect, it's difficult to say whether my experience differed from my expectations. My first impressions with the newsroom, the studio and the staff were basically what I expected, based on what I've seen in movies and on TV shows, so there was no real surprises there. I'd have to say that the newsgathering and reporting were not exactly what I expected; however, I really didn't know what to expect — I was completely naive to the workings of a radio station, so the whole experience was truly enlightening and educational. One thing I didn't realize was that when we hear those on-scene broadcasts, they may not really be live at the time we're hearing them — many of them are live-on-tape. It seems that most, if not all of the information is gathered and processed at one time, then spread out over the course of hours by using bits and tapes. Another thing I noticed is that some information is "withheld," or not fully reported, during the initial covering of the story — sometimes this is because the information simply is not known at the time, while in other situations the public is spoonfed only small pieces of information at a time, thus leaving room for expansion and future updates, even though there has been only one information-gathering interview.

I must say that I did not expect, and was pleasantly surprised, when Steve put his pad and pencil, and tape recorder, aside for off the record conversation. I think it's a great technique, and the detective seemed suitably impressed; the whole mood of the conversation became even more relaxed, friendly and cooperative than it already was. While it may have been a small gesture, it certainly added to trust, rapport, and respect during the interview — Steve respected the detective's request, and I know the detective respected Steve's integrity. I applaud Steve for his handling of the matter, and I think it would be a good rule of thumb for reporters to show such respect, especially when it doesn't take much effort, as in this case. Simple, courteous and respectful gestures as this may make a big difference in a police-press relationship, and I think matters such as this should be emphasized in police-reporter training.

Costa's Report

At 3:40 A.M., on 4-30-85, I arrived on the 44th floor of the Prudential Center to meet Steve Sbraccia from WEEI Radio News. Steve has been with WEEI for three years and with WHDH Radio for the previous four years.

During my short stay in the newsroom I observed many things. At first I was overwhelmed at the amount of equipment that was in the office. I noticed police scanners, teletype machines, copying machines, reel to reel recorders, television sets, radio base units, and other types of equipment. There were three other people in the office at this time besides myself. I'm not sure what their titles were, but they were responsible for editing taped material, writing reports and keeping some type of log, listening to the scanners and dispatching reporters to the scenes of various incidents. At this time of the morning Boston was relatively quiet.

Quite a Car

At 4:05 A.M., I met Steve in the lobby of the Pru and proceeded to his vehicle which was parked in the garage. From the outside it appeared like any other Chevy Caprice. However, from the inside, it was a totally different machine. In the vehicle, in addition to the two-way radio, there were three scanners which contained the frequencies of Boston Police, Metropolitan Police, T-Police, State Police, and numerous other local police agencies. Also included were Boston Fire Department and other metro-fire department frequencies.

In addition to this equipment, there was a portable scanner, a portable two-way unit, and a cellular phone. Also in the vehicle were various codes and breakdown of call numbers taped to the dashboard. There were numerous maps of the city and metro-area as well as a code book which contained addresses of the various fire alarm boxes in Boston. When an alarm box is activated it sends a series of beeps over the scanner. After the beeps are counted, they can be looked up in the code box for a corresponding address. The last, but not least important part of his equipment, was a portable taperecorder without which he could not function as an on-the-scene reporter.

Watching the Interviews

By 4:15 A.M., we had arrived at University Hospital to check out a water main break. At this point it was under control. I observed Steve interview what I thought to be a maintenance worker at the hospital. Steve approached the worker, identified himself, and then proceeded to question him. At first they were close in stance. Then the worker started to shift from side to side and appeared hesitant to give out any information that wasn't already known. Then when Steve asked him some specific questions about how much water was lost, or what was the damage, he walked away.

We left the scene at 4:30 and due to low police activity we stopped for coffee and doughnuts. In these early hours of the morning I observed very few vehicles on the streets. There were no people walking about, nor did I observe any police vehicles. It was an extremely quiet morning as far as police activity was concerned. Even though there were many transmissions over the police frequencies, most turned out to be false alarms or minor incidents.

Steve next received a radio call from base instructing him to proceed to Quincy Shipyard to cover the General Dynamic layoffs. We arrived at the shipyard at 5:30 A.M., and parked across the street from the entrance. Upon arriving, I noticed that we had attracted the attention of the security guards at the front gate. We received some curious stares from the guards as well as from the general public. We remained at this location until 10 A.M.

Steve made live broadcasts approximately every half hour with statements from some workers. I observed him, from the vehicle, interview six to eight workers. The interviews were conducted in the street, on the sidewalk, or in a small diner near the front gate. They lasted anywhere from one minute to five minutes. It appeared that the workers were not inhibited with Steve's presence or his interviewing. I observed a reporter get escorted off General Dynamic's property after attempting to interview workers. There were also reporters from WRKO, and WBZ Radio. I observed friendly contact and sharing of information between Steve and the other reporter from WRKO, even though they were competing to get the story on the air before the other.

We left Quincy at approximately 10:00 A.M. and proceeded back into Boston. We did respond to a couple of EMT calls, but they were minor incidents such as one involving a diabetic who forgot to take her medication.

During the shift, since there were few police calls, I had the chance to ask Steve about police/media contact, and his own views and experiences on the subject. Steve stated that whenever the police and the media come together someone is going to get hurt; whether it is the victim, the offender, or the police. The real skill is trying to minimize the hurt.

'Green' Reporters Hurt Police

He stated that there is a great need for police and media cooperation. He believes the police show a great willingness to talk to reporters and release information. However, he feels problems arise with the young, "green" reporters. They want to know everything about the incident and participants at that instant.

They are too pushy and do not know when to back off. They forget the rules about getting information such as: criminal records, names, ages, etc. They want everything but are not willing to give anything. He stated that he personally knows of police officers getting "burnt" after releasing confidential information to reporters, only to have it show up in the papers, radio, or television. This type of reporter is a great source of stress and frustration to the officer.

Steve feels police are even willing to talk about sensitive issues such as the prospect of drug testing in the Boston Police Department. However, they fear not the media, nor the public, but have a greater fear of their colleagues if they are discovered. The police fraternity can and does exert more pressure on an officer than the public. This is an added stress that is not seen by the media or the public when an officer refuses to talk to the press.

Common Sense Needed

Steve stated that there is a need for more responsible reporting. The best quality that a reporter should possess is good common sense. The reporter should know what the limits are in any situation. The reporter should be sincere and willing to give as well as take. The reporter should ask questions related only to this specific incident and not go off on tangents.

Steve feels the direction of police/media relations appears optimistic. The police are hiring better educated men and women who can see the need to cooperate with the media more than the older personnel. He said that he has a very good relationship with area police, who see him as sincere and straightforward.

WHOM DO I ALIENATE — THE COPS OR MY EDITOR?

Lisa M. Pane

At a major metropolitan daily newspaper such as *The Boston Globe,* copy flow means the involvement of sometimes up to three reporters, two story (or assigning) editors, two copy editors, and various upper-level editors. Here's how a typical story is prepared:

By listening to police scanners located in both the photo department and on the city desk and the news radio stations, and by watching the wire services for stories, the story editor on the city desk develops a "budget" of stories to be covered by the general assignment and police/courts reporters. These stories are assigned by story editors to one — and sometimes more than one — of the approximately 100 reporters assigned to the city desk. The degree to which stories are covered is determined by the assigning editor and overseen by the "Glass Houses," those editors at management level such as managing editors and executive editors;

The Reporter's Job

The reporter then either covers the story by phone or by driving to the scene(s). Not all the sources needed for some stories are available at the scene(s), so reporters may have to finish calling sources once they've returned to the office;

Once at the office, the reporter checks in with the assigning editor to let the person know the drift and direction of the story, the space needed for the article, etc. This is also one of the many times when an editor might suggest other sources that should be contacted for comment, questions that should (or should not) be asked, and suggest story direction;

After finishing the writing end of the article, the reporter sends (electronically) the story to the city desk where it is edited for style, factual and grammatical accuracy;

While all of the above is taking place, in the back of the editors' and reporters' minds are the deadlines within which they must work. At the *Globe,* a morning paper, a reporter must have his/her story sent to the city desk by 6 P.M., to be edited in time to send to the copy desk so it can make publication for the first edition of the paper. Second and third edition copy should be sent to the city desk by 7 and 8 P.M., respectively;

The copy desk consists of approximately 10 copy editors and a "slotman"—the head copy editor who assigns what stories each editor is to work on. Copy editors write the headlines and determine the size of the headlines, write photo captions, determine which pictures are to be used at what size. They also design/layout the page, determining which stories will go where and how long they can be. Copy editors are supposed to check for grammatical errors, and doublecheck city desk editors' efforts at avoiding libelous and slanderous articles and other content problems;

As articles are edited, headlines and photo captions written, and layouts completed, these items are sent down to the composing room where they come out as "cold type" contact sheets ready to be "pasted up" on grid sheet boards the size of a printed *Globe* page. Each page in the *Globe* is pasted up on these boards, a negative made of it and transferred to a plate used to print the paper;

Certain copy editors are assigned to go to the composing room where the pages are being "made up," to ensure the layout is being followed and the headlines and captions match the assigned stories and pictures. Generally, they are supposed to catch those mistakes that occasionally get through the computer system from the copy desk to the composing room. If time is short, many errors may go unnoticed; and even if time is not tight, there are bound to be errors that slip by.

Deadlines Need Respect

Often the most difficult part of covering a police-related story is the lack of understanding that deadlines must be met. It is a particularly trying time when deadline is nearing and calls to police sources (inevitably) are made when shifts are changing. This usually occurs on late-breaking stories or stories that occurred earlier in the day but of which we were unaware.

I can't count the number of times I was told that all "records of that incident are locked up in the records department and cannot be retrieved until the next morning." Unfortunately, neither editors nor readers can wait that long for the information to be released. But equally as unfortunate is that the reporter is at the officer's mercy. The reporter can neither argue with the officer, thereby alienating the source, nor can he/she remain passive and accept such lines thereby alienating his/her editor. What ultimately follows is just one big game of negotiations that could be avoided if both parties understood the time restraints and pressures under which they work.

POLICE VS. THE PRESS:
THERE'S ALWAYS TENSION

MICHAEL KIERNAN

JOHN KATZENBACH, a reporter for the *Miami Daily News,* had a sensational story. For two months the press had known of a major breakthrough by Miami police in solving one of the city's most controversial murders, but authorities had refused to disclose any details. Now Katzenbach, with the help of a tip and some recently filed court documents, had come up with the name of the key witness: Jan Cleveland Thurston, a 28-year-old freelance artist and temporary laborer, who in a court deposition named two men as the killers of Victor Butler, a Miami police officer gunned down in an unprovoked street ambush in February 1971.

"I was excited when I learned about the court deposition," said Katzenbach, recalling his story of last December. "I hurried back to the office and wrote the story quickly for the next day's paper." Then, said Katzenbach, he began to have second thoughts. Would his story destroy an eight-year police investigation? Did the prosecutor know his star witness would be on page one the next day?

Concerned, Katzenbach called the prosecutor to warn him of the story. The prosecutor, in turn, immediately dispatched two detectives to Thurston's home out of fear that the story might alarm the star witness. Meanwhile, another *Miami News* reporter went to Thurston's home to get a first-person interview.

Michael Kiernan, who has worked as a reporter for columnist Jack Anderson and the *Washington Star,* is currently an executive producer in charge of series and special projects at WRC-TV News in Washington, D.C. This article originally appeared in the July, 1979 edition of *Police Magazine,* a publication no longer in print. The interviews with the well-known police beat reporters appeared in the same issue.

What happened next has not yet been clearly established. But one thing is certain: The next day Thurston had vanished, out of reach of both the press and police. Several weeks later a tape recording surfaced in which Thurston denied everything he had said in his earlier deposition.

"I don't blame either the press or the police for what happened," said Richard Katz, the state prosecutor handling the case. "But I do think there's a definite correlation between the witness vanishing and the reporter showing up at his house. I think they probably spooked him. By the time the detectives got there, Thurston was gone."

Said Katzenbach: "There's always tension between police and the press because our jobs are different. Sometimes there's no practical effect of our conflicting roles. But in this case the press appeared to have an impact on the case."

Each day, in fact, the press has a profound impact on police work. At any given moment somewhere in the country an exchange is taking place between these two venerable American institutions. Often, it is no more than an exchange of information—a simple question by a reporter, a straightforward answer by a police spokesperson. Other times, as the Miami case suggests, relations can become strained. Tensions rise. Words are spoken. The result: mutual distrust. Such conflict, in differing degrees, is now occurring in major cities across the country:

- In Los Angeles the press recently filed a lawsuit to force the police department to release records of shootings by police dating back to 1976. The newspapers are trying to discover the disposition of the cases and any possible pattern in the shootings.
- In Philadelphia relations are so strained that officers at the scene of a crime risk disciplinary action if they are seen talking to reporters. Some newsmen have resorted to meeting off-duty police officers in bars or at their homes to find out details of a particular crime.
- In Maryland's Prince Georges County police have publicly singled out the news media—particularly *The Washington Post*—for creating an environment of hostility toward police that culminated last April when a jury acquitted of murder a 16-year-old black youth who had shot and killed two officers in a police station. The youth, who told the jury that he was beaten by police before the shooting, was instead found guilty of manslaughter. "It's all your fault," an officer told reporters after the verdict. "You have blood on your hands. . . . "

- In San Francisco, two former police officers and a former prosecutor successfully sued the *San Francisco Examiner* for libel after the paper published allegations that while working for the city the three had harassed and coerced a murder suspect. The jury ordered the *Examiner* and two reporters to pay $4.5 million in damages.
- In Miami two newspapers have sued Dade County Public Safety Director E. Wilson Purdy for refusing to release investigative files on alleged police misconduct.

The police and the press are more at odds than ever these days. "We're the enemy," said Pat Collins, a television reporter for WDVM-TV in Washington, D.C., who has covered crime in the nation's capital for ten years. Added Megan Rosenfield, a reporter for *The Washington Post* who covered the District of Columbia police for more than a year: "They [the police] hate us. . . . For one thing, we come from such different worlds."

But are the police and the press really such enemies? What, indeed, is the relationship between the two? Are reporters covering the police any differently today than, say, a decade ago? And are police departments responding to such coverage any differently?

To answer these questions *Police Magazine* interviewed police officials, prosecutors, community activists, and reporters from both the print and the electronic media in seven major U.S. cities: New York, Chicago, Los Angeles, Boston, Philadelphia, Miami, and Washington, D.C.

One fact that these interviews made very clear was that the press and the police have more than a little in common. There are, in fact, some striking similarities. Both are powerful, visible institutions. Both are highly structured and assign personnel specific "beats" for which they are responsible. Both prize ingenuity, individual effort, and investigative skills. Both have attracted large numbers of ambitious young men—and increasing numbers of young women—to their ranks in recent years. Both are often secretive about their methods of operation and frequently must rely on anonymous sources for information. Both espouse high ideals and speak often and publicly of their importance to the community. And when it comes to criticism, neither appears especially adept at acknowledging its own failings.

Despite their similarities, both reporters and police officers have long viewed each other in simplified, stereotyped terms. This appears to be changing somewhat as younger, better educated men and women join each institution. Still, the stereotypes of the hard-bitten, cynical reporter and the tough, sometimes brutal cop are sufficiently prevalent in some cities to disrupt efforts at improving police-press relations.

"Right now *The Boston Globe* does not have the trust and confidence of the rank-and-file members of the police department," said David Nyhan, the *Globe*'s metropolitan editor. "One reason is that Boston's is an older police department. Many of the men are in their mid-40s. They're pretty set in their ways and they're not about to change their attitude toward the press even though we'd like to improve relations."

Police chiefs often play key roles in setting the tone for police-press relations. As a general rule, they are extremely wary of the press. "The power of the press in police politics is awesome," writes Patrick V. Murphy, former New York police commissioner and now head of the Police Foundation, in his book *Commissioner*. "A bad press can quickly bring down even a good chief. A good press can keep a bad chief in power. A capable chief, even if he has the respect and support of the mayor or city manager, can become a political liability if constantly under fire from the news media. A chief who is intensely disliked by the mayor or the city manager may nevertheless be invulnerable to removal if the department continues to receive rave reviews in the press."

The press is generally respectful, if not laudatory, of police chiefs in most cities. Even in Miami and Los Angeles, where the press is suing for the right to examine internal police records, editorial writers have made a point of explaining to readers that in general they think the chiefs are doing a good job.

Rank-and-file police are also wary of the press. Police officers, in fact, often test reporters—sometimes they even put them through a kind of initiation rite—before confiding in them. One reporter recalled that, during his first days covering police headquarters, officials "would try to gross you out to see if you could take their kind of life." Recalled Rosenfeld of the Post: "When I first went to D.C. police headquarters, the homicide detectives showed me pictures of some very gory murders just to see how I would react. I looked at the pictures, which were awful, and just made a face. They laughed and accepted me after that."

Sometimes the test is given to determine whether a reporter will keep his word. "I've been tested several times," said Neal Hirschfeld of the *New York Daily News*. "A new detective you meet will deliberately tell you something off the record just to see how you use his information. If you use it in a way that gets him in trouble, you've double-crossed him in his eyes and he'll never talk to you again." Reporters who pass such tests are often given inside information about ongoing investigations. The problem is that under this system reporters often will not write about investigations until authorities have given them approval. "Sometimes you wonder who you're working for," said one veteran police reporter. "But at the same time no one wants to blow an investigation."

Media coverage of police tends to be sporadic and inconsistent—positive one week, negative the next—often without apparent reason. Such coverage is one factor police cite to explain why they mistrust the press. "You don't know what to expect from reporters," complained one D.C. detective. "One day you'll see a story praising you to the hilt for a successful 'sting' operation. The next day the same reporter will be tearing down the department with a story about officials retiring on disabilities."

Reporters have similarly mixed feelings about police officials. *Washington Post* reporter Ron Shaffer, who recently wrote a book about the D.C. "sting" operation as well as a series of critical stories about police retiring on questionable disabilities, complained: "Several ranking police officials including the District's police chief [Burtell Jefferson] have an obvious, personal dislike for me because for my stories on disability retirements. They can't understand why they should cooperate with a reporter who has criticized the department. They simply ignore the fact that I spent a year writing a book about a police accomplishment. That's all forgotten. They only remember the negative stories."

Those negative stories can be more painful than ever to police, now that the electronic media are a dominant force in local coverage. Police officials in many large cities say they are spending more time dealing with radio and television reporters than newspaper reporters. In Chicago, for example, police officials estimate that 65 percent of their news inquiries come from television and radio stations. At police headquarters in Boston during a recent month, queries from television and radio stations outnumbered those from Boston's two daily newspapers four-to-one.

Recognizing the potential impact of expanded local news coverage by the media, police departments are revamping their public information offices to accommodate the electronic media. In Chicago, Capt. David M. Mozee, director of the police department's news affairs office, spent a year interning with a local television station to learn the ropes of the television news business. Last year New York Police Commissioner Robert J. McGuire chose Ellen Fleysher, a 34-year-old correspondent for WCBS-TV, to head New York's sprawling police public information office.

"The police really cater to the media these days," said Al Lewis, veteran police reporter for *The Washington Post*. "They don't care about the print press that much anymore. When they hold a press conference, they hold it for the television people. If the television people are late, they'll delay the press conference and wait for them. The police are very accommodating."

Despite, or perhaps partly because of the competition from TV and radio stations, the nation's daily newspapers seem to have become less interested in providing day-to-day coverage of crimes, unless they are particularly bizarre or heinous. When a crime breaks, the TV reporters will almost always "scoop" the newspapers, simply because they can get a camera there immediately and flash the news onto the TV screen within minutes, while newspaper readers have to wait until the following morning.

The de-emphasis on crime coverage also has to do with changes within the newspaper industry. As newspaper competition continues to dwindle in most U.S. cities, successful newspapers no longer are depending on sensational crime stories bannered across their front pages to boost street sales. As a result, said Lee Dye, assistant metropolitan editor for the *Los Angeles Times*, "the rape or murder that used to appear on page one ten to fifteen years ago now sometimes doesn't get into the paper at all. We have reporters who do police reporting, of course, but we don't have anyone who covers the Los Angeles Police Department full-time."

Editors in other cities echoed Dye's contention that newspapers' day-to-day coverage of crime is not what it used to be. *The Boston Globe, The New York Times* and the *Washington Star,* for example, no longer assign reporters full-time at police headquarters to cover crime. In Boston, in fact, there is no longer a press room for reporters at police headquarters. The time-honored practice of reporters inspecting crime blotters at station houses for news has given way at many newspapers to periodic telephone checks with police headquarters to keep track of breaking crime stories.

Not all newspapers are de-emphasizing their daily coverage of crime and police. The *New York Daily News,* for example, still has six full-time staffers who cover the New York City Police Department and its 24,000 sworn officers. Moreover, even those editors who say their newspapers are toning down crime coverage acknowledge a continued fascination with what one editor calls "the super-crime story . . . the Son-of-Sam crime . . . the kind of crime that has all the elements of horror and suspense." The consensus, among police and reporters alike, is that readers will always remain interested in such stories. As one public information officer in New York's police department put it, "The press isn't really de-emphasizing crime. They're just becoming more selective."

One crime the media repeatedly selects as newsworthy is the hostage situation. The media's enthusiasm for covering such crimes, in fact, has created new tensions between the police and the press. In the District of Columbia, for example, police officials complain that during the past five years the press has complicated their handling of three separate hostage situations: the two-day take-over of a basement cellblock in the U.S. District Court House by two prisoners in November 1974; the three-hour seizure of a fashionable Georgetown men's clothing store by three armed gunmen in November 1976, and the three-day seizure of three Washington buildings by a Hanafi Muslim sect in March 1977.

In each instance, police officials said, reporters tied up phone lines trying to interview the gunmen and greatly complicated police efforts to negotiate a surrender.

While many newspapers have lost interest in the latest burglary or armed robbery, they have pursued another kind of crime story with Watergate-inspired zest. There is hardly a major city in America where there has not been some recent investigation and coverage of alleged police brutality or corruption. This is now, as it always was, the stuff of which Pulitzer Prizes are made, and the new breed of reporter will pursue such stories relentlessly.

Reporters in several cities have resorted to using local freedom of information act provisions—"sunshine" laws—and even lawsuits to pry loose documents on alleged police misconduct. "For me, the lawsuit was distasteful," wrote John McMullan, executive editor of *The Miami Herald* last March after his newspaper had gone to court demanding access to police disciplinary files. But, he added, "the disciplining of police cannot be left as a purely internal matter, handled only by fellow police.... The *Herald* wants a look at the closed disciplinary files we feel the public has a right to see under the sunshine law. We are not seeking the files of current inquiries into alleged misconduct, since such revelations conceivably hamper ongoing investigations."

Some reporters and police officials fear that such lawsuits threaten close, informal relationships between individual reporters and police officials. "I don't need a lawsuit to find out what's going on in the department," said one veteran police reporter in New York. "That kind of thing would only help button my sources up."

Police rightly complain that the press takes too much interest in their sins and not enough interest in their accomplishments. In fact, most newspapers make almost no attempt to analyze the day-to-day performance of police departments—any more than they do of any other government institution. Few newspaper readers—and even fewer television viewers—will ever be exposed to information on the latest investigative, forensic or patrol techniques. Neither will they learn how effective their police department has been at curbing crime, except when the FBI publishes its quarterly Uniform Crime Reports, and UCR statistics are at best a very crude measurement of any police department's effectiveness.

In Atlanta, for example, of 135 newspaper articles on police issues published by the city's two major newspapers from February 1978 through February 1979, only one article addressed police performance. That article, written by Ken Willis and Barry King of the Atlanta *Constitution,* attempted to link a reported increase in crime with a "manpower crisis" in the Atlanta Police Bureau. The other 134 stories—most of which dealt with budgets, pay disputes and a police cheating scandal—certainly had significance for readers, but the articles did little to inform the public about how local police were protecting Atlanta citizens.

Reporters in other cities noted similar shortcomings in their coverage of police. "We cover crime very well, but we cover the police department very badly," said John Katzenbach about police press coverage in Miami. "It's extremely rare that you see a really incisive behind-the-scenes look at how the department is being run or what impact it has on community life." Added Thomas Crosby, a ten-year veteran at the *Washington Star* who now covers criminal justice: "If I had to characterize in one word our coverage of the police in Washington, I would say it's shoddy. Neither *The Washington Post* nor the *Star* are very consistent in their coverage of police issues."

One newspaper that has made a major attempt to assess police performance is the *Los Angeles Times,* which published a lengthy 20-page section on the Los Angeles Police Department in December 1977. The special report, entitled "The LAPD: How Good is It?" included 21 articles on various aspects of police work. One article discussed arrest and conviction rates. Another compared police in New York with police in Los Angeles. Still another took an in-depth look at the political clout of top Los Angeles police officials at City Hall. The *Times* also commissioned a poll that showed that more than two-thirds of the populace approved of the way the police were doing their job.

While the *Times* section represents one of the most impressive efforts to date by a newspaper to evaluate police performance, it has not started a trend among other papers. One reason is the expense. To produce the section, the Times assigned 11 reporters full-time to the project for three months. Publishing and payroll costs amounted to well over $125,000. Besides the expense of such projects, reporters at other newspapers question whether readers are interested in such large "take-out" sections on issues like police performance. "I couldn't get through it all myself," said Hirschfeld of the New York *Daily News* about the special police section. "And I cover the police."

Harvard professor and criminologist James Q. Wilson viewed the *Los Angeles Times* special section as a rare event in the press's coverage of police. "The press isn't in the business to tell the public how our major institutions work; their basic interest is relating unusual events of public significance." As a result, said Wilson, "the press usually offers a very vague and largely inaccurate view of day-to-day police life." Even its coverage of crime is "sporadic," said Wilson. He added that the public would benefit if the press more frequently followed up on crime stories and traced people through the entire criminal justice system, from arrest to trial to sentencing. "If newspapers did only that on a more routine basis, it would improve the quality of debate about crime in the cities," Wilson said.

Police officials say they would welcome efforts by the press to publish more stories about day-to-day problems in their departments, but that reporters generally appear more interested in stories they can do in a few hours than stories that require several days or weeks of research.

"The press is under a lot of pressure to get results fast, just like we are," said Albert Knuipis, a police public information official in Boston. "Sometimes you don't have a lot of time to think about what's going on. You have a job to do, and you do it."

COVERING THE POLICE BEAT

MICHAEL KIERNAN

AL LEWIS, 66, may be the dean of police reporters working for major U.S. newspapers. Joining *The Washington Post* as a cub reporter in 1935, he has covered the Washington (D.C.) Police Department ever since—44 years, through eight Presidents and nine chiefs of police. All told, he has worked on more than 100,000 crime stories, sometimes as many as a dozen a day. Though now in semi-retirement, Lewis still reports crime stories for the *Post* three days a week from his desk at police headquarters. "Uncle Al is incredible," said one ranking police official. "He's been here longer than most of us have been alive." Following are excerpts from an interview with Lewis.

On covering homicides in the early 1940s: "Back then you'd never go to the scene of the crime without a bottle of booze in your pocket. It often came in handy. On a murder case, you'd hang around outside waiting for the homicide detectives to finish their initial inspection of the scene and you'd strike up a conversation with one of the uniformed police officers who was first on the scene. After a while, you'd take the officer aside, offer him a swig or two from your bottle and ask him for all the details. It nearly always worked. By the time the homicide unit was finished, you were on the phone to the city desk with the story.

On police corruption: "Twenty years ago in the fifties in *The Washington Post* led a lot of crusades against police corruption. It was always my job to get comments from the chief about our latest story. It wasn't easy, I'll tell you. I remember one chief we had back in the 1950s was a real bully, a very rough guy. We had tied him to a $100 million gambling operation and were trying to get him canned from the force. Every time I'd walk into his office trying to get a comment from him, he'd be behind his door waiting for me and he'd cuff me on the back of the neck a couple of times and scream, 'What do you want now, you

Jewish son-of-a-bitch.' I'd tell him, 'It's not me, chief. It's the *Post.* I just work for 'em'. As the stories got rougher, so did the chief. He sent police officers to my home town in Connecticut to check me out. He threatened men with dismissal if they talked to me, but a lot of them did anyway. It was amazing how many people disliked him. Finally, when things really started to boil, my publisher ordered me to go to Europe for a vacation. He was afraid I was going to get killed. When the guy finally resigned, I breathed a lot easier.

On the press room at headquarters: "This used to be a pretty busy place 30 years ago when we had five newspapers in town. There was always a card game going on until a good story broke. Now some days I sit alone here. You don't see a reporter until the chief calls a press conference. Then all the media boys show up with all their paraphernalia. When the press conference is over, they all disappear.

On what makes a good detective: "Oh, several things: unlimited stamina, a good memory, some luck and good informers. Most of all you need good informers.

On his most memorable day: "It was February 25, 1958, I think. I had a story on nearly every page of the paper, including the two lead stories of the paper and two stories on the local front page. One story was about a rapist who called me up at home and said he wanted to surrender to me. He was afraid the cops were going to kill him. We took pictures of the guy to make sure he wouldn't be beat up and I personally handed him over to one of the department's top detectives. The next day, the publisher came to the newsroom and said, 'We're going to dedicate today's paper to Al Lewis.' "

On his ulcer: "I love this beat. I have no regrets, really. But there is one bad thing about it. You're always working in an environment of hostility. The police are your adversaries. They're always worried you'll expose them. Your fellow reporters are your adversaries. They're always worried you'll scoop them. So, from the time you come in 'till the time you go home, you're tense and nervous. I guess that's why I've had an ulcer all these years."

David Burnham, 46, a Washington correspondent for *The New York Times,* covered the New York Police Department for the *Times* from 1967 to 1974. He is still regarded as one of the most aggressive reporters ever to cover New York police. When officers David Durk and Frank Serpico decided to make public facts about police corruption in New York, they turned to Burnham, whose stories led to the creation of the Knapp Commission and major police reform. Today, Burnham covers federal regulatory and law enforcement agencies, which he describes as "bigger, more complicated police departments." Following are excerpts from an interview.

On joining the *Times:* When I came to the *Times* in 1967, I had just worked two years for President Johnson's Commission on Law Enforcement and Administration of Justice in Washington. I had spent my two years at the commission doing little else than reading about criminal justice. I was by default probably the best-informed crime reporter in America. So I didn't let any official talk me out of a story. I knew what I wanted, and the information I got shook people up. I began to feel how powerful it is to cover police for *The New York Times.* It was really exhilarating. And it was easy, too. It was like shooting fish in a barrel.

On police officers as victims: "Cops are as much the victims of the criminal justice system as they are the monsters who keep it going. So many times a young person will join a police force with all the right motives and get chewed apart in the daily grind. No one else in society sees the abuse of power as often as a police officer. No one else is so often tempted to become corrupt.

On bureaucracies: Cops are not necessarily bad, but police departments are. The reason: Police departments are bureaucracies, and all bureaucracies are bad. It doesn't matter whether it's a federal bureaucracy like The New York Times. They're all bad. They all have an inherent tendency to screw up.

On advocacy journalism: "I don't believe in it. I don't believe a reporter should deliberately slant his story. But at the same time I don't think reporters should restrict themselves to reporting only what a politician or administrator says is going on. His job is to report what actually is going on. Often, there's a big difference.

On his most memorable story: "The single story I wrote for the *Times* that most caught the public eye was a front-page story in 1968 on 'cooping,' the department's time-honored expression for sleeping on duty. A copy boy named Leland Schwartz had a camera and we prowled the docks, alleys and parks of New York in the morning from two to six o'clock in search of the evidence. Many New York policemen were enraged when the story was published. But I remember one *New York Daily News* reporter complaining to me that the cooping story was not a story at all because 'everyone' knew it went on. He underlined what I considered a fundamental truth about journalism: Most important stories concern widely known and generally accepted practices.

On district attorneys: "I gave the cops and the judges of New York City a hard time, but I failed in any systematic way to examine the district attorneys of New York. I think they got off too easily. If I had my six years to do over again, I would concentrate less on police and more on the prosecutors. District attorneys have tremendous power, which is often expressed in negative ways—by what they don't investigate, by whom they don't indict. The most serious fault in the press coverage of the criminal justice system is the failure to examine the power wielded by city prosecutors.

THE COP WATCH

A Top Item on City Budgets, the Police Often Get Low-Grade Coverage. A Look at the Turf—And How to Dig Into It

DAVID JOHNSTON

IN 1974 the Chicago Police Department began periodically releasing statistics showing *reported* crime declining, declining at such a rate that by 1982 then-Mayor Jane Byrne, citing an FBI report based on data supplied by local police agencies, proclaimed the Windy City, "the second safest" of America's fifty-seven largest cities. For eight years Chicago news organizations routinely reported these statistics. Then one reporter began to wonder why, if crime was truly on the wane, more and more people she knew were victims of crime. The reporter was Pamela Zekman, who had done outstanding work as an investigative reporter at both of Chicago's dailies before joining WBBM-TV, the CBS-owned station in Chicago, in 1981. She decided to check out the reality behind the statistics.

In November 1982, after five months of digging by WBBM's Channel 2 investigative team, Zekman reported that "thousands of crimes [are] routinely wiped off the books as though they never happened"; this was done by simply stamping "unfounded" on initial crime reports. More than half of the rape reports and one-third of the robbery and burglary reports examined had been "killed" in this manner by detec-

---

*David Johnston joined the staff of the *Los Angeles Times* in 1976 in San Francisco, California and came to Los Angeles in 1979 to work on the *Times* Metro desk. He currently covers the politics and economics of nonprofit organizations. He is the recipient of two national prizes for investigative reporting, including a George Polk award, shared with another *Times* reporter, Joel Sappell, for exposing intelligence gathering abuses by the Los Angeles Police Department.

†Reprinted from the COLUMBIA JOURNALISM REVIEW, September/October, 1983. Reprinted also with permission of the author.

tives who, it seems, thought their superiors wanted them to make the city's crime statistics look good.

Zekman's five-part series, titled "Killing Crime: A Police Copout," brought into question the credibility of the Chicago Police Department. At the same time, it pointed up a serious flaw in the way many news organizations cover the police: while most public statements are checked against the views of others and the public record before inclusion in a news story, statements about crime statistics and individual crimes are almost never checked out. This occurs despite the fact that the police often have a vested interest in the version of the story they tell and despite the fact that judges, juries, and even prosecutors frequently find it hard to accept the police version of events.

The public deserves more careful and critical coverage. So, too, do the police, one of the most powerful and, at the same time, least examined components of American society. In many large cities the police-department appropriation is the biggest item in the municipal budget, yet journalistic examinations of how efficiently the police use taxpayer funds are rare. The intelligence-gathering activities and investigative techniques of the police also merit—but rarely receive—attention. And, finally, while the police make life-and-death decisions in at least three areas—shootings involving officers, investigations of violent crime (which may determine whether a dangerous criminal is caught), and traffic enforcement—these areas are seldom subjected to press scrutiny.

Jerome H. Skolnick, a professor of law at the University of California at Berkeley, who has just completed a study for the American Bar Foundation on "police accountability and the media," believes that news organizations "focus too much on events in which the police are participants and not (enough) on how police departments operate as organizations." Police departments, he adds, are relatively easy to study, "because they are almost perfect hierarchical organizations." The police chiefs he interviewed, Skolnick says, complained that reporters asked simplistic questions about crime statistics and what it means when reports of one crime go up or down over a short period of time. "In a way," says Skolnick, "the police chiefs I interviewed argued that coverage of their departments wasn't deep enough."

A first step to improved coverage is learning to see the police not as blue knights fighting criminals but as bureaucrats with guns. For, despite the image perpetuated by television shows, most police work does not involve crime but the more humdrum business of settling disputes, maintaining order, and enforcing regulations. Particularly in big cities, the police generate enormous mounds of paperwork that can be mined to learn much about how well the police protect and serve.

Zekman's exposé dealt with the most elementary level of covering the police as an institution. News organizations often carry stories on the latest crime figures that lack the simple, but crucial, qualification that the data reflect only reported crimes. In most instances, of course, the actual level of crime is higher than the reported level. How much higher depends on such factors as whether the police respond quickly and take reports in the field or make citizens go to a precinct house and wait until they're called; whether citizens believe that making a police report is worth the effort; and, in cities with large populations of illegal immigrants, whether the immigrants fear the police too much to report crimes committed against them.

"Crime stats are very tricky," observes David Burnham, whose pioneering reportage a decade ago in *The New York Times* is widely cited by criminal-justice experts as a model of the genre and who has written a guide to help reporters understand crime statistics. "Most of the figures," Burnham adds, "don't mean anything."

Statistics on reported crimes in one city can be compared to reports from other comparable cities. Zekman, who did just that in her WBBM exposé, learned that the Chicago police classified crime reports as "unfounded" from six to fifty times as often as did the police in New York, Los Angeles, and St. Louis. Such statistics can also be compared to data collected by the U.S. Census Bureau in its periodic victimization surveys.

Stories on the *crime rate* based on the FBI's eight major "index crimes"—murder, rape, robbery, aggravated assault, burglary, automobile theft, larceny, and arson—are often misleading because in this computation one cold-blooded murder counts the same as one theft of an unlocked bicycle. Two years ago Los Angeles television stations frequently referred to a "crime wave." An examination of Los Angeles Police Department statistical summaries, however, revealed that the entire increase in reported crime in the first ten months of 1981 was due to burglaries from locked cars and thefts from unlocked cars, the usual aim being the removal of expensive automobile stereo sound systems.

"Crime statistics tell you more about the police than about crime," observes Professor George Kelling, who studies policing and teaches at Harvard University's John F. Kennedy School of Government. Kelling says that reporters looking into clearance rates—the percentage of reported crimes that result in an arrest or the amassing of enough evidence for an arrest that, however, cannot be made for one reason or another — should use them as a guide to finding out where the police focus their efforts. "A high solution rate may just mean the police are arresting a lot of suspects," Kelling points out, "while a low solution rate may actually be a good thing if it means the police are concentrating on, and are getting, convictions in the cases they do solve."

Reporters also need to keep in mind that police tend to focus on street, not white-collar, crimes, and thus their statistics may present a skewed picture of a community's crime problem. In addition, police often cite total arrest figures as an indication of their workload without noting how many arrests resulted from sweeps of prostitutes and drunks rather than the apprehension of more dangerous lawbreakers.

Zekman followed up her initial series with a second exposé last February which showed how Chicago police had manipulated data to make it appear that they were solving an unusually high percentage of crimes. The bureaucratic technique employed was to claim that suspects caught in one case had confessed to several other crimes for which they could not be prosecuted because the other victims declined to press charges. Zekman obtained copies of police reports from her sources, then showed them both to the criminals who had supposedly confessed to the other crimes (they denied having done so) and to the victims, who said they had never been asked to press charges.

Richard J. Brzeczek, who was superintendent of the Chicago police at the time the program was aired, initially denied that the police were manipulating crime statistics. But in his final press conference, after the mayoral election last April, he conceded that "there were, in fact, problems in the integrity of our [crime] reporting system" and that Zekman's estimates of its understating of data were accurate.

Other reporters whose stories offer tips on how to cover the cops include:

- Burnham, who in 1972 revealed that New York's finest had adapted to a wasteful state law requiring the same number of patrol officers to be on duty at all hours by systematic "cooping," or sleeping on the job, in the wee hours. The story, the idea for which Burnham says a deputy editor at the *Times* initially rejected, resulted in major changes in police patrol staffing across the nation. In subsequent pieces, published in 1973, Burnham used a sample of 100 murder cases and 100 robbery cases as a basis for analyzing such factors as the location, time of day, and race of the perpetrators and victims to give New Yorkers a better understanding of crime patterns in their city. ("Trend analysis will tell the public what they need to know; stories about individual crimes won't," says Lawrence Sherman, research director of the nonprofit Police Foundation, which does research and encourages the adoption of innovative police techniques.)

- Jonathan Neumann and William K. Marimow, whose 1977 *Philadelphia Inquirer* series "The Homicide Files" drew on court documents relating to more than 400 murder prosecutions to establish that detectives frequently beat confessions out of suspects, one of whom was hospitalized for twenty-eight days. Judges ruled that the police had acted illegally in eighty of the cases; court records yielded x-rays, medical reports, and testimony about the beatings, some of which lasted for twenty-four hours. Neumann and Marimow's reporting won their paper a Pulitzer Prize.
- Wayne Satz of KABC-TV in Los Angeles, who in 1977 began investigating shootings by Los Angeles police officers, especially of unarmed citizens. The police ignored Satz's written request for a list of officer-involved shootings so he began showing up at one shooting scene after another to interview witnesses. Satz rarely encountered other reporters until a police sergeant shot a naked, unarmed man who, it later turned out, may have been under the influence of a powerful hypnotic drug called PHP. Eventually, an officer agreed to appear on the air, his face and voice disguised, and tell about his fellow officers' attitudes toward shootings — prompting an unsuccessful police investigation aimed at identifying the individual whom then-Police Chief Edward M. Davis, called "the lying Masked Marvel." In 1979, after another police shooting drew other media into the story, the civilian Police Commission ordered a massive study and made major changes in how police shootings are investigated. The county district attorney also created a special team to investigate officer-involved shootings.
- Richard Morin, a *Miami Herald* reporter specializing in computer analysis, who examined 1,391 brutality complaints filed against Metro Dade County Public Safety officers between 1974 and 1980 and, with other *Herald* reporters, located victims whose partially investigated complaints had been dismissed by the police despite compelling medical and other evidence of brutality. The *Herald*, which in 1979 ran a five-part series on police brutality that was based on civil court records, had to sue to get access to the files on closed brutality-complaint investigations. The computer analysis showed that the police acknowledged as legitimate fewer than one in twenty complaints

made by non-Latin whites and fewer than one in forty made by blacks. The series also established that in two-thirds of the proven police-brutality cases officers who were witnesses "testified that they saw the brutal cop do nothing wrong."

- Bob Zeller of the Long Beach, California, *Press-Telegram,* who in 1981 read 289 damage claims filed over the course of six years against the city's 600 police officers and reported his findings in a series called "With Undue Force." The series showed that most brutality complaints are filed by ordinary citizens, not criminals: that no claims had been brought against 75 percent of the city's officers; and that nine of the nearly 900 officers who served on the force during the six-year period were involved in nearly one-fourth of the claims. Zeller's articles also showed that some citizens agreed to drop brutality claims in return for dismissal of charges that they had assaulted officers. (Police critics have often made the point that victims of police beatings are charged with assaulting officers in order to deflect investigation of the officers' conduct.)
- Athelia Knight and Benjamin L. Weiser of *The Washington Post,* who, after spending six months with their city's Third District Police, produced a seven-part series titled "Street Cops" that documented how police arrested people they regarded as undesirable on petty charges in order to harass them. The July 1982 series also showed how some officers were punished if they failed to meet an arrest quota by being given unpopular shifts and assignments, and included the tale of one officer who got "the West Point silent treatment" after reporting that fellow officers had beaten a handcuffed narcotics suspect. The series was an object lesson in how much information can be obtained from police sources rather than documents.

By and large, press coverage of the police shows a lack of sophistication. Professor Skolnick says that, while he was conducting his research for the American Bar Foundation study, police executives repeatedly said that the superficial way reporters examine complex issues discouraged them from disclosing information. Other police executives say they think reporters should study police-science texts and departmental manuals, especially if they are planning to write about such controversial issues as police shootings. Such homework, they believe, might help reporters understand that the issue of how many shootings occur is less significant than a consideration of whether the shootings were necessary.

Police executives also say that reporters need to keep in mind that departments are frequently forced to use their resources in ways that reflect not their own professional judgment but public demands that may be irrational. In many cities, for example, the police are obliged to respond to every burglar alarm even though studies indicate that 97 percent of these calls are false. In Los Angeles the result of meeting a perceived public demand to respond to every burglar alarm — in effect, a huge subsidy to the alarm industry — is that in 1981 the police spent more money on chasing after false alarms than on investigating homicides.

Policing abounds with interesting and important stories. Getting those stories isn't all that hard. For reporters it requires a willingness to crack a few books; for editors, a willingness to treat the police as they would any other interest group; and, for their employers, a willingness to provide the time to examine how well the police are using the taxpayer's money to protect and serve the public.

IF YOU COVER POLICE, LEARN OUR PROCEDURES

JAMES C. SARTORI

"I DON'T KNOW whether or not you have aspirations to be with the news media here in Massachusetts, New England or elsewhere, but that decision will be yours after graduation. I am quite sure there are some of you who are interested in what we call police beat hard news. Going back a little in history, the police beat reporters who lived at police stations seemed to be police chasers, and that's not the case; but they were aware of what was going on, and in order to get the proper story perspective, they had to be present. So they worked many crazy hours that police officers, like firefighters, have to work. The key to the whole thing is that they had to establish credibility, reliability and accurate sources.

Cops: Basically Cynical

"Police officers basically are cynical people. You wonder why? Why are cops cynical? You're just dealing with people. You're trying to help people. That's the name of the game. A police officer in his duty, whether it be two years of highway patrol, detective work, street beats, in that course of time, sees more death and destruction, injury, hurt, misery that any one of you, fortunately, will ever see in your lifetime. Thus a cop becomes cynical.

---

*Staff Sgt. James C. Sartori is the commanding officer of the Massachusetts State Police Public Relations Unit. He is a 20-year veteran of that police agency and has been with the unit for five years. Much of his policing career has been spent on road patrol.
†(EDITOR'S NOTE: Sgt. Sartori addressed an audience of journalism majors in 1985 at Northeastern University, Boston, Massachusetts. His appearance was videotaped, and this article is an edited excerpt made, with Staff Sgt. Sartori's permission, from the tape.)

"He sees it. He sees the victims. He may see the defendants walk away laughing at the court system, laughing at depriving victims of their rights. No remorse. Yet the cop has to be the nice guy on the block, has to fill out the paper work, etcetera, and the man walks out. And maybe when he comes back to the courts, finally, for some kind of trial—a slap on the hand.

"You sitting here could be a victim. You as a reporter have an absolute function to protect the rights of the accused person. And you have to turn around and also consider the rights of the victim. Why? Because in this great country, we have a Constitution. We may not like it on certain points, but believe me, ladies and gentlemen, it is by far the best in the world. So it's better sometimes to let a guilty person actually slide through the system as opposed to just saying, point-blank black and white, 'that's it. You're guilty, you're gone.'"

Learn the Job

"What you have to learn as a reporter is how to deal with a police agency. No matter what agency you cover, you have to take it upon yourselves to earn a police officer's trust. Any unknown reporter that comes up to me, or any new reporter—they can ask me a question about any crime we've investigated or an accident. They are going to get, just like the old Jack Webb Dragnet days, 'yes, ma'am, no ma'am, just the facts.' They don't even get a story. Enough maybe to print, but they may not get all the information, and they are going to say, 'Gee, those cops, especially troopers, they don't want to say anything.' There is no sense, really, in my being put in a situation that might compromise an investigation.

"Within the State Police, we have a rule and regulation, a policy and procedure that covers every function of an officer from how he should handle a homicide case, accident case, up to and including, believe it or not, how he should take a coffee break while on patrol. It may sound foolish, but we want our officers to be uniform; we want them to be professional and trained, and what most reporters aren't aware of, we also have complete, distinct rules that explain what is our role, our obligation, in giving out information to the media.

Right to Know

"The public has the right to know, but, at the same time, can I, as a police officer, tell you everything? One of the questions that sort of upset me was by a professional reporter very recently from one of the two major newspapers here in Boston, who kept pressing me about a Mr. MacTavish (reference here to Craig MacTavish, former Boston Bruins forward arrested by Massachusetts State Police on vehicular homicide and drunken driving charges in connection with the motor vehicle death of a Maine woman)—on whether he did in fact take a breathalyzer test after an accident that resulted in the death of a young lady.

"And no one could understand why I could not give that information. And as we stand here today, I will still not give you that information, because it is against the constitutional rights of any person to acknowledge whether or not he has taken any kind of test. And if he has taken the test, I can't tell you whether he passed it or failed it, because you compromise the investigation; you compromise that man's rights; you also then unintentionally tried him in the newspaper on presumption.

Specific Procedures

"I'd like to go over a few of those particular procedures that we have for the information that may not be released to the news media. We cannot release to any person or persons the existence or contents of prior criminal record of the accused. I can't offer you the character or reputation of the accused, the existence or content of any confession by the accused, the performance of any examination or test, such as a polygraph or breathalyzer; or the accused's refusal to submit to such examination, and/or the results of any such examination.

"It is not my job as a police officer or public relations officer to reveal the possibility of a guilty plea, the opinions as to his guilt or innocence, the opinion as to the quality of evidence that has been gathered for that case. I cannot tell you the identities of witnesses or prospective witnesses, statements of testimony.

"Photographs are not available at all times, though, as an exception, many times in trying to locate, possibly, the accused, convicted, we would probably call upon the news media to assist us by the use of a photograph. You then become eyes and ears. We do not want to compromise your position, get you involved as an investigative agency. It is very important we eliminate you from doing that, but that is something done for public safety.

"Now here is the information that can be released if certain conditions are met: photographs of the person sought by police, the arrest and journal items to legitimate news media personnel, as long as the release of the information does not jeopardize the department investigation or the subsequent judicial process.

"What I can tell you are the facts and circumstances surrounding an arrest, the identity of the investigating officers, except for undercover, the length of the investigation, the description of the physical evidence seized, five pounds of coke, two firearms, etcetera. I can give you the identity of the accused and place of arrest if he or she is age 17 or over. I can give you the age and sex of a person, not a name, if that person is under the age of 17. I can tell you the nature of the charges. I can tell you the fact that the accused denies the charges. And I can tell you the schedule or result of any stage of initial process before we go to court.

Press Rights

"And now what are your rights? The rights of the news media personnel? Your primary responsibility is to report the news by obtaining information and photographs. Since the opportunity to do so is extremely limited at an emergency scene, an officer should not unnecessarily obstruct you from the performance of your duties. However, members of the news media are not exempt at any scene from any municipal, state, federal statute. With the permission of authorities, you can enter the scene; once you enter, we have no protection for you.

"Many people think that news media people can just walk into a scene, but you can't sometimes. It can be an instance where a S.W.A.T. or S.T.O.P. team is involved. You may have a deranged person with a firearm. Media people may photograph or report anything they may see or observe at an emergency scene. When such coverage would interfere with an investigation or place a victim, suspect or other person in jeopardy, withholding publication is dependent upon a cooperative press. Under such circumstances, officers should advise the news representative or superiors of the possible consequences of publication. Officers may not, however, interfere with news media personnel, as long as their activity remains within the confines of the law.

"Photographing prisoners by news media personnel is a very key issue. And this is by a Supreme Court decision. News media personnel have the right to photograph persons in police custody; however, officers will not pose prisoners for news photos, nor will they allow prisoners to be photographed by the news media inside departmental buildings.

"You ask, well, that is sort of difficult. You say I can photograph, then maybe I can't. You again, unfortunately, try a suspect by setting these scenes or scenario. As a defendant is brought into a police station, he is under arrest. He is handcuffed. He is brought to the detention center, normally with a background that is adjacent to cell areas, clearly identifiable by the viewer. At the same time, also, he will go through a process of being photographed and printed by an officer. The inference you give from a photograph inside that kind of building is, positively, guilt. You've associated a person, and he may be innocent.

Police Protect Accused

"See, the police responsibility is to protect the rights of the accused, because it's his life, his freedom that are jeopardized. But we can't do it all by ourselves. We have to ask the news media to cooperate.

"Have you heard of Don Batting, WBZ Radio; Charles Austin, WBZ TV; Steve Sbraccia, WEEI Radio; Kevin Cullen, Boston Herald? Why do I pick these men out? Don probably has 25 years plus experience as a professional police beat reporter. Charlie has 10, maybe more. Steve and Kevin are basically new kids on the block. But they are police beat reporters.

"I singled them out for one purpose. They are excellent. They know as much about police operations as police officers. They are probably privy to a lot of information that none of us in this room will ever learn. Why? It's a friendship? No, it's not. It's trust, confidence, credibility. Any police officer, if he is burnt by an erroneous story, false information, information that could compromise a case, he would be a fool to talk to you again. Now I don't know how you go back to your editor and say, 'Gee, the cops won't talk to me.' First thing he looks at is your time slip and figures, let's get someone who can.

'I've Been Burnt'

"I've been burnt. Nothing serious so far, but my career is not over yet, either. If somebody is new, I give him what information is legal, and I watch then how it is reported. These four gentlemen I mentioned took a little time to learn the procedure for police officers effecting an arrest, in going after a suspect, in booking a prisoner. They made themselves available to ride in our cruisers to see what it is like to hear these calls, see what an officer is supposed to do.

"It's like anything. How can you possibly expect, if you come out of high school, to be a reporter without being here. Just walk into a newspaper and say, 'I want to be a reporter.' Maybe tomorrow, 'I want to be a brain surgeon.' You get fundamentals right here. So you have to learn the intricacies of what makes a department run. Why can't they do this, or why can they do this? If you understand what we can do and what we can't do, your job is very easy. You then have actual information.

"It's not uncommon for us over the years to be sitting with some reporters and we'll discuss the case just as if it were a bunch of cops at the jail. And just talk about everything, stuff you'll never see in the press; but it helps that reporter as he's following that case to know all these little things. What's happened during the investigation? What's going to happen after the investigation? So no matter how he writes his story from day to day or once a week or once a month, it's positively right on the dollar, right on the button. You can't compromise each other.

Media Blacklist

"In my office, I, unfortunately, have to maintain a list of several people in the news media whom I just can't deal with. Take the MacTavish case. That reporter, day in and day out, wanted to know, did he take a breathalyzer test, did he take a breathalyzer test? Many times I explained to her, you are compromising the case, you're putting your newspaper up to a chance of having it litigated by the deceased's family. And she kept coming back and back and back until, finally, as easy going as I try to be—time! You're not going to get the information. I told you why several times. And I said, I don't even want you to call on a day to day arrest, 'cause if you call, I'm too busy to talk to you.

"Now, she has a problem. She can't call our department to find out what is going on. Anybody else from that agency can call, fine, they get it. She can't. I'm not out to hurt this woman, no way. She was out, unintentionally, I thought at the beginning, and now, bottom line is, I think she was out to compromise the case, for whatever reasons. She knew better. She's not a new kid on the block. She's what I consider a professional.

Arrest Procedures

"What does happen to a person if he's placed under arrest? First of all, he has to be placed under arrest before he is advised of his rights. He will be placed in handcuffs, normally behind his back, placed in the front seat of a cruiser, seatbelt put across him. He is then transported to the nearest barracks or police facility lock-up and booked. If the crime is a felony, automatically a photograph is taken, along with prints. Misdemeanor, that is not done. Misdemeanors are crimes that have fewer than five years state prison penalty, felonies have five years or more. He has a right to make a telephone call at his own expense. He then can make bond, depending on the circumstances of the case, contacting a bondsman. He is brought to the very next sitting of the next available court day for his arraignment. The judge will set a bail, if any, for his appearance at a later date for the trial, giving him the opportunity to retain an attorney. We can back up a bit.

Any of You Arrested?

"Have you ever been arrested. Have you? Would you feel a bit upset if for some reason a police officer were to stop you and find an outstanding speeding ticket or parking ticket? That's pretty common today. The court has ordered your arrest for not paying that. Pretty minor.

"What would your attitude be for that outstanding parking ticket now with my arrest procedure? I just told you what's going to happen to you. He'll stop you. Check you out. Goes back to the computer; there's a warrant from the court. Parking ticket. I'm going to put the handcuffs on you, the seatbelt. Not too good a feeling, huh? This is where we have problems.

"You say, Gee, why are the cops so rough on these people? Why? It's personal safety. I just saw you for the first time today. I don't know who you are. You could be a deranged person. You might have committed a serious crime prior to my stopping you. And if I, as a police officer, come up to you with a nice attitude, 'Hi, how are you, would you mind getting in the car?' and we drive along, I'm liable to be dead. It can happen. Most cops, by the way, tend to get killed in the line of duty on routine motor vehicle stops, percentage-wise. Second is responding to domestic calls. Man beating up his wife, police officer enters. Now the wife and the guy jump on the cop, and that's it. So you can't. As much as you'd like to have all of us in society love each other, we do have an obligation.

"I'm a father of three boys, whom I love dearly, and my wife, I love even more. But when I deal with you on the street, I have to take a different attitude. I know nothing about you, and you should probably be a little apprehensive about me, because you don't know if maybe I'm a deranged police officer. How would you like to have that for a reverse?

"Now the idea of my job is not to go out and harm people. I always thought when I came into the department a little over 17 years ago, public servant I am, to help and serve. And that's been my intent. It's still my goal and daily function. I do have to pull patrol one day a week, and I get a little mixed up. I am the public relations guy. I'm supposed to come here positive and say everyone's okay, and the department's great, and everybody's happy, and we love everybody. And one day a week, I'm out there giving speeding tickets. You know, you have to sometimes change, but that goes with the turf.

Resisting Arrest

"You'll have the case of the person who, in fact, didn't want to go, and you hear 'resisting arrest, police brutality, two cops jumped on the guy, they did this and they did that.' The point is that to place somebody perfectly under arrest, you have to touch a subject and basically say, 'you are under arrest.' And now he turns and says, 'I don't want to go.' Put yourself in that same position.

"Maybe if a person is drunk, he doesn't want to go. Or like I say, a little matter like you are saying to yourself, 'I can't believe this. I'm in the United States. I'm in Massachusetts. And this big burly cop is coming up (of course I am not that big burly guy; I'm only five nine and one half) and he's going to take my arms, and he is going to put handcuffs behind me, he's going to throw me in the car like a common criminal. And all I am is a student at Northeastern University. I've always been decent. I just made one mistake.'

"Thus, you get the reaction: 'Hey, I don't want to go.' Well, I'm a police officer. I have a court order. In plain English, come hell or high water, I can't let you walk away. At some given point, we're going to become physical. And if that be the situation, and that's what people don't understand, that picture is worth a thousand words.

"The more the officer keeps grabbing you, the more you resist. Then he is going to have to do as he's trained as a police officer to do, to embrace you somehow, knock you to the ground. You are still not going to go along with him to the point of being knocked down until he's going to get you all the way to the ground, and there might be three or four police officers come, and they are all now holding you to the ground. You are kicking, screaming, yelling, hollering. But they are going to have to cuff you. Now comes Mr. Reporter. Walks down the street, sees the officers jumping all over you. Click, click. Police brutality. We got a good shot here.

"It can happen. And I'm not saying that it doesn't happen. I'm not so naive or over-protective to say that cases of police brutality never occur. You see how easy it is. But if you understand police procedure and have seen arrests, after the fact, have seen people who have resisted, you can, basically, as a professional, determine what is the resist and what is the brutality.

Address Brutality

"And if there is brutality, you then have the right, and you have the obligation to address that. We're not perfect. We're human. I don't know if any of you have ever gone down a street and been spit at in the face and had things thrown at you, people try to kick you. I have. It's not a nice feeling at all. That goes with the turf. I don't think any of you in your professional lives will ever have that happen to you.

"The point I go back to — you have to learn police procedure, whether or not you deal with a smaller town or large departments. And if you don't understand our procedure and you portray me or any other police officer in a bad light, we don't want to talk with you again because you've declared yourself as being anti-police, you are declaring yourself without knowing why, or the reasons, or the how to it.

Drunk Driving Arrests

"The other common arrest we have right now is a drunk driving arrest. Procedure for a drunk driving arrest is tentatively the same type of procedure, but the officer has to use probable cause at the time of meeting, such as maybe at a roadblock, or you may get stopped for a motor vehicle violation. Certain criteria have to be present: an odor of alcohol, glassiness of eyes, sometimes slurred speech, unsteadiness of the feet, maybe physical appearance, attire, jacket all over the place, whatever.

"At that point, you'd be treated as any other arrest and advised of your rights, handcuffed, put into the cruiser, transported to the barracks. You would also have been advised enroute you have the right to a breathalyzer test. A breathalyzer test is not a secret space-war invention that the police have hidden away into the building, especially today's. The Model 200 Smith and Wesson, small suitcase. That's all. No surprises, state of the art, computerized, all done by digital printouts. There is no way, absolutely no way, a police officer can even be accused of tampering with the machine. A tape is fed into it; it is warmed up; the machine registers it, will be operational and non-operational by codes.

"It's within .02 percent of complete accuracy on a breathalyzer reading. This new state of the art has also incorporated a defense for police. On the old machine, acetone could never be detected. People who are diabetics, whether hidden or known, appear to be drunk when they have an attack; the odor of an alcohol substance emits from their breath. They are usually glassy-eyed; their behavior changes to belligerence, or they become passive. They can't walk.

"And the unknown diabetic is a sad sight, because that poor person has never even realized that he has the disease. But he is apt to get caught by police because of erratic operation or a motor vehicle accident. Within the past two weeks, one of our officers arrested a young man. No question in the officer's mind—drunk out of his mind: belligerent, and a physical restraint had to be used to get him into custody. And the tirade that happened at the barracks was just a horror show, screaming, yelling, kicking, banging around.

"He was given the breathalyzer test. It came out with what they call a code four. That indicates to the machine that there is an acetone presence. It's not blood alcohol. The officer got a bottle of coke and forced it on the man. Within about five minutes, the man calmed down to about as normal as we are here and asked where he was, what was he doing here. Diabetic, an unknown diabetic. It's a very common thing. It used to be a defense for some people when they were actually drinking.

"For your information on alcohol: if you take a breathalyzer test and your reading is .05 or less, you are released from custody forthwith. Over .05, it is not presumed that you are driving under the influence, but you will be charged, and the court will decide. At .10, which in foreign countries is half that, you are presumed to be operating under the influence of alcohol, and you are detained for court and charged as such.

Whose Right Is It?

"You may not like the idea of a breathalyzer test. Granted, you don't have to take it. That's your right. We will take away your license for 90 days for not taking it—we collectively means Registry of Motor Vehicles. But the breathalyzer test might protect your individual rights to drive on any state highway, secondary road, city or town street without the fear of running into a drunk driver. So look at the other side of the coin here. It's not somebody's rights being fooled with, challenged by taking the test. Your rights are automatically being protected. I don't think we should have to go out on the street and have a fear of being hit by a drunk driver.

Case in Point

"I know the case of a local police officer, with several years on his department, who, one night when we were on patrol, he and his partner met with me in a turn-around spot to shoot the bull for a minute, as many cops would do. All of a sudden, his radio came on to say there was an accident, head-on collision in the roadway about an eighth of a mile from us. They turned around in their local cruiser. We returned to the highway, and since everything was quiet there, we went to give them a hand. At the scene of the two-car accident, a woman was decapitated, a young woman, a 22-year-old school teacher. And there was the fellow who had been driving on the wrong side of the roadway.

"And the police officer was going through what you would say was police brutality, with his feet, his nightstick, trying to get his firearm out to put this driver out of business. His partner was trying to hold him back, and he yelled to us for help. The three of us knocked down that fourth officer. Well, you might ask, why was he doing this? Was this woman related to him? No, that patrol car had just stopped that drunken operator less than half an hour ago. Although the young man driving the car was drunk, 23 or 24 years old, being a father of three kids and a truck driver, he said it was important for him to maintain and retain his license; he couldn't afford to lose it on a drunk driving charge.

"The police officer—some people think they are inhuman—said, 'Give me your keys, by the time I'll be back in four or five hours, you will be sober and can go home.' Too bad he didn't check the kid's wallet for a spare ignition key. The police officer is convinced to this day that he killed that young lady. Did he? You tell me. Do you want to be the judge? It's a human moral issue, gray line, black or white—you have to find the spot. You can have luxury of gray line decisions. I can't. That police officer today—I hope he doesn't stop you with a drink on your breath, because no matter who you are, you are gone. And that's a true story. I was there.

No Gray Line for Police

"While you try to do your job, you have to watch your back, with lawsuits coming down. Why cops are cynical is that they have seen so much, and you have to watch your back. Our Supreme Court—some of the decisions that have come down have been great decisions, some of them to protect your rights because in years past, police officers like myself did abuse them—rubber hoses, lights, the whole bit. But there are other decisions that have come down that I don't like. But I can't say just because I don't like a ruling, I am going to ignore it. That's what makes the profession so hard.

"As a police officer, we can do no wrong. But a police officer, in a given situation of imminent danger has a split second to make a decision up to and including the use of his firearm. When all this is settled, someone may lie dead. There is a case being appealed now in Supreme Court, and the hooded individuals, and I don't knock them, have had two years, the opportunity to sit down for two years and go over every single bit of evidence and decide what they think should not have been done. And if I, as a Monday morning quarterback, decide I have made a mistake, my home, my job, my freedoms are at stake. I don't think any of you have that problem.

My Closest Call

"I'd like to tell you how close you can come to taking a person's life and still come out on top. One night I was patrolling Rt. 1 northbound by what they call the jug handle lights. Heavy traffic. This guy was moving along about 75 miles per hour, pretty quick in Friday night traffic. I chased him and finally stopped him, and according to policy and procedure, I positioned my cruiser in such a way that I was angled off, so that if I alighted from my car, if a car were to slide in toward me, hopefully it would deflect off my fender and not run me down. I was very aware now, lights flashing, heavy moving traffic, people coming in and out of businesses, motels, restaurants. I was trying to watch them, trying to see the man in the car, whether anyone else was in the car, was half-blinded by lights. And a man comes out of the car from the driver's position, like this (Sartori simulates the driver, bending over, back-to and reaching inside his jacket in the upper left, shoulder area). I saw that, and as a police officer, I am yelling 'freeze.' And I am going for my firearm in defense, because I figure it is him or me.

"And through the din of the traffic, I hear, 'passport, passport.' I stopped. This guy stopped, and now he was waving something in his hand. I walk up to the man. He hardly speaks English, been here maybe for a month on the international driver's license. He told me that when he went through customs they said to him, if you ever get stopped by the police, get out of the car and show them your passport. Meanwhile, I am upset at this point because I know how close I came to just blowing this individual away.

"And would you believe me the next day when you saw this guy on the ground with his passport? That I thought it was a gun? I doubt it. I really, truly doubt it. You had to be there. But if I had shot that man, and it went to the Supreme Court, the court would have said, 'Well, officer, you should have waited until you were positive.' How positive can you be? If there was a firearm, some trooper would knock on my door and say, 'Jim's not coming home, are there any outstanding bills?' That's the end of it. Inside my stomach was turning like it never did before in my life. I didn't even give the guy a ticket.

"Scared, Absolutely Scared"

"I was scared, absolutely scared for the first time in my life. With that, I told the guy to slow down, and if a police officer approaches you, do what he says, don't come jumping out of cars like that. He didn't know what the heck I was talking about. From there, I just drove up to a wooded area, it was 7 o'clock, and I got off at midnight. But I just sat there smoking cigarettes. I did not go on the highway again; I did not respond to any calls, look for any accidents, look for any disabled cars. I didn't do the police function at all, just sat there and said, 'Oh, Jesus,' thinking about how close I actually came to doing it. What if I had killed that guy?

"And sometimes, when it does happen, a cop will say, 'I thought it was a gun.' Let's face it, we are reasonable, prudent people. How can you think a passport was a gun? If I could simulate for the court, for the jury the complete circumstances, the lighting, etcetera, then maybe you could see the resetting of the situation, then you might believe it. But you will never see the same situation, and it can happen. That's why cops are cynical."

POLICE NEWS:
CONSTRUCTING AN IMAGE OF CRIME

MARK FISHMAN

NEWS ORGANIZATIONS know of the world they report almost exclusively through legitimated institutions (Fishman, 1980; Tuchman, 1978; Roshco, 1975; Sigal, 1973). A good deal of what we see in the news is the result not only of what journalists do, but also of accounts which other agencies produce in the course of enforcing laws, rescuing survivors, negotiating treaties, investigating corruption, and trading stocks. The possibilities of news are set by some as yet unanalyzed "bureaucratic mode of story-telling" (Tuchman, 1976). While a growing literature on newsmaking has shown the considerable extent to which media accounts are first formed outside news organizations, that literature has not tackled the question of how routine sources construct accounts for the press. This article is an attempt to help fill that gap in media research by addressing the issue of how one legitimated institution, the police, produces accounts which become the journalist's raw material for news.

As *the* routine source of crime news (Gordon, 1979: Sherizen, 1978: 210-211; Fishman, 1978: 538; Chibnall, 1977, 1975), law enforcement agencies formulate for journalists what is "out there" and what can be

---

*(AUTHOR'S NOTE: This is a revised version of a paper presented at the 1979 Annual Meeting of the Society for the Study of Social Problems. I wish to acknowledge Antonio Valderrama and Israel Rios for their invaluable research assistance, and Pamela Fishman for her help in formulating several points in this article.)

†Mark Fishman is an associate professor of sociology at Brooklyn College, City University of New York. His publications include *Manufacturing the News* (1980).

‡Mark Fishman, "Police News Constructing an Image of Crime," *Urban Life,* Vol. 9 No. 4, January, 1981, pp. 371-94. Copyright © 1981, Sage Publications, Inc. Reprinted by permission of Sage Publications, Inc.

said about it. News organizations may choose what crimes to report, but the pool of occurrences from which they draw is preselected and preformed within police departments. Thus in this study, the issue of how the police make news for the press does not mean analyzing the relationship of individual crime reporters and police sources,[1] but examining how these sources get *their* accounts. To study this is to examine the organized ways a law enforcement bureaucracy keeps tabs on itself by continually monitoring what its officers are dealing with moment by moment in a community. This article reports research on such a monitoring system in the New York Police Department. It will be shown that the police crime-reporting apparatus systematically exposes the media to incidents which perpetuate prevailing law-and-order themes in crime news. It will also be shown how the monitoring system is vulnerable to news promoters (Molotch and Lester, 1974) who attempt to publicly formulate new social problems.

The Police Crime Reporting System

For the most part, crime news is news of individual occurrences. Thus, almost anywhere one finds crime news, one finds police departments supplying news organizations with an assortment of crime incidents every day. In towns and small cities this assortment often consists of all crimes known to the police in a 24-hour period. But in large urban areas journalists must rely on the police for a "summary" of daily incidents.[2]

In New York City this daily summary is known as the "press wire."[3] Each of the city's major media has a newsroom teletype which receives crime dispatches from the NYPD. This press wire types out from 12 to 25 messages per day. It is the main means by which news organizations first learn of crime in the city.

To determine the origin of the press wire and the nature of the decisions made in selecting information for it, in-depth interviews were conducted with twenty-two police officers at two levels of the NYPD. Fifteen were patrol and supervisory personnel in three different precincts. Seven officers were connected with the sections of headquarters that control the press wire. In addition, NYPD crime figures, the records of one precinct, and participant observation data from an earlier study of a New York City television newsroom (Fishman, 1978) were analyzed to examine the role of the police in the construction of a crime wave.

The press wire originates from a unit in the police department known as the Operations Section. In essence, this is the NYPD's central command post which surveys what is happening throughout the city, moment by moment. Reports of incidents are funneled into the operations room from two major sources: an "incident log" and "the field." The press wire is made up in the process of monitoring these two sources.

The incident log is a teletype which continuously prints brief summaries of emergency phone calls from citizens who have dialed "911" for police assistance. Because it produces an enormous volume of messages (about 6,000 every day), this source is very quickly scanned for only a few types of incidents: certain "serious crimes" (mainly homicides) and emergencies that either require rapid mobilization of large numbers of police, e.g., looting, plane crashes, or require notification of other city agencies, e.g., power failures, delays in subway service. However, the main source of incidents for the press wire are reports received from "the field."

The NYPD requires officers to report any "unusual occurrences." Thus, the field consists of precinct police who, in the course of their work, look for events that the Operations Section would want to know about. A telephone call, later followed by a written report,[4] would be made from a precinct to the office of its local area commander, who in turn, would pass on the news to the Operations Section in headquarters.[5] If the Operations Section has any doubts about reporting an occurrence to the press, they would contact the Office of Public Information, which has the final say in such matters.

Although the police department issues official guidelines as to what constitutes an unusual occurrence, the police acknowledge that these are too vague to be of use in actually deciding whether any given happening is unusual or not. Instead, both precinct police and officers in the Operations Section use a set of informal criteria for identifying unusual incidents and thus, for deciding what occurrences to transmit to the news media. Before discussing these criteria, a few things first must be said about routine police work. It is within an environment of "ordinary occurrences" that police officers perceive unusual happenings.

On Policing the City

In large urban areas like New York, crime is perceived as a monolithic problem. It is seen as an enduring blight that resists every effort to reduce or control it. "Crime control" is a term little used by veteran officers, because they see their efforts as having little effect on the overall situation. As one put it:

> We could double our arrests and it probably wouldn't solve the problem in New York. I think a lot of our leaders in this job realize that. Therefore, the amount of arrests really doesn't count. All they do is cost the city more in terms of manpower and money.

And when the law enforcement officers speak about policing the city, they do not talk in terms of enforcing the law when they see it broken. If conceived in this way, their job would overwhelm them.

> (At our precinct) we could make arrests practically anywhere we turned every night of the week, if we chose to. But we don't. You have to use discretion.

In this context, the use of discretion when making arrests does not mean deciding on a case-by-case basis whether to make an arrest. It means deciding where, in the first place, to look for trouble.[6]

The police want to save their limited resources for intervening in what they view as the worst cases (LaFave, 1965: 5). And worst cases almost always mean threats to public order, i.e., troubles in public places and crime between strangers.[7] For precinct police, such cases typically include muggings, bank robberies, stickups of small businesses, auto theft, burglaries, homicides, and gang fights. At the level of police headquarters, where crisis management is the explicit concern of the department's top commanders, offices in the Operations Section scan their sources of information looking for even larger disruptions of public order than precinct police ordinarily see. These include bombings, looting, riots, demonstrations, attacks on the police, and all civil disasters (large fires and floods, train and plane crashes, storage tank explosions, and the like).

In contrast, the police would rather not be bothered with incidents which they view as not endangering relations in public. These typically include troubles between intimates, friends, acquaintances, and neighbors, as well as the so-called victimless crimes: drug use, numbers running, prostitution, bookmaking, most rapes, and all family violence falling short of homicide or hospitalization. At the Operations Section of headquarters, reports of these matters would be ignored unless they appeared to involve murder. At the precinct level, police officers view these matters (particularly family violence and rapes) as essentially private or interpersonal troubles which only incidentally involve law-breaking. Police in precincts do not seek out these situations, and when called into them, they prefer not to pinpoint a wrongdoer and make an arrest (Walker, 1979; 26, 64, 206-210; Brownmiller, 1975: 364-368; Shearing, 1974: 84). Speaking about family violence, one officer said:

> Historically, in my 16 years in the department, we've always really stayed away from family disputes. At least we try to. . . . When called into a dispute, we try to handle the situation by asking one party to leave—and not necessarily the male, either—for a cooling-off period. . . . And these things tend to blow over. I think very rarely is a complaint ever taken. . . . [The police] realize these things tend to iron themselves out, and to take a complaint where a detective will call three days later when it's a dead issue—it might just further aggravate the situation.

In the police view, disturbances in the private sphere are best left alone to work themselves out, while crimes in the public sphere are seen to require police intervention (see Reiss and Bordua, 1967: 29-31). It is important to note, though, that disturbances in the public sphere excludes such matters as price-fixing, political bribery and corruption, environmental pollution, tax, evasion, and unsafe food, drugs, housing, and work conditions. The police generally are not concerned with these because other agencies are responsible for their enforcement. From the outset, these kinds of crime are excluded from consideration as candidates for the press wire.

Whether in a precinct or at headquarters, the police are geared to look for disruptions in the flow of business as usual in the city. It is with reference to this conception of social order that the police see unusual happenings and report them to the news media. This means that public-order crimes will be considered as either usual or unusual instances of their type. But disturbances in the private sphere fall outside such evaluations. The police will consider whether any given robbery is unusual, but the question will not even arise for family disputes, unless homicide is at issue.

Deciding What's Unusual

Public-order crimes were evaluated as unusual on the basis of three considerations: the frequency with which the police encountered a type of incident, their estimation of its seriousness, and their anticipation of its newsworthiness.

Frequency

Police officers did not keep count of how many suicides they had seen, how many muggings they had dealt with, and so on.[8] But they did show a general concern with the frequency of particular types of incidents, by using such phrases as: "This kind of thing happens every day of the week," or "We see these things by the dozens." As one might expect, it is with reference to this sense of "normal crimes" (Sudnow, 1965) that officers noted unusual incidents.

The perception of unusualness (in the sense of the frequency of occurrence) varied from area to area. The commander of a Brooklyn precinct pointed out:

> What's unusual in one place is not unusual in another. For instance, if you go out to the 75th precinct (one of the highest crime areas of the city), a stickup is not unusual. In Parkville (a low crime area), if you get the same stickup there, they want an unusual.

Despite this variation among precincts, something can be said about what kinds of troubles in the public sphere generally were reported to headquarters as unusual.

Some types of incidents were considered uncommon no matter where they occurred. Homicides,[9] bombings, bank robberies, hostage situations, looting, and race riots did not happen every day in any one precinct. Thus, if an incident could be seen as one of these types, it would be telephoned to the Operations Section simply because it was one of these types, and they, in turn, would place the incident on the press wire.[10] The process was virtually automatic.

Other types of incidents were considered common in most precincts as well as in the Operations Section. These included muggings, robberies of businesses, burglaries, vandalism, larcenies, arson, auto theft, rape, and other nonfatal assaults. To be seen as an instance of one of these types was not enough to ensure the incident would be reported as unusual to headquarters and placed on the press wire. Bombings did not happen everyday; muggings did. There had to be something special about the mugging for it to be unusual.

Seriousness

Among other things, this "something special" involved the police officer's sense of the seriousness of an incident. In most precincts, only muggings with extensive injuries would be serious enough to warrant an unusual report. Similarly, only robberies and burglaries involving large sums of money and other valuables would be reported as unusual. In contrast, a bombing would be reported as unusual whether or not there were injuries or extensive damage. Generally, the police sense of seriousness was based on the most visible or quantifiable consequences of an incident: the number of deaths, the extent of injuries, the dollar amount stolen, the number of alarms for a fire, the size of an area flooded, and so on.

Newsworthiness

Interestingly, I found it difficult to get police to give even ballpark estimates of how much money stolen made a theft unusual, or how extensive the injuries had to be for a mugging to be considered unusual. The police would not or could not give such estimates because they could think of too many exceptions whenever they proposed an answer. One reason for this was that many officers knew that the delineation of seriousness varied from precinct to precinct, just as frequency varied. But another reason was that unusualness did not simply depend on the measurable consequences of an incident. Newsworthiness was also involved. For example:

PO: In our precinct, a typical unusual would be a serious assault or a major robbery.
MF: Major in terms of dollar amount taken or extent of injuries?
PO: Yeah.
MF: Is there roughly a dollar amount? If there's a robbery in a supermarket, and you're getting up into eight, ten, twelve thousand dollars. . . .
PO: I'd say if it was in a supermarket, you'd probably have an unusual. Then again, probably politics enter into it. I've never really given it much consideration. If your Walbaums is knocked over, they'll probably be an unusual—probably, not always. I don't know. It also is discretionary on the part of the sergeant who responds; does he think it's unusual.
MF: What is he thinking when he's thinking, "Is this unusual?"
PO: More than likely, if the borough (commander) doesn't know about it and the newspapers pick it up, then, will there be static for them not to have done the unusual?
MF: You also said serious assaults would be unusual. Does serious injury mean hospitalization or that the injury would look serious enough for hospital treatment? Is that the dividing line?
PO: Ahhh [sighing and thinking] serious injury. You could have a stabbing on Jerome Street in the 75th precinct, where the perpetrator is known, and there'd be no unusual on it. Let's say it's two friends, drinking beer, hot summer night. You know. Typical. The department considers it nothing newsworthy. It's normal and routine for that area.

Any incident which the police anticipated the news media might want to report was considered unusual regardless of whether the incident met the other criteria of frequency or seriousness. As long as the occurrence looked like the kind of thing the media might pick up, precinct police felt it imperative that headquarters be notified immediately, even if they also felt that the incident was fairly common in their area or that it was not very serious. Thus, newsworthiness had priority over other criteria for judging the unusualness of an incident.

The police anticipation of media interest was based mainly on their reading of newspapers and viewing of television. Like any other news consumers, the police inferred that the press was interested in any bizarre or ironic incident, as when a man intending to commit suicide jumped off a 12-story building into an open automobile, killing another man who was riding in the funeral procession of a friend. Similarly, the police inferred that any crime involving a celebrity was of interest to the press, as was apparent when the *New York Daily News* featured on its front page the arrest of John F. Kennedy's brother-in-law for refusing to pay a 60-cent cab fare.

Most of the time, however, the police provided the media with newsworthy incidents of a different sort. All officers were aware of current themes in criminality and law enforcement being covered in the print and broadcast media. For instance, as examples of unusual incidents several officers indicated types of crime that were receiving moderate and heavy publicity at the time of the interviews: crime in the subways, robberies of taxicabs and diamond merchants, and crimes against the elderly. Incidents which could be seen as instances of these types of crime were placed on the press wire by the police in the Operations Section. Before discussing the consequences of this, let us first examine why the police attach such importance to the possible news value of the incidents they deal with.

The police motivation for identifying unusual occurrences on the basis of what the media seemed to want was not intended in quite the spirit of charity that it might appear. If an unusual report were not made for an incident which had already come to the attention of journalists, then a wave of unanswered questions could sweep through the NYPD's chain of command. Reporters would call the Office of Public Information with questions. If this office knew nothing of the incident, a public information officer would telephone the Operations Section. If Operations was unaware of the event, an officer in that unit would call the office of the relevant area commander, who in turn would call the relevant precinct commander, who then would contact the sergeant in charge of patrol, who finally would talk to the offending patrol officer. No subordinate wanted to be in a position of not knowing what his superior would hold him accountable for knowing, and — even worse — not being able to find it out from subordinates.

The system of unusual reports is meant to obviate this problem by anticipating those matters about which the police might get inquiries. Moreover, the system supplies headquarters with a pool of incidents that could be given to the press before journalists even knew of any specific happenings. If journalists then call for more information about an incident they had seen on the press wire, the police already would have an available account (based on the unusual report). Thus, the system of unusual reports allows the police department both to define for news organizations the set of possibly interesting crimes of the day and to formulate for reporters "what happened" in any one of these incidents. This gives the police considerable control over their own image in the press. Not only could the department publicize examples of "good police work" to the media, but they would be prepared with explanations of potentially embarrassing incidents.

From the individual officer's standpoint, unusual reports offer some protection from potential troubles. More importantly, from an institutional standpoint, unusual reports not only maintain the police department's image as a competent bureaucracy, but also strengthen the dependence of media organizations on the police for accounts of crime. In general, the system of unusual reports is the way an urban police department cements its relations with the media and maintains its position as a routine source for news.

Controlling Changes in the Image of Crime

The anticipation of newsworthiness as a criterion for transmitting incidents to the press has a curious effect on the overall crime-reporting system. On the one hand, a police officer explained the perception of unusualness in these terms:

> An unusual [report] is predicated on what the media itself feels is newsworthy. So I guess *they* really determine what to us is unusual.

On the other hand, in the television newsroom I observed, the selection of crime news was predicated on the assumption that the police supplied the press with only the most important crimes of the day. Without this assumption, journalists would not have taken the press wire seriously enough to make it their main source for crime stories.

Thus, the press selection of crime news is based on what the police make available to them. And what the police make available is, in large part, based on what the press reports. Crime news recreates itself.[12]

One might be tempted to conclude that the sorts of incidents available to the press do not change, and therefore crime news continually reproduces the same image of crime. But crime news does change, within limits. New kinds of crime appear briefly in the media, and, periodically, new categories of incidents receive continuous and heavy publicity. That is, crime waves occur which impress upon the public's new social problems and which insure the existence of new categories of crime for years to come. To see how this occurs, let us look at the history of a recent crime wave.

Crimes Against the Elderly

From October to December 1976, New York City experienced a major crime wave. For seven weeks all the city's media were filled with reports of crimes against its elderly citizens. News stories formulated a new kind of crime with typical victims (poor elderly whites who had not yet fled neighborhoods in transition) and typical offenders (black and Hispanic youths with long juvenile records). The crimes involved were largely homicide, robbery, and purse snatching.

Interestingly, the police department's figures for crimes against the elderly do not indicate that a surge of violence aimed at senior citizens was taking place. Homicides against the elderly for 1976 were down 21% over the previous year (and down 2.5% for the whole population). Even more detailed figures for robberies and purse snatchings reveal that the wave of publicity was occurring in the midst of a general decrease in the reported rates of crimes against the elderly. (See Appendix A. See also Hoyer, 1979: 9; Braungart et al, 1979: 24.)[13] What, then, accounts for the crime wave in the media?

Promoting a Crime Wave

This crime wave can be traced back to October 24, 1976, when a series of feature articles on crimes against the elderly appeared in the New York *Daily News*. The reporter who wrote this series told me that he received "considerable help" from the Senior Citizens Robbery Unit (SCRU), a newly formed police squad specializing in robberies and assaults on the elderly. On October 7 the reporter first wrote a story on two crimes with elderly victims, which had appeared over the press wire the same day. At that time an editor thought it would be a good idea to do a series of feature stories on "this kind of crime." (Other news organizations had done such features in the past.)

While researching these stories, the reporter was in frequent contact with SCRU. This police unit let him know it felt beleagured, understaffed, and that it was fighting a battle that deserved more attention. After he finished the feature stories, the reporter was able to follow up the series with several reports of specific incidents because SCRU officers were calling him whenever they knew of the mugging or murder of an elderly person. This kept the issue alive in the *Daily News,* and soon the theme of crime against the elderly began to catch on in other news organizations.

One incident in particular brought all the city's media into covering the theme. Police from SCRU, in a phone conversation with the *Daily News* reporter, complained that the courts were releasing juvenile offenders almost as fast as they were apprehended. The reporter replied that to write about this problem he needed to know of a specific incident. The police told him about a recent case of a black youth who was released on $500 bail after being charged with beating an 82-year-old woman. This story was published. Upon reading it in the *News,* a state legislator (who sat on a juvenile justice subcommittee) obtained access to the youth's record of prior offenses and found that one of these was a homicide. The legislator telephoned several of the city's media, who then publicized this latest development. Seeing the kind of coverage his case was receiving, the youth promptly jumped bail. That event quickly made headlines throughout the city. At this point, the mayor called a press conference and "declared war" on crimes against the elderly. He denounced the juvenile justice system, advocated harsher punishment for young offenders, and allocated more money and manpower to the Senior Citizens Robbery Unit. (This, too, was heavily covered in all media.)

In these early days of the crime wave several things occurred which underlay its growth. The most obvious of these was the active promotion of a new social problem by parties with interests in it: the state legislator on the juvenile justice subcommittee, the mayor (just beginning to run for reelection), and the Senior Citizens Robbery Unit (established only months before and concerned about budget cuts in the police department). All strategically used their power to make news (Molotch and Lester, 1974) as a way of formulating the problem and discerning what could be done about it. Thus, some actual occurrences of crimes against the elderly plus the statements and actions of local newsmakers generated enough stories to begin a "crime wave dynamic" in New York's community of news organizations.

Constructing a Crime Wave in Newsrooms

My observations in a television newsroom at the time of "crimes against the elderly" indicated that a crime wave is little more than a *theme* in the news which is heavily and continuously reported. Editors use news themes not only to give their program or newspaper a presentational order, but also to sort through and select a few stories from the masses of news copy they receive every day. Moreover, journalists depend on other news organizations for a sense of "what's news today," i.e., which themes to look for in raw materials for news. This means that judgments as to what is a current news theme can spread quickly throughout a community of news organizations all watching each other. Within the space of a week, a crime theme (such as "crimes against the elderly") can become so "hot," so entrenched in the news community, that even journalists skeptical of the crime wave cannot ignore reporting each new incident that comes along.

But no matter how much journalists expect to see a certain theme in the news, they cannot continue to cover it without a steady supply of fresh incidents. In part, local news promoters served this function. But the NYPD's press wire apparently provided the bulk of incidents which made the crime wave possible after it arose in the last week of October.

Unfortunately, no records of the press wire for the period of time in question could be obtained for analysis. But there is enough indirect evidence to confirm that when the wave of publicity had just begun, the press wire suddenly started to report incidents of the new problem in far greater numbers than it ever had. Journalists interviewed after the crime wave recalled suddenly seeing "a run of crimes against the elderly" on the press wire. And the police in the Operations Section and the Public Information Office remembered that more of these types of incidents than usual were placed on the press wire "because the media was interested in them."

Even more significant was the fact that when the mayor "declared war" on crimes against the elderly, an unpublicized part of his "battle plan" included a policy directive which affected the system by which the police monitored unusual occurrences. Operations Order 96/76, issued on November 4, required precinct police to make unusual reports for the new category of crimes against the elderly, and it told officers in the Operations Section to place instances of these crimes on the press wire. But the order was just temporary. It specified that all precincts were to specially monitor crimes against the elderly only from November 1976 to January 1977.

As it turned out, the crime wave died down in mid-December. Thus, it does not appear that the expiration of the police order was directly responsible for the end of the crime wave. But it does appear that, in conjunction with the early news coverage of crimes against the elderly, the departmental directive led police suddenly to see a new kind of crime as unusual in greater numbers than they had, and thus increase the flow of incidents over the press wire. The records of one precinct show that when the policy order was in effect, the number of unusual reports on crimes against the elderly suddenly increased even though the amount of crimes known to that precinct did not (see Appendix B). Therefore, the mayor and police officials not only promoted the new social problem directly to the media through their public statements, but in a far more powerful way, they indirectly nurtured the growing crime wave by institutionalizing a new category of unusual incident. Their seemingly innocuous act of "keeping better track of this new kind of crime" led to a flood of news stories for weeks to come.

Summary and Conclusions

The system by which the police report incidents to the news media reflects two concerns: managing order in public and managing the image of the police department. Incidents that satisfy these concerns become the journalist's raw materials for news.[14]

The department's concern with containing crime's worst cases" results in a system which is fixed on monitoring troubles in the public sphere: crime in public places, crime between strangers, and disruptions of the flow of business as usual in the city. Thus, the system of unusual reports provides media newsrooms with a steady diet of the most extreme examples of street crime (large gang fights, brutal muggings, and the like) punctuated every now and then by even larger disturbances of public order, such as bombings and violent demonstrations. Because they rely on the police for raw materials, journalists convey an image of crime wholly in accord with the police department's notion of serious crime and social disorder.[15]

But just as journalists implicity adopt a police perspective on crime, so do the police adopt a journalistic perspective. The department's concern with managing its image and remaining the media's routine source for crime news results in the use of "newsworthiness" as a means for deciding which incidents are unusual. Police officers develop a journalist's eye for crime, viewing some incidents not only as "good busts," but also as good stories. Because their criteria for newsworthiness are inferred from media coverage, the police continue to provide the press with the same types of incidents that have been reported in the past.

Thus, contrary to the assumptions of previous research (Sherizen, 1978; Roshier, 1973; Antunes and Hurley, n.d.), the selection of crime news is not located exclusively in media organizations, nor are judgments about the newsworthiness of crime strictly a function of the conventions of journalism. Rather, crime news is mutually determined by journalists, whose image of crime is shaped by police concerns, and by police, whose concerns with crime are influenced by media practices.

During periods when new crime issues are not being promoted in the press, the police reporting system on its own continues to provide the media with incidents that reiterate old law-and-order themes. But when moral entrepreneurs begin to promote a new type of crime, the crime-reporting system can amplify coverage of the issue. Entrepreneurs who have the power to make news can promote coverage of a new social problem by calling press conferences, issuing news releases, leaking information, and arranging dramatic coverage for TV film crews. In the case of New York's "crime wave," favored news sources (like the mayor, the state legislator, and SCRU) increased the number of stories about crimes against the elderly by exploiting their routine access to the press. This kind of news promotion has been noted by other researchers not only in crime reporting (Chibnall, 1977; Tillman, 1976), but in all forms of news (Tuchman, 1978; Schudson, 1978; Roshco, 1975; Molotch and Lester, 1974; Sigal, 1973; Boorstin, 1961).

But this study has shown that another, less-recognized form of news promotion can occur in crime reporting. The power to construct social reality rests not only with those who promote their public statements as news, but also with those who can control the media's raw materials for news. A police department's system for monitoring unusual occurrences can be altered so that reveals new kinds of crime to the media. Once police start keeping track of a new category of crime, as long as there are some occurrences every day that can be seen as instances of the category, then a previously invisible form of crime suddenly will appear as a crime wave to journalists. Those who have the power to define what the police monitor have the power to publicize new social problems.

The number of such problems that await discovery in this fashion are vast because there are an indefinite number of conceivable types of existing public order disturbances, e.g., muggings of tourists, crime in buses, schoolyard crime. The specific ones that emerge at a given time reflect the politics of newsmaking in a region, as particular interests vie for power in a community or particular police units seek to increase their importance within a law enforcement bureaucracy.

But the police crime-reporting apparatus will not sustain any social problem that makes its way into the news. As long as the routine sources for crime news are police departments, whose enforcement net is fixed on troubles in the public sphere, the press reinforces a climate of opinion that keeps the police concerned with "crime in the streets." Particular social problems may come and go, but law-and-order news is here to stay.

APPENDIX A

Crimes Against the Elderly as a Percentage of Crimes Against the Total Population (Robberies and Purse Snatchings Only)

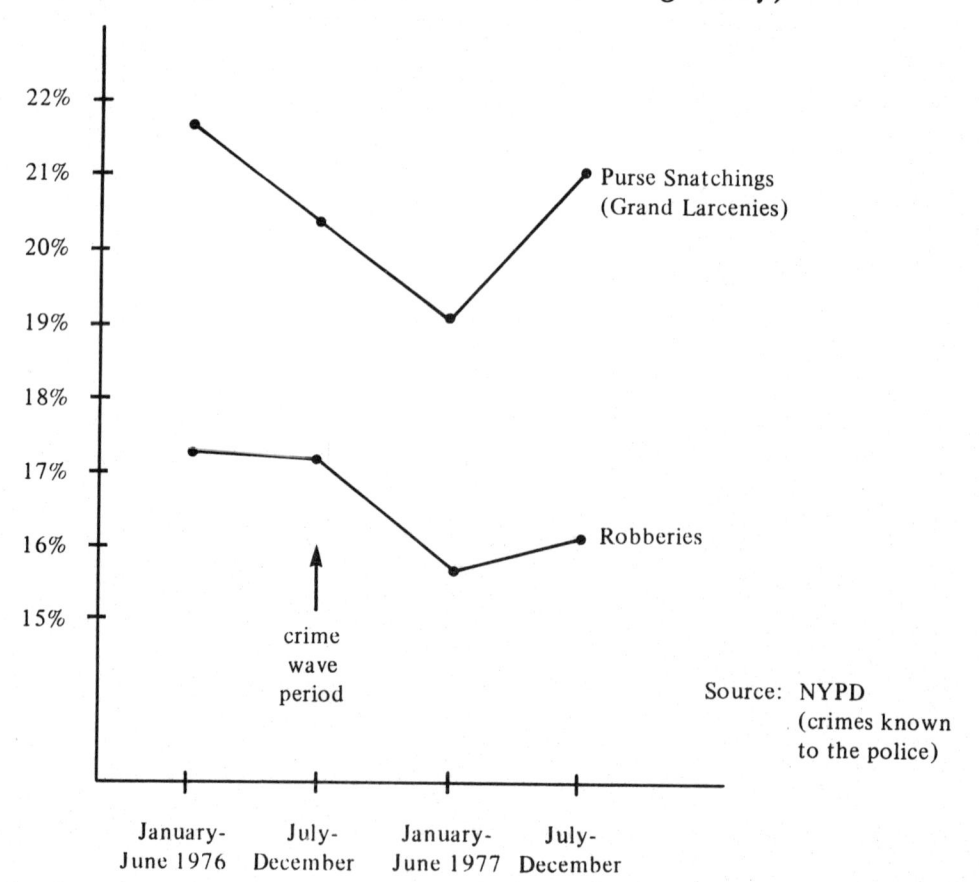

APPENDIX B

As a way of testing whether the publicity on crimes against the elderly and the departmental directive concerning these crimes affected the system for reporting unusual occurrences, the records of one police precinct were analyzed.[16] The number of unusual reports for crimes against the elderly were compared with the number of crimes against the elderly known to the police (as indicated by complaint forms) from February 1976 to September 1977. Because there were so few unusual reports involving elderly victims in this precinct, frequencies were tabulated for four-month blocks of time. October 1976 to January 1977 was the crucial period which included the crime wave and NYPD policy order.

Crimes Against the Elderly in One Precinct: Crimes Known to the Police and Crimes Reported as Unusual

	Unusual Reports	Crimes Known to the Police	Percent of Unusuals Out of Crimes Known
February-May (1976)	1	43	2.33
June-September (1976)	1	30	3.33
October-January (1976-77)	3	36	8.33
February-May (1977)	2	27	7.40
June-September (1977)	1	45	2.22

The small number of unusual reports involving elderly victims in this precinct makes any conclusions highly tentative. Nevertheless, the figures do indicate that the police increased their unusual reports for crimes against the elderly in just the period we would expect. The table also shows that the variation in the number of elderly victimizations known to the police would not account for the increase in unusual reports.

ENDNOTES

1. For studies of police beat reporters and their relationships to the law enforcement bureaucracies they cover, see Fishman (1980), Sherizen (1978: 209-213), Chibnall (1977, 1975), and Tillman (1976).

2. Even in communities where there are a few enough incidents for journalists to know of all crimes known to the police in one day, newsworkers still depend on someone in a police department (usually a press officer) to provide some kind of summary of the "most important" crimes of the day. Not only does this method simplify the newsgathering process for reporters, but also these sources often have more recent information and can provide more details about a case.
3. Journalists refer to this teletype as the "police wire" and call its messages "squeals." Police refer to it as the "press wire" and call its messages "principal cases." Although I used the journalist's terminology for the teletype in an earlier study (Fishman, 1978), I shall follow the policeman's terms here because the focus of this article is on the police department.
4. Unlike other official forms which the police fill out in the course of taking complaints, doing investigations, and making arrests, the "Unusual Occurrence Report" has no legal status and plays no role in the processing of a case in the criminal justice system. As one precinct commander put it, unusual reports are "strictly informational, for internal department use only."
5. The office of an area commander would not screen unusual reports. All would be passed on to headquarters. Apparently, precincts do not directly call the Operations Section because area commanders expect their precincts to keep them informed of all unusual happenings.
6. The sense I am interested in police discretion here differs from most discussions of the issue which usually focus on the individual officer as a decision maker (Skolnick, 1975: 71-90; Bittner, 1970: 107-113; LaFave, 1965; Piliavin and Briar, 1964; but see also Cicourel, 1968; Reiss and Bordua, 1967). Instead I am concerned with discretion as an organizational phenomenon wherein priorities of enforcement are initially set by the distribution of manpower, the specialization of subunits in a department, the known policy of superiors, and the like. For example, if its informal department policy "not to go out of one's way" to arrest customers of prostitutes, or if manpower is deployed in a way that makes such arrests unlikely, then we can speak of discretion being exercised at an organizational level.
7. I say "almost always" here because there is one notable exception: homicide. Any suspicious death (or assault likely to result in death) was considered a "worst case" whether it occurred in public or private and whether it involved stranges, acquaintances, friends, or intimates.
8. See Sudnow (1967: 36-42) for a discussion of the significance of counting occurrences and the conditions under which professionals will keep count of the matters with which they deal, e.g., nurses counting deaths witnessed in a hospital.
9. There is some question that this is true of homicides. One officer maintained that homicides happened "every day of the week" in a precinct in the South Bronx where he had worked, and claimed that not every murder would be considered as unusual and reported to headquarters. Nevertheless, officers in the Operations Section considered all homicides unusual, and because they monitored the 911 emergency phone calls to the police, they were likely to know of murders even if local precincts did not bother to report them as unusual.

10. Often the Operations Section would already know of these occurrences before a precinct called to report them because this unit monitored 911 phone calls.
11. Incidents would not immediately be reported to the press in the event that (a) the police were in doubt about the authenticity of the incident as an instance of its type, e.g., discovering a bomb was fake, or (b) the police felt that publicity might hamper their operations or escalate the incident e.g., encourage more looting. In both cases the Office of Public Information was contacted and they decided what to do.
12. For a detailed discussion of the circularity of all types of news, see Rock (1973).
13. The police data is offered here only to point up the problematic character of what was happening "on the streets." In fact, NYPD crime data is not a reliable indicator of actual amounts of crime and thus, should not be taken as proof that there really was not a "behavioral crime wave" (see Fishman, 1980: 157-158).

    Actually, a case could be made — albeit a weak one — for the existence of more crimes against the elderly at the time of the heavy publicity. If one measures the crime rate in terms of victimizations per 1000 elderly, one finds a moderate increase (3.4%) in the robbery rate over the previous six months. (However, one also finds a 4.9% increase in reported robberies for the general population. And one still finds decreases in the rates of homicide and purse snatching for both the elderly and the general population.)

    The point here is that no one at the time of the publicity knew — or still knows — if there was a sudden increase in victimization of the elderly. Given this state of indeterminacy — typical of social problems in their early stages — I am raising the question of how a crime wave was formulated in the press.
14. It is important to note that the generality of the findings of this research are at present at an open question. This is so not only because this study deals with a single police department, but also because smaller law enforcement agencies may employ somewhat different mechanisms or monitoring "what is happening" in their communities. Even if this is the case, it is possible that the NYPD crime-reporting apparatus represents one of the most bureaucratically developed systems toward which smaller law enforcement agencies may be moving as they expand their public information functions and formalize the reporting of unusual occurrences.

    Research on the routines of crime reporting in small cities (Fishman, 1980: 38-46; Tillman, 1976: 61-63) indicates that police beat reporters to a large extent rely on official "summaries" of daily incidents provided by headquarters through a variety of means: the comments of a public information officer or other centrally located person, e.g., a dispatcher or desk sergeant; a clipboard, blackboard, or other crime blotter in the dispatcher's room; and a telephone "newsline" with a prerecorded message on the few "most important" crimes of the day. It seems likely that some kind of system similar to New York's for defining "unusual occurrences" underlies these devices.
15. In discussing the content of news from television networks and news-magazines, Gans (1979: 57-58) notes: "The frequent appearance of disorder stories suggests that order is an important value in the news, but order is a meaningless term unless one specifies what order and whose order is being valued. For one thing,

there are different types of order; a society can have violence in the streets and a stable family life at home, or public peace and a high rate of family instability. . . . Social disorder (in the news) is generally defined as disorder in the public areas of society."

16. This one precinct was chosen because its records were accessible. (The NYPD does not centrally compile statistics for unusual reports and, in general, the police do not make such records available to the public.) There is good reason to think that the precinct studied was fairly typical in the amount of crimes against the elderly that most precincts would have dealt with. It ranked close to the median precinct in the amount of elderly victimization reported by all precincts for 1977.

REFERENCES

Antunes, G. and P. Hurley (n.d.) "The representation of criminal events in the metropolitan press." Univ. of Houston. (unpublished)

Bittner, E. (1970) The Functions of the Police in Modern Society. Rockville, MD: National Institute of Mental Health.

Boorstin, D. (1961) The Image: A Guide to Pseudo-Events in America. New York: Harper & Row.

Braungart, M., W. Hoyer, and R. Braungart (1979) "Fear of crime and the elderly,: pp. 15-29 in A. Goldstein et al. (eds.) Police and the Elderly. New York: Pergamon.

Brownmiller, S. (1975) Against Our Will: Men, Women, and Rape. New York: Simon & Schuster.

Chibnall,. (1977) Law-and-Order News: An Analysis of Crime Reporting in the British Press. London: Tavistock.

— (1975) "The crime reporter: a study in the production of commercial knowledge." Sociology 9 (January): 49-66.

Cicourel, A. (1968) The Social Organization of Juvenile Justice. New York: John Wiley.

Fishman, M. (1980) Manufacturing the News. Austin: Univ. of Texas Press.

— (1978) "Crime waves as ideology." Social Problems 25 (June): 531-543.

Gans, H. (1979) Deciding What's News. New York: Pantheon.

Gordon, M. (1979) "Some costs of easy news." Presented at the annual meetings of the Society for the Study of Social Problems, Boston, August.

Hoyer, W. (1979) "The elderly: who are they?" pp. 1-14 in A. Goldstein et al. (eds.) Police and the Elderly. New York: Pergamon.

LaFave, W. (1965) Arrest: The Decision to Take a Suspect Into Custody. Boston: Little, Brown.

Molotch, H. and M. Lester (1974) "News as purposive behavior: the strategic use of routine events, accidents, and scandals." Amer. Soc. Rev. 39: 101-112.

Piliavin, I. and S. Briar (1964) "Police encounters with juveniles." Amer. J. of Sociology 70 (September) 206-214.

Reiss, A. and D. Bordua (1967) "Environment and Organization: a perspective on the police," pp. 25-55 in D. Bordua (ed.) The Police: Six Sociological Essays. New York: John Wiley.

Rock, P. (1973) "News as eternal recurrence," pp. 73-80 in S. Cohen and J. Young (eds.) The Manufacture of News. Beverly Hills: Sage.

Roshco, B. (1975) Newsmaking. Chicago: Univ. of Chicago Press.

Roshier, B. (1973) "The selection of crime news in the press," pp. 28-39 in S. Cohen and J. Young (eds.) The Manufacture of News, Beverly Hills: Sage.

Schudson, M. (1978) Discovering the News. New York: Basic Books.

Shearing, C. (1974) "Dial-a-cop: a study of police mobilization," pp. 77-88 in R. L. Akers and E. Sagarin (eds.) Crime Prevention and Social Control. New York: Praeger.

Sherizen, S. (1978) "Social creation of crime news: all the news fitted to print," pp. 203-224 in C. Winick (ed.) Deviance and Mass Media. Beverly Hills: Sage.

Sigal, L. (1973) Reporters and Officials, Lexington, MA: D. C. Heath.

Skolnik, J. (1975) Justice Without Trial. New York: John Wiley.

Sudnow, D. (1967) Passing On: The Social Organization of Dying. Englewood Cliffs, NJ: Prentice-Hall.

— (1965) "Normal crimes: sociological features of the penal code in a public defender office." Social Problems 12 (Winter): 255-276.

Tillman, R. H. (1976) "The police reporter: a study in strategic interaction." M.A. thesis. Univ. of Oklahoma.

Tuchman, G. (1978) Making News. New York: Free Press. — (1976) "Telling stories." J. of Communication 26 (August): 93-97.

Walker, L. (1979) The Battered Woman. New York: Harper & Row.

SECTION II

THE ISSUES WHICH DEFINITELY DIVIDE AND/SOME TENTATIVE SOLUTIONS

SHOOTING DOWN TV'S COP SHOWS

Experts Deplore the Sloppy Procedures That Turn Up on Prime-Time Police Dramas

DAVID JOHNSTON

WORKING undercover as a sidewalk vendor, Mick Belker, the dirtbag detective on *Hill Street Blues,* waited until the dope dealer completed his illegal business and ordered a hot dog before growling, "You're under arrest, dogbreath." The dealer slammed the steaming cart lid on Belker's hand and ran, prompting a wild foot chase that Belker lost.

Great entertainment? Sure. Great police work? No way.

Watching such scenes troubles me because that's not the way it happens on the streets. To viewers whose freedom to stroll their own neighborhood during prime time has been restricted or even taken away by fear of random crime, the sins of TV's police may go largely unnoticed within the reassuring, false premise that the cops usually catch the bad guys. But if real police officers acted like the fictional cops we see on television, they could never do their work, would probably be fired or sent to jail, and might even get killed. Says retired Los Angeles deputy police chief Lou Reiter: "Most of what passes for police work on television is just plain embarrassing."

Reiter's complaint may seem trivial. After all, police dramas are just entertainment. But life often imitates television, and millions of people get distorted images from police dramas. That's bad for the police and bad for society.

---

*(EDITOR'S NOTE: Biographical information about David Johnston appears with his article titled "The Cop Watch," which is also part of this collection.)

†Reprinted with permission from TV GUIDE® Magazine. Copyright 1983 by Triangle Publications, Inc. Radnor, Pennsylvania. Reprinted also with permission of the author.

Practically all police dramas hire police officers as script consultants. But usually their roles are limited to technical matters. When entertainment and reality conflict, reality loses. As Jesse Brewer, a Los Angeles deputy police chief who is technical adviser to *Hill Street,* notes: "I take exception to a lot of what they do, but in the end they do exactly as they please."

What results are scenes like Belker's chase—scenes that make Jim Fyfe cringe. Fyfe, a retired New York police lieutenant who used to patrol Brooklyn and Times Square, is now an associate professor of justice at The American University and a nationally noted expert on police tactics. "Chases are exciting, but no well-trained police officer would have handled it that way," Fyfe observes. "I'd have collared him from behind, had my gun on him and then announced he was under arrest. I would have had the cuffs on him before he had a chance to run or be a danger to anyone—including me."

Hill Street co-creator Steve Bochco admits Belker "didn't do it by the book or even the way most cops would." But Bochco says dramatizing the emotional impact of policing is more important to *Hill Street* than faithfully depicting "the mechanics" of policing. "The point of that scene wasn't whether Belker caught or didn't catch the bad guy; the point was Belker's depression at being too old to outrun him," Bochco says.

Hill Street's characters at least actively debate the ethics and merits of some of their conduct. So do the characters on *Cagney & Lacey.* But how many viewers realized questionable tactics were being depicted when detectives Chris Cagney and Mary Beth Lacey, hot on the trail of six Asian gang members wanted for bank robbery, slipped into some alluring clothes so they could snuggle up to the suspects in a crowded Chinatown restaurant and bust them?

"The gang members could have shot Cagney and Lacey under the table," complains Lou Reiter, the former chairman of LAPD's Use of Force Review Board, which passes judgment on officers' tactics when they use guns, batons, and other weapons.

"By arresting the bandits inside, those two created a possible hostage situation, endangering the lives of other diners," Reiter notes. "They should have waited for the gang to come outside after their meal and arrested them on the street."

That's how FBI and Federal drug-enforcement agents acted when they arrested one of maverick auto tycoon John Z. De Lorean's alleged partners on charges of cocaine trafficking. The G-men let the associate finish his meal at a posh restaurant and step safely outside before slapping the cuffs on him.

Free-lancer Brian McKay says he never thought about such dangers when he wrote that *Cagney & Lacey* scene. "I had to go sexual to make it work," McKay says, explaining that portraying the pair provocatively caught the gang members off-guard. "When you do this kind of show," McKay adds, "it's tough to have it be totally credible and work as drama."

It may be tough, but no one ever said writing was easy work.

T. J. Hooker portrays some of the most amateur police tactics on television. That's ironic because William Shatner, in the title role, plays a police-academy instructor who also offers his "expert" guidance to rookies while patrolling the streets. In one episode, a rookie and his veteran partner race to a corner grocery where a bandit has murdered the owner. They fail to clear the crime scene of gawkers, who could damage vital evidence. Then the rookie mouths platitudes to the tearless widow until his partner runs up shouting they must leave immediately because "we've got a radio call." With that, the two blue suits abandon the crime scene even though homicide detectives have yet to arrive. In real police work that's called neglect of duty. It's enough to get a cop suspended, perhaps fired.

Later in the episode, Shatner and two rookies spot a crazed sniper atop a building. Valiantly, the trio draw their six-shooters and race to the rooftop—without radioing for backup units. On the roof, one rookie, his service revolver drawn, jumps the madman, wrestling him to the ground. Luckily it was television, so the gun didn't go off and kill anyone.

Rick Husky, *Hooker*'s creator and supervising producer, acknowledges the officers should have cleared the murder scene and waited for detectives to arrive before leaving. And before pursuing the sniper, he concedes, they should have radioed for more officers as well as holstered their weapons before any hand-to-hand combat.

But, Husky says, "the show has to bow to the demands of our audience" to be entertained, as well as to the realities of a seven-day shooting schedule. "You write a script; the technical adviser goes over it. It's late in the day, an exterior shot; you're over budget and running out of light and you can't come back to that location the next day," Husky explains. "So sometimes mistakes are made. . . . You can't put these shows under a microscope and have them hold up."

The issue is not how closely these shows are examined, though, but how faithfully they portray reality. Husky and other television people interviewed for this story all said they want to help the police. But police-drama producers who really want to support instead of exploit the police should harken to Deputy Chief Brewer's observation that "many people assume what they are seeing is proper and accepted police behavior."

Of course, real police don't always do what they are taught in police-academy classrooms either, as documented in a 1982 *Washington Post* series about how cops on the street sometimes step outside the law. Abundant evidence of less-than-perfect police performance can be found in Los Angeles, where, in the past three years, more than two dozen police officers and deputy sheriffs have been arrested for armed robbery, cocaine smuggling, burglary, brutalizing suspects, shooting a pregnant woman and other misdeeds.

While Husky and others say their shows portray police positively, Dr. Lawrence Sherman, research director for the non-profit Police Foundation, says police dramas often do just the opposite. "There are lots of illegalities, especially illegal searches of suspects, on police shows," Sherman explains.

In 1976, Ethan Katsh and Stephen Arons, two University of Massachusetts legal scholars, watched one episode each of 15 police dramas, including *Hawaii Five-O, Starsky & Hutch, Kojak, Police Woman* and *Baretta*. They identified 21 clear violations of constitutional rights, seven possible violations and 15 instances of police brutality or harassment. "Even the most blatantly illegal and unconstitutional behavior of police is glorified by an endless stream of police dramas," they concluded.

"Things are pretty much the same on the new shows," Katsh says. "Even on *Hill Street Blues*, which is a bit different from the usual police show, they pay only lip service to the Constitution."

There's nothing wrong with showing police breaking the law. But there is something seriously wrong when programs fail to clearly identify such conduct as illegal or improper. Routinely depicting the police running roughshod over the very laws they are paid to enforce, and especially glorifying misconduct by associating it with hero figures, builds disrespect for the police and the rule of law. And our free society depends on voluntary support to our system of laws.

Police dramas also fail to take into account the major policy and tactical changes that most large police forces have made in the past decade to avoid unnecessary shootings, minimize risks to officers and calm distraught people so that minor incidents don't explode into violence. Cops today are taught to think first, then act. But on television, cops use their guns instead of their heads to solve problems.

"On television, the gun is out all the time and it just isn't realistic," Fyfe says. He should know. After analyzing every shot fired by New

York's finest over a five-year period, Fyfe found the average cop in the Big Apple would have to work 60 years just to shoot it out once with the bad guys.

In Los Angeles alone, police shootings are down one-third from the mid-'70s, but fans of trigger-happy TV series about police would never know it. April Smith, a former story editor at Cagney & Lacey, says that among police-show writers, "everyone's assumption is that you have to have death. It creates tension and jeopardy and suspense that people love."

But that assumption is an erroneous one. "Television is missing a great opportunity to educate people about the law, their responsibilities and how to act when a police officer stops them," says Los Angeles Police Chief Daryl F. Gates. He believes that police dramas foster the false idea that people have a right to flee when a police officer orders them to stop. Why? Because on TV, suspects do it all the time.

Even real cops can get mistaken notions about their work from watching television. "Many recruits think police work is *Starsky & Hutch,* swinging from fire escapes and chasing people in their private cars," observes Capt. Tom Hays, commanding officer of the Los Angeles Police Academy.

In Culver City, Cal., Police Chief Ted Cooke tells recruits that behaving like cops on television will get them in deep trouble with him.

Growing up watching television cop shows can leave young officers with the impression that police always race, sirens wailing and red lights flashing, to crime scenes. Or that they pull guns on everybody who just might be a bad dude. "We have a structured program to de-train them," Cooke says.

Don Reierson says he observed few problems with police drawing and using their firearms when he became director of San Diego County's police academy in 1969. But a few years later, as police dramas became popular, "it seemed like everybody was pulling their guns all the time like Starsky and Hutch. We learned you've got to untrain officers, sometimes even officers working the streets, from the perceptions they get from TV."

Adds the Police Foundation's Sherman: "An exciting television show is much more powerful in influencing behavior than a boring lecture from a sergeant."

Police dramas can portray model tactics and still entertain. "The old *Dragnet* and *Adam-12* shows were pretty much accurate right down the line," recalls Jesse Brewer, the technical adviser to *Hill Street.* "Many of Joe Wambaugh's old *Police Story* shows were accurate because he insisted upon it."

Indeed, one Police Story episode, "The John Wayne Syndrome" is widely used to train recruits about the dangers of acquiring an unrealistic sense of their own power and importance just because they wear a badge and carry a gun. And the California Highway Patrol believes the squeaky-clean image created by *CHIPS* helps to attract good officers.

More faithful portrayal of model police conduct might even improve police action on the streets. A decade ago, Culver City's Chief Cooke, then an LAPD lieutenant, spent two months in New York on an exchange program. To his dismay, Cooke repeatedly observed what he considered sloppy tactics by his New York colleagues.

Then, one day, "I watched two New York blue suits conduct a perfect by-the-numbers traffic stop on three guys in a stolen car. I asked how they learned to do it that way and they opened up a notebook," Cooke recalls. "It was filled with tips they got from watching *Adam-12*."

POLICE AND THE MEDIA: DEBUNKING THE MYTHS

PATRICIA A. KELLY

THE RELATIONSHIP between police and the media has traditionally been a hostile one, chilled by conflicts, real or imagined, which inhibit the flow of information that the public has both the right and the need to know.

David M. Mozee, Sr., management training specialist for Institute of Police Technology and Management, University of North Florida, assigns a shared culpability for the contentions.

"Both groups perpetuate the myth that the other group is the enemy," says the 28-year veteran of the Chicago Police Department, who has served as its director of news affairs. "In reality, they should be working toward the same end—good government, justice, public confidence and equal treatment of all citizens."[1]

My work as a police reporter, my interactions with police officers, both as a student and a teacher at the Florida police training institute, and experiences related by my journalism majors as they covered police agencies convinced me that the "myth" as defined by Mozee flourishes. Further, in fact, it is often responsible for making instant adversaries of the keepers and seekers of information, who could sometimes share cooperative ground in the common good.

Psychiatrists, psychologists and researchers who treat or study the physiological and psychological effects of job-related stress on police frequently cite the relationship between police and press as one of the principal, negative profession-induced anxieties. For example, in "Job Stress and the Police Officer: Identifying Stress Reduction Techniques," Terry

---

A portion of this article appeared in the summer, 1986 issue of *Journalism Educator*, a publication of the Association for Education in Journalism and Mass Communication.

Eisenberg includes among his six major categories of stressors, distorted press accounts of police incidents.[2]

When asked to categorize the career-based stressors they have encountered most often in their police training and counseling, the heads of the psychological services units that function for the major police agencies in Massachusetts were unanimous. High on their condemnation list was a media they claim deliberately portrays police in a poor light and sacrifices the truth of event to the selling powers of sensationalism. Patrolman Edward C. Donovan, founder of the Boston Police Department's Stress Unit, recalled his anger at what he termed slanted coverage of an anti Ku-Klux Klan demonstration in Washington, D.C., complaining that an isolated police behavior received a biased play, while the provoking aggressions from protesters went virtually unremarked. "The front pages showed pictures of policemen in windows with clubs, maybe the only time in the six-hour fracas they used clubs," he said. "But they just had to show that, not some guy kicking a cop."

My years in newsrooms and on police beats have convinced me that both sides have been about equally to blame for keeping the antagonisms at kindle. I have certainly have known reporters who believe that all cops accused of wrongdoing are guilty until proven innocent (in which case, their reasoning generally goes, they are probably, really still guilty). I have known an editor or two dedicated to the proposition that a good cop makes bad copy, a bad cop makes good copy and news judgments should be made along those guidelines.

But I have also walked into many a police station on assignment and been verbally lashed with a litany of all that is supposedly most base about my profession, sometimes before I could even ask a question.

And the cold war between police and the media shows little signs of thaw. In addressing an audience of 50 police officers gathered from across this country and Canada in 1985 on the subject of ethical considerations in the press' coverage of rape, it took all the classroom control maneuvers I could muster to prevent the question and answer period from degenerating into a one-upmanship swap of "worst-reporters-I-have-ever-known" stories. In fact, one veteran officer quietly commiserated later, "It took great courage for you even to get in front of us."

Unfortunately, it is most often the public that ultimately is a kind of faceless corporate victim of these deeply-rooted tensions. In teaching our journalism students the structure of police systems, the terminologies of law enforcement and the basic how to's of crime coverage, we legitimately strive to give them a technical competence. But such proficiency tends to become a kind of moot skill when mutual mistrusts affect access to and dissemination of news in the public interest. Enmity between police and press at its most intense can also seriously compromise the effectiveness of a law enforcement investigation, the rights of a victim of crime, a complainant and a defendant, and therefore neither serve the common weal nor the cause of justice.

Less Heat, More Light

What, as educators, can we do to lower the heat and increase the light? My goal was to design a course that would work on attitudinal changes within both groups. What better setting than an undergraduate classroom shared by future journalists and law enforcement professionals? This seemed like optimum timing—before half-truths become entrenched and estranging fictions.

The existence of both a department of journalism and a College of Criminal Justice at Northeastern University made the population of such a course possible. With the support of a modest grant from the university's instructional development fund and the collaboration of a seasoned police officer, I created an upperclass, inter-disciplinary elective that was piloted in the spring term, 1985. When those twelve weeks has ended, we had several police officers-to-be very much surprised at what they had learned of the journalist's job and some aspiring reporters equally as amazed at the gap between their expectations and the realities of the police function.

There were dramatic conversions in attitudes of majors from both disciplines, marked by a respect for the rigors of the respective professions. And the conclusion that they had perhaps been most unprepared for at the seminar's beginning was a pleasantly ironic realization that reporters and police officers are far more alike than different. This group of soon-to-be working journalists and law enforcement personnel had participated in a learning experiment that I believe has much to teach us about the origins of these cross-suspicions and antagonisms and maybe even about the possibilities for their reduction.

The administration of our Criminal Justice College was enthusiastic about the course entitled "Police and the Media" and encouraged their undergraduates to take this first class to be shared by that particular student mix in the history of the university.

The enrollment of twenty-one was nearly evenly split between the two majors, and the course was co-taught by myself and Trooper

Richard E. Kelly, co-director of the Massachusetts State Police Psychological Services Unit (Stress Unit), who is a veteran trooper, teacher and police stress awareness specialist.

A Trio of Causes

We narrowed our focus to three causes we theorized were the major catalysts in the breakdown of the police and media relationship: (1) the naturally adversary function of the media's objective to disseminate information to serve the public's right to know, and a law enforcement agency's often juggled objectives to protect privacy of victim and victim's family, the welfare of informant and complainant, the rights of the accused and the integrity of an on-going investigation (2) a preconception, historically deeply-rooted and widely-held on both sides that the values and attitudes of police and press are mutually exclusive (for example, the generalization of "liberal" is often used derogatorily by police to describe journalists, and the term "conservative" is often used in the same intention by journalists to describe police (3) the negative stereotypical views that police officers and journalists hold of one another's professions.

Our goals were to: (1) soften the rigidity of the image of police as unreasoning strangleholders of information and journalists as self-serving raiders on their fortress (2) to debunk occupational stereotypes (3) to examine the areas in which both groups are justifiably likely to remain adversary and those in which they might work more harmoniously for the public benefit.

We sought to accomplish objective no. (1) primarily through provision of information where misinformation had prevailed. In lecture and through written materials compiled into a special notebook which each student was permitted to keep, we outlined public records laws and privacy statues in Massachusetts and guidelines typical in other states regarding publication of law enforcement agency-held data. We examined both the black and the white and the gray or discretionary areas in information release and withholding, exploring the ethical considerations from the police and the press perspectives.

In addition, police reporters from the two Boston dailies, an editor of a weekly heralded for its balanced community police coverage, and the public information officers for the Massachusetts State and the Metropolitan Police appeared for panel discussions. Topics included the generation and outline of official police/media relationship policies, ethical dilemmas posed to journalists during crime coverage and advice from both sides on how to improve the inter-personal contact between reporter and police source.

The class was assigned to read articles gathered from newspapers and journals, analyzing clashes that have occurred between police and press during the fact-gathering process. They were shown a videotape of a hostage-taking incident in Jasper, Arkansas, in which a television reporter was asked by law enforcement officials to become part of an action that eventually included an on-camera murder and suicide. They also saw the follow-up newscasts of local outlets in which police were alternately chastised and defended for their conduct.

In their critiques of what they saw in that footage, students agreed that the dialogue between law enforcement personnel at a crisis scene, their performance of their duties, their decision-making machinations and strategy deliberations and their reactions to the bloodshed they both tried to prevent and precipitated did not mesh well with television and cinematic versions of the same.

Misleading Images

It is the image of police actions as projected on the viewer screens which Trooper Kelly addressed in one of his classroom presentations. He dissected movie and television shows which both diminish and inflate the profile and the role of the police officer. On one hand, he said, there is the depiction of the cop as inept, callous and crude, and on the other, its bi-polar counterpart which paints him as Herculean. He described both representations as artificial and explored how the negative feelings engendered by the former and the unrealistic expectations fostered by the latter can be stressful to the police officer.

There were a few students who said they did have a larger-than-life conceptions of a police officer, derived from these television and wide-screen models. They saw cops as superhuman beings, with the machismo-mettle of a John Wayne and the talents of marriage counselor, forensic expert and psychologist, all rolled into one demi-god.

But the majority of majors from both disciplines expressed precisely the prejudiced images of one another's professional personas that we had anticipated when devising the course's goals.

Stereotypes Abounded

Journalism majors largely saw police officers as cynical, overly-aggressive, rigid, paranoid, insensitive to human needs and often at least verbally abusive to the public they were charged to protect and serve. Criminal justice majors shared visions of journalists as also overly-aggressive, as well as arrogant and abrasive. They saw them as cop-haters who slanted stories for personal interest or "to sell papers," sensationalizing coverage of law enforcement, eager to promote anti-police subjects and having little care for a victim's right to privacy or the efficacy of a police investigation.

Some of our students even felt at the start of the "Police and Media" seminar that these negative attitudes they believed flourished in the real world of cops and reporters were reflected in the microcosm of the class itself. As one criminal justice major phrased it, he sensed "some animosity between the criminal justice students and the journalism students."

We sought to discredit jaundiced perceptions and cliche visions by: (1) analyzing the origins and perpetuation of the presumptions which created them (2) acquainting each group with a realistic picture of the working world of the other—the respective ethics, goals, limitations, frustrations and unique, stress-inducing demands. We used two teaching approaches, one passive and one active, one in which the class members would be presented information from which to draw conclusions, the other requiring them to be both observers and participants in that heretofore foreign work world of one another's discipline.

Prior to performing their so-termed action projects, they were exposed to: (1) lectures on psychological and physiological reactions to stress, including a presentation by a psychologist (2) video material, including police training films and a documentary entitled "The Police Tapes," chronicling the nightshift performances of Bronx, N.Y. patrolmen as two broadcast journalists accompany them, recording interactions between police and criminal and police and public.

The students were also required to read *The Choirboys* and *The New Centurions* by Joseph Wambaugh. These novels by the former detective sergeant for the Los Angeles Police Department have been praised particularly by law enforcement professionals as a realistic rendering of the police officer's world, both private and public, from an insider's point of view. One journalism major, a senior who has had considerable experience as a general assignment reporter, wrote and distributed to the class a paper describing in detail copy and assignment flow at *The Boston Globe*, where she was employed as part of the university's cooperative work plan. She furnished valuable insights on the tension injected in the police/press relationship by the pressures of deadlines.

The Action Projects

At the completion of the information-presentation phase of the course, class members were asked to participate in exercises designed to stimulate them to reach, through personal experience, conclusions that would be vivid and enduring than if only reinforced in lecture or written material.

They were exposed to one another's work worlds in two steps, one exploratory and on the sidelines, the other far less tentative, in which they would be playing the principals, not the spectators.

The first was an out-of-class project, assigning criminal justice majors to spend at least one shift accompanying a police reporter on his or her job, and journalism majors to do the same with a police officer. The second was an in-class videotaped role-playing in a staged, crisis situation, in which criminal justice majors acted as reporters and journalism majors as police officers.

In their follow-up reports on their in-field excursions, the students were unanimous in their assessment that watching a law enforcement or a media professional at work game them insights more graphic and solid in impression than had yet been conveyed.

Many journalism majors perceived the strains on police officers that original in those officers' perceptions that they essentially operate in a system of non-support, seeing their own administrations as unsympathetic, the legal system as a mockery and their so-termed noble purpose of protecting and serving the public as actually degenerating into a role of caretaking humanity at its unrelieved worst.

Said one student who spent an evening shift with police in a poor industrial city with a large population of non-English speaking residents: "How you can deal with people that are so drunk they fight anything that moves . . . you can't really forget about the fights, the drunks or even the drug pushers, without it affecting some part of your personal life. Who would want this job? Not me."

He was shocked when one patrolman complained, "We have no stress unit or counseling in this department. A lot of the guys are alcoholic. I guess that's their way of beating it." He added that of the twenty-seven men who joined the force ten years ago, "nineteen of them are either divorced or separated."

Some Graphic Lessons

Another journalism major, who rode with an officer in a suburb west of Boston expected to spend most of the evening drinking coffee and making routine checks. Instead, he found himself experiencing a "strong fear" as he clung to the passengerside door handle of the cruiser as the patrolman pursued a stolen car in a high-speed chase which ended in the crash of that vehicle and injuries to the offending juveniles. Our student received an on-the-scene impromptu lesson in police cynicism with the court system. He reported: "The consensus of the officers seemed to be that the kids in the car got what they deserved. While I didn't expect an outpouring of sympathy for them, I was surprised at the apparent lack of concern about their condition. While nobody said anything, I sensed that several of the cops felt that this was a sort of justice. The court system would only slap them on the wrist. At least now they had paid for their crime."

That night's experience in few ways had conformed to this student's expectations. "In four short hours, I had witnessed three accidents," he recounted. "I had not prepared myself for anything like what had happened. I realized that it must be very difficult for police officers to ride around all day performing their usual tasks, yet still be prepared for anything to happen."

One class member who, by comparison, spent a humdrum tour of duty in one municipal police station, was intuitive enough to observe that the human relations task of policing have their own kind of heroics.

"Even though I was unable to go out in a cruiser, I still saw enough of the work officers must do in the department to change the way I perceived the police officer and the job he does," she wrote. Watching as the in-station personnel quelled a family argument, interceded in a lovers' quarrel over a so-reported stolen engagement ring, and pacified a crying teenager, she "discovered that they were not macho-tough guys, but people with feelings, just like the average person on the street."

And some of the criminal justice majors who had been most vocal about their projections of journalists as abrasive, arrogant and self-serving had to admit they were impressed by the ethical concerns exhibited by the reporters they accompanied on the police coverage rounds.

Referring to a reporter for a suburban Boston daily whom he accompanied on a police station to police station tour one busy Friday night, one student noted, "I believe that there is a definite necessity for trust to be greatly developed between police and media. A responsible press is the beginning of that relationship. It was obvious that Anton had developed a trust relationship on his shift. It is apparant that law enforcement agencies are willing to give information to the press, if the press, in turn, acts with integrity."

A criminal justice major who paired up with a Boston radio station reporter expressed amazement that the journalist "was honest and frank and not pushy."

"I must say," he continued, I did not expect and was pleasantly surprised when Steve put his pad and pencil and tape recorder aside for the off-the-record conversation . . . adding to the trust, rapport and respect during the interview. Steve respected the detective's request and I know the detective respected Steve's integrity."

Their assignment on the peripheries of one another's professional worlds was the prelude to prepare them for the simulation exercise. It was through this final event, staged approximately three-quarters of the way through the term, that class members agreed they learned much about human reaction under pressure, about the complexities of task faced by professionals on both sides, and about themselves.

The Role-Playing

"My reactions to this role play were so overwhelming, I have talked about it extensively for the past week," a senior journalism major wrote in his final assessment paper. For a few intense minutes, in a "crisis" situation, the criminal justice majors played reporters, and the journalism majors played police officers. Trooper Kelly fabricated the crisis scene, intending his preparation of the student players to be "as non-specific and as non-directive as possible, to make their reactions more realistic."

The class was divided into two primary groups, with subgroups within those divisions. The incident was to enacted twice, allowing each student to: (1) play a role (2) be a spectator for a segment of the action in which he would not be directly involved. This latter provision provided the scene with onlookers or a crowd presence to intensify the tension of interplay between police and suspect, police and media. Participants were instructed not to compare or share information, unless appropriate to their roles. There was no opportunity for rehearsal and only minutes given to each to absorb his assignment.

The drama unfolded in three segments:

Scene I: The setting is an office in a small college in a small town (my office at the university was used). The situation: a person identifying himself as a college security guard notifies local police by telephone that a woman is being held at knifepoint by a man in that office. The two responding "police officers" will learn as the scene is played that the hostage is a female employee and the suspect is her estranged husband.

They are parents of a two-year-old son, and the husband, denied visitation rights by the court because of assault and battery convictions against his wife, threatens to kill her is he cannot see their child.

Trooper Kelly instructs: (1) the suspect to consider his own safety and the goal of access to his son (2) the victim, to consider his own safety and ultimately the safety of her son (3) the patrolmen to consider the safety of all and bring the crisis to resolution, by whatever method they deemed fitting.

Also at the location is a reporter from the local newspaper who has heard a barebones report on her newsroom scanner. She is instructed by me to get as much information as possible in preparation for writing a story.

Scene II: After enactment of the hostage-holding, two interactions are simultaneously played out in separate rooms. The police chief is briefed by his patrolmen as to their versions of what has occurred — a prelude to a press conference which will be convened on the incident. The reporter who witnessed Scene I briefs a fellow reporter on her version of what happened, because she will be unable to attend the conference.

Scene III: The press conference itself, during which the chief and the chairwoman of the board of selectmen field questions from the local reporter and out-of-town press on such delicate topics as the arrest of the reporter (in one enactment) and the failure of the two officers to receive back-up manpower (a theme extemporized by one of the actors).

We contrived Scenes II and III to involve multiple relays of information so players could measure the accuracy of news gathering and dissemination under pressure.

The journalism majors assigned the patrolmen's roles donned Massachusetts State Police uniform jackets and carried prop guns, which they were to regard as loaded service revolvers. The suspect's "knife" was a letter-opener. All players were asked to treat the camera as invisible.

In both enactments of Scene I, the escalating verbal and physical conflict between the estranged husband and wife ended when police persisted in using persuasion, rather than force, and talked the suspect into surrendering. Although the police guns were drawn at times during both encounters, no "shots" were fired.

In the first staging, the reporter minimally interfered with conduct of police duty. In the second, she disobeyed repeated warnings from the officers to stay on the perimeter of the scene; she entered the office several times, directly addressed both suspect and hostage, and was subsequently arrested for "obstruction of justice."

In their post-mortem performance evaluations, the majority of players agreed they were not influenced by the camera's presence.

"I felt myself actually believing I was a reporter," said one criminal justice major. Another noted, "I forgot about the camera, I became so wrapped up in my role that I actually began to feel this was a real situation."

In fact, the students did become so absorbed in their parts that passersby in the hallway stopped in dismay, believing that the hostile encounter was actually occurring.

The more "real" the situation was perceived to be by the actors, the more intense were their psychological and physiological reactions to stress. All participants said through their role-playing they had discovered pressures and complications involved in the execution of both the policing and the reporting functions they had not anticipated. Some of these perceptions were confirmation for them of theory they had been introduced to during the classes; some they discovered for themselves.

Journalism majors playing police said their high anxiety levels were rooted in the complexity and the critical consequences of their duties and actions. Said one actress: "I was trying to worry about too much at once, the safety of the hostage, the safety of the suspect himself, the potential hazard the onlookers might create, the presence of the reporter—how much is she allowed to know? How close is she to get? . . . While trying to control the crowd and the reporter, I missed a lot of what was going on with the actual hostage situation . . . and that could have been fatal."

The stress created by control, jockeying for it, fearing to lose it, was cited by every student as a consideration in every role.

One "suspect" admitted he was "having fun at the center of attention and control," and he "did not want to relinquish it." He was distressed when "police invaded my space" and felt "degraded to be led away under someone else's control."

A see-sawing struggle for power a bit more subtle developed between and among the principals at the press conference.

One "police chief" said his goal there was "to establish complete control," and, "being in control at the press conference, I ended it as soon as my authority was questioned."

The "selectwoman" recalled, "I felt the tension in the air as the reporters were trying to get as much information as they possibly could, while the chief and I were limiting the output."

Students were unanimous in their experiencing of one or more of the physiological symptoms of being under acute stress—symptoms which Trooper Kelly told them had been described to him many times by police officers he counseled after they had been involved in traumatic incidents. Sense of time became warped for many who estimated that the eight-minute hostage-holding segment had actually lasted a half hour or longer. One participant reported feeling "tremendously hot," and another, "exhausted when the scene was over."

Still another noted, "anxieties flowed constantly," and one student said, "my adrenalin was up one hundred percent." Two students, both having played police officers, recorded a vivid experience of what Trooper Kelly had defined as "tunnel vision." One was dismayed to see, when viewing the tape later, that her partner had actually dropped his gun. "Tunnel vision had taken over," she explained, "and I never noticed it." Even the "patrolman" who had fumbled that weapon had not himself realized he had done so. Ironically, he was a journalism major who had been very critical of police and skeptical about the stressful nature of the occupation.

Criminal justice majors who played reporters learned that a journalist's job has its own anxiety-inducing factors and its own pressures of accountability. One recounted feeling overwhelmed by the complexity of task, being expected to "get sufficient information for a story," while vying with the "competition present" for recognition at the press conference, ultimately having to "answer to my boss and the public who would want to know what happened."

Another complained about the "impossibility" of framing questions, listening to answers, recording responses and devising a fresh question—all seemingly in a matter of milliseconds. And a third "reporter" who covered the unfolding crisis defined an ethical dilemma, saying she was caught between "not giving the officer a hard time" by barraging him with questions while he tried to handle a life-threatening situation, and "having to get the story."

Criminal justice students also agreed that a journalist's dedication to fairness and conveyance of facts was a critical, but not-so-easily-recognized avocation. That insight came after they viewed the tape and listened to information become mutated as it was passed from eyewitness reporter, to a second reporter and from patrolman to police chief, to selectwoman and finally to a congregated press.

According to the journalism majors, among the graphic lessons were: "a policeman's job involves a great deal of instant decision-making" and unrealistic expectations that he can be "a psychologist and a mind reader;" it is defined by a fearsome unpredictability created by "never knowing what would be found when answering a call."

It was clear that stereotypes had been shattered.

In fact, the consensus of our students was that all phases of the instruction had contributed to major attitudinal changes, including a realization which could create empathy where estrangements now exist. For in addition to becoming aware of some of what Trooper Kelly had early on labelled as "stressors" peculiar to each profession and appreciating the complex nature of the job functions, majors from both discipline began to perceive similarities between their two worlds and the characteristics that contribute to competent performances in each.

"I found [in the police world] many parallels to the journalist's world," wrote one journalism major, citing a shared need of reporter and police officer to often use "the same means of achieving control or order — the gathering and processing of information." He also saw a similar "unpredictability" in the work of each, "a certain amount of tedium, broken by short stretches of pandemonium."

When asked to describe the "perfect police officer and the perfect reporter," one criminal justice major concluded, "surprisingly enough, they share many of the same attributes." He itemized some, including a highly-defined sense of responsibility to the public, "good writing, interviewing and verbal skills," and a strong sense of "fairness and compassion and concern for the people you deal with."

Among other common characteristics defined were: a need to possess "good people sense, common sense, the ability to remain clear-headed under adverse conditions, to perform extremely well under pressure, to be objective and gather all the information available." An especially well-worded wrap-up was offered by a senior journalism major who graduated to become a police reporter on a Massachusetts suburban daily. He described mutual needs to be: "sensitive to people's needs and feelings, but not susceptible to serious emotional wounds," to be observant and inquisitive, to be "able to maintain a noble view of the human race against all odds, to have sympathy for people without sentimentalism, to be able to quickly strike up rapport with all kinds of people."

All students said in a final assessment paper that their respective attitudes toward police and media had changed dramatically since the beginning of the course when they had many misconceptions about each other's professions.

We hope they will apply their new insights to their careers. One of the senior journalism majors who enacted the part of the police chief accepted a slot on a small daily as its police reporter. He contacted me recently and said he was establishing a sound working rapport with his area police agencies.

"What transpired reshaped my thinking of what police must go through," said another senior journalism major, now employed by a wire service in New York.

Perhaps the goal expressed by Trooper Kelly as motivation for his interest in the inter-disciplinary venture is being realized in individual instances that can make a collective difference.

"We hope," he said, "that such a course can help seed the fields of law enforcement and journalism with newcomers who will not allow myths and imaginary conflicts to put wedges in police-media relationships."

ENDNOTES

1. "Police/Media Conflict," *Law and Order.* 30:23-25 (February, 1982), p. 23.
2. "Job Stress and the Police Officer: Identifying Stress Reduction Techniques," in Kroes, W. H. and J. J. Hurrell, Jr., eds., *Job Stress and the Police Officer: Identifying Stress Reduction Techniques; Proceedings of Symposium, 1975* (Washington: U. S. Government Printing Office, 1975).

POLICE/MEDIA CONFLICT

DAVID M. MOZEE

SOME AMOUNT of conflict between police and media is bound to occur because both groups have responsibilities that sometime "seem" to be at odds. Members of the media think they must get all of the facts and get them right now. Police believe they must protect the scene of any incident from all intruders, protect the principals from unnecessary bother from others, and keep all of the facts to themselves so as not to hamper the investigation of the incident, whatever it might be.

Both groups see their mission as "the most important" and judge the arguments that support this opinion as valid. Both also perpetuate the myth that the other group is the "enemy" when in reality they should be working toward the same end — good government, justice, public confidence and equal treatment for all citizens.

Neither the police nor the media seem to recognize that they are basically doing the same type of job — gathering and reporting facts. The police officer must obtain and report all facts known about an incident from as many reliable sources as possible. He then assembles these facts into some logical sequence so they will eventually lead to the solution of the incident and the apprehension of the offender, if any.

The job of the newsperson is to get all the facts about a situation from the most reliable sources available, as soon as possible, and assemble

---

*David M. Mozee Sr. is management specialist for the Institute of Police Technology and Management, University of North Florida. In that position, he is responsible for development, coordination and presentation of management and supervision related courses to police agencies in the United States and abroad. He served 28 years with the Chicago Police Department in various capacities, including commander of its 3rd Police District and director of news affairs in the office of the superintendent.

†Reprinted with permission of the author and of *Law and Order* Magazine. The article appeared in the February, 1982 issue of *Law and Order.*

these facts into some logical pattern to make an interesting and honest story that will keep the public informed. The similarity between the work of the two groups can be readily seen.

Another similarity can be found between two occupations. Newspeople are faced with routine, non-demanding tasks most of the time. Their jobs are not as super-exciting as most people think, so when something out of the ordinary comes along, they want to take full advantage of it. They rush to get all the information they can and then rush to get it into print or on the air.

Most newspeople are responsible journalists trying to do a good job. But, they also realize that a real good story might earn them a bonus or an award or, at the very least, earn them accolades from peers and supervisors.

Police officers are also often faced with routine, non-demanding tasks. Like newspeople, they do not have the exciting job that most people think they have. When something out of the ordinary comes along they rush to the scene to apprehend the offenders or gather information that might help them quickly apprehend the offenders.

Many officers are dedicated public employees that perform well because they like their job. But they too realize that a real good case, handled swiftly and professionally, might earn them an award or promotion or, at the very least, earn accolades from their peers and supervisors. Note how much alike the two groups are.

These pointed similarities might be a key to the resolution of conflict. It has been my experience that once a newsperson and a police officer really made an attempt to understand the other's point of view, cooperation is usually the result. This is not to say that they will become "buddy-buddy," but they do allow the other to do their job without interference and hostility.

Typically, conflict develops when an officer refuses a reporter access to an incident scene or when media thinks the police are trying to "hide" something from them . . . or when the police think media is either "out to get them" or is misquoting them. Tensions that result from real or imagined abuses often develop into vendettas that either group can ill-afford. Both groups need each other, one to gain and keep public confidence and the other to keep the public truly informed.

Meetings between police and media personnel to discuss policies and procedures relating to media and access to information and scenes may prove beneficial by eliminating many minor conflicts. Areas that have been "gray" for years can be wiped out by such meetings, and if media has input into the policies that they have to live by, the policies will be far more palatable to them. The key to any meeting however is honestly and genuine desire to make cooperation a fact.

Making newspeople aware of the potentially serious consequences that might arise from allowing them entry onto a scene that has not been thoroughly processed is one way to gain their cooperation. The police, however, must also grant entry as soon as possible after processing has been completed, and not drag their feet doing the processing.

Media should be allowed to take whatever visuals they can from any vantage point outside the prohibited area. They should also be given the opportunity to interview a responsible police person as soon as that person can provide some basic facts.

Valid Reasons

One of the best ways to prevent conflict is to have valid reasons for doing the things we do, and explain it to responsible media management. Arbitrarily denying a request because we do not like the media generally, or the particular requestor specifically, or denying a request because "we have always done it that way," is looking for trouble. In my experience media people will oblige if we have valid reasons. If we don't get cooperation, then we are on solid ground to respond to any charge leveled by them.

A wise policy is to have the Public Information Officer (P.I.O.) review any internal investigation brought about by the complaint of a newsperson. The P.I.O. should be familiar with both sides of the issue and be in a good position to determine the validity of the complaint. The P.I.O. should also handle any complaint police have against the media. The P.I.O. should have enough rapport with the media to be able to resolve most complaints. News executives normally do not want their employees creating trouble or ill-will, even though at times it may not seem that way to the police.

An "open door or open telephone" policy between the media and the P.I.O. is a must if a meaningful relationship is to develop. If the P.I.O. hides from the media; will not take a stand, no matter how unpleasant the task; is afraid to take a chance and innovate, then there is little sense in having a media policy or a P.I.O.

Valid Interest

The best P.I.O. in the world and the best written policies in existence are useless if the department hierarchy does not have real interest in good media relations. Interest must start at the top of the organization and filter down to the greenest recruit. If the job of media relations is left to one or two people "somewhere in the organization" without the backing of the department's high command, nothing positive will occur. Ideally, the P.I.O. should be direct staff to the Chief Administrator and have his/her trust and confidence.

No one should be misled into believing that good relations means that media will not print or air stories about inadequacies or abuses they find in the department. Good media relations simply means that newspeople will deal fairly with the department and present both sides of a story. Possibly they will also give the department the opportunity to improve their public image by writing some positive pieces about the police.

Credentials

Some on-scene conflict might be avoided if working members of the news teams are given credentials by the department, or if they have their own that are recognized by the department. Officers on duty at the scene of an incident cannot be expected to know by sight every news team member. Newspeople understand the need for credentials because it makes their job easier if only credited people are allowed access beyond barricades.

In most routine cases, reporters are on a tight schedule and do not want to be at a scene longer than necessary. They need some basic questions answered and a few visuals. The sooner the police can satisfy these needs, the sooner media will leave the area and the less likely the tensions and conflicts will arise.

Quick Action

When conflict does occur, and it will occasionally, the P.I.O. should handle it promptly and decisively to prevent a smoldering feud. Police personnel should be educated not to show preferential treatment. An officer may think that he is winning friends, but he is not and should be advised that he is not. "Media friends" recognize that they may be the next on the "not preferred" list, or that the officer might be moved to some less sensitive position . . . and the buddy system will continue without him being the "buddy." Most will welcome equal treatment as they are adept at getting their own stories and developing informants.

A similarity that causes a lot of conflict; newspeople are good investigators, they have to be, and sometimes their investigations lead them into areas previously the exclusive domain of the police. Occasionally newspeople solve cases prior to the police, and occasionally they mess up a case so bad it is impossible to get conviction. Both cause bad feelings.

If relations are good, the media will work closely with police in fighting crime . . . but they have to feel confident that their efforts will be recognized. In my own experience newspeople have given me information that led to good arrests and helped clear crimes.

All conflict probably cannot be eliminated, and we should not think that it can. Conflict can be reduced to where it presents no serious problems, however. The solution is to have a policy both groups can live with and function within. If either group feels "put upon" the policy will not work.

Management of both groups must be dedicated to viable relations and insist that subordinates respect the job of the other group. It would benefit both if an exchange program could be worked out so that both management groups could see how the other works and what they need to do their job effectively. It might be an eye-opening, and interesting experience.

BOTH BLAMED: POLICE, MEDIA RELATIONS—A NEW LOW

DAVID SHAW

(Joke making the rounds in local law enforcement circles:
First cop: "Do you know how to save a drowning newsman?"
Second cop: "No."
First cop: "Good.")

HIS NAME IS George Fry. He is 51. He has white hair, and he wears glasses. When he was much younger, he thought fleetingly of becoming a cop. But at 5 feet 8 inches, 125 pounds, he was too small. So he became a photographer instead.

For the past 22 years, as a photographer for The *Times,* Fry has been in frequent—almost constant—contact with the Los Angeles police. And sheriff's deputies. And Highway Patrol officers. He has ridden in their squad cars, attended their roll calls, worn their gas masks; he has socialized with them—and voted with them.

Throughout the 1960s and 1970s, when the police were under attack for their treatment of blacks, Chicanos, anti-war demonstrators and campus activists, Fry consistently defended law enforcement and critized some of his more liberal colleagues in the news media. The police, he often said, had a difficult and dangerous job to do. Anyone who gave them problems had to expect trouble.

---

*David Shaw is media critic for the *Los Angeles Times*. He has received 13 first-place awards from the Greater Los Angeles Press Club for his work, as well as awards from the American Bar Association and the American Political Science Association. He also holds the Lowell Mellett Award for Media Criticism, 1982 and the Greater Los Angeles Press Club Award for Reporting on Media, 1983. His publications include: *Press Watch* (1984), *Journalism Today: A Changing Press for a Changing America* (1977), *The Levy Caper* (1974), *WILT: Just Like Any Other 7-Foot, Black Millionaire Who Lives Next Door* (1973).

†Copyright, 1979, *Los Angeles Times*. Reprinted by permission.

But last month in Beverly Hills, shortly after Iranians had seized the American Embassy in Tehran, Fry was covering a demonstration by Iranians hostile to the deposed shah. When the Iranians were attacked by American counter-demonstrators, police declared an unlawful assembly and ordered everyone to disperse. Fry tried to photograph the melee. Police ordered him to stop taking pictures and to go away. Fry protested.

"The cops half-shoved, half-yanked me out of the way," he says. "It felt like my right coat sleeve was going to come right out of my jacket."

Several days later Fry's arm still was badly bruised. But he was more angry — and confused — than he was injured.

"I've covered all the big demonstrations," he said. "I've worked with the cops on them. They have their job to do and I have mine, and there's never been any real problem. But this time they were pushing the press around, trying to keep us from doing our job. I actually had the feeling they were going to beat these (Iranian) guys up and just didn't want us around to see it.

"I don't understand it."

Fry is not alone. A number of reporters, photographers and television cameramen at the demonstration also said law enforcement officers interfered with them — sometimes rather roughly.

One veteran reporter said he is accustomed to "a certain amount of pushing and shoving (between police and the press) at all these demonstrations, but it was different in Beverly Hills. They were scary. They actually seemed to enjoy giving us a bad time."

One photographer said a Beverly Hills police officer put a baton against his neck and forced him to the ground. Other journalists said they were pushed and jabbed by police batons. Doug Dare, a 60-year-old KTTV cameraman, said he was "whacked in the stomach with a billy club — twice."

Dare, like Fry, has sympathized with law enforcement throughout his 39-year career: "I've had cops protect me from getting roughed up by demonstrators . . . in Watts and Century City and UCLA," he says. "I don't think you can find a more pro-cop guy than me."

But Dare, like Fry, feels personally betrayed by what happened in Beverly Hills. "There was just much more (police) hostility toward the media than ever before," he says.

Two of Dare's KTTV colleagues — reporter Judi Bloom and soundman Johnny Walker — were actually handcuffed and taken into custody briefly that day. Bloom was almost jerked off her feet, then almost pushed to the ground; Walker was handcuffed so tightly, he says, that his left hand was still numb the next day, and his wrists bore cuffmarks for several days.

The sheriff's office says Bloom and Walker refused to leave when the crowds were ordered to do so. Bloom and Walker say they were leaving—conducting interviews as they retreated. But they were not backing up as quickly as sheriff's deputies would have liked, and their interviews probably did somewhat delay the dispersal of that particular group of people.

Therein lies the crux of the resultant dispute between the media and the local law enforcement.

Law enforcement contends that the media interfered with them, impeding the breakup of a violent, illegal demonstration. The media contends that law enforcement officers interfered with them, preventing them from reporting and photographing the demonstration for the public.

Both sides seek refuge in the law. Law enforcement officials cite the California Penal Code sections prohibiting anyone from interfering with them or disobeying their orders during an emergency. The media cites the Penal Code section that prohibits peace officers from stopping "duly authorized representatives" of the news media from entering any area closed to the public in a "calamity."

In at least one case, the courts have ruled that the specific permission granted the media takes precedence over the general exclusion of the public.

Police argue that the media should have no such special consideration, but the U.S. Supreme Court has ruled: " . . . The press has a preferred position in our constitutional scheme . . . to bring fulfillment to the public's right to know."

Of late conflict between police and the press over press access to riot, crime, accident, and disaster scenes has been escalating. The confrontation in Beverly Hills is not an isolated incident.

In a recent survey 42 members of the Press Photographers Association of Greater Los Angeles said they have had problems with law enforcement officers this year. In San Diego a television newsman was actually tried—and, ultimately, acquitted—on charges of interfering with the police at the scene of a plane crash. In Hollywood a photographer was arrested for taking flash pictures during a sheriff's narcotic arrest. He was released; no charges were filed.

To many, these incidents are a natural if unfortunate by-product of mounting tensions between the police and the press. Over the last five years or so, says Sheriff Peter J. Pitchess, " . . . a strong, deep-rooted suspicion of the media (has developed) in our field personnel."

Why?

"The performance of the media," Pitchess says.

"They've given us cause for suspicion."

Los Angeles Police Chief Daryl Gates says:

"We keep getting hit over the head by the media, and we start to wonder if their role is just to cut us up."

Recent stories on police-involved shootings and charges of racism and high-level ties to organized crime in the LAPD have only exacerbated these feelings.

Stephen Reinhardt, president of the Los Angeles Police Commission and now a nominee for a federal judgeship, thinks police are "just overreacting to long overdue questions."

"Historically," Reinhardt says, "the press has not done an adequate job of investigating law enforcement in this city. Until the last two years or so, the press here has been a patsy—a press agent—for the police.

"Having been immune to criticism by the press for so long—and being sincerely convinced that they (the police) are the guardians of the public welfare—they just can't understand why the press is now subjecting them to the same rigorous examination they give any other institution in public life," Reinhardt says.

But the press has written critically about the police here since the mid-1960s—most particularly in covering their actions in Watts and East Los Angeles and during a 1967 anti-war demonstration in Century City. Other stories on improper police behavior so enraged former Police Chief Edward M. Davis that he once said a *Times* editor was the Police Department's "public enemy No. 1."

Lt. Dan Cooke of the LAPD press office remembers that Davis used to become so upset with the press that he would say reporters should have full access to any crime or disaster scene because " . . . newsmen have the constitutional right to get themselves killed in the pursuit of a story—and in Los Angeles, we're long overdue."

As Reinhardt says, "Police traditionally get their views from the chief. If he says the press is the enemy, they think the press is the enemy. Not that they aren't capable of independent thought, but they have some of those basic concerns themselves to start with, and those are confirmed and exaggerated by sweeping statements that appeal to their emotions."

When Gates attacked the press earlier this year, the Police Commission was so alarmed that it drafted a statement urging the media to "continue to do its job vigorously." But by the time the wording of the statement was agreed upon by all five commissioners, the furor had died down and the statement was never officially released.

Gates shares Reinhardt's concern about the impact of his statements on his officers. In fact, he says, after reading about the problems the press had at the Beverly Hills demonstration, he reflected on his own recent criticisms of the press and called in Cmdr. William Booth, his top press relations officer.

"I was worried," Gates says. "I've been blasting the media and I was afraid that might filter down and the guys would think, 'Gee, the chief is hitting the media. Why can't we? Maybe he's giving us a sign.' "

Gates says he told Booth to pass the word that there was no change in the department's longstanding policy of cooperating with the media.

Nevertheless, Gates says, "There is more hostility toward the media among the rank-and-file police officers today than just a few years ago," and his criticisms of the media are intended to give official voice to those feelings. Some think they may also be intended to counter recent charges within the department that he has not been as outspoken as Chief Davis in defending LAPD against the press.

Conflict between the police and the press is not new, of course. Police-press relations first began to seriously deteriorate in the 1960s.

Until then most contact between law enforcement and the media had involved traditional street crime—murder, robbery, kidnaping. The journalists who covered those stories were generally experienced police reporters who liked and admired the police.

But the sociopolitical upheavals of the 1960s changed all that. Suddenly the police were no longer the heroes, making the streets safe for women and children. Often they were accused of bigotry, brutality, murder.

Newspapers began to change in the 1960s, too. The increasing complexity and contentiousness of society—and the increasing competition from television—required newspapers to be more probing and analytical, more comprehensive than ever before. Editors wanted more interpretive and investigative stories, and police often found themselves confronted by more liberal, more skeptical reporters than their police-beat predecessors. Newspapers no longer were satisfied with just the police—or the City Hall or the White House—side of the story. Police-press relations became polarized, embittered.

Most court decisions involving the press during this period gave the police little comfort. In the last two or three years, however, the press has not fared so well in the courts. Decisions on libel, privacy, confidentially of sources and access to prisons have all gone against the press. The Supreme Court has even ruled that trials can be closed to the press—and that law enforcement officers may search a newspaper office without advance notice or court hearing.

These court rulings have contributed to a general climate in which many law enforcement officers, long resentful of the press, may finally feel emboldened (even officially sanctioned) to act upon that resentment—to disrupt and restrict normal press activity.

Police probably also feel that widespread public criticism of the press further legitimizes their own feelings. People are more afraid of crime than ever before, and that may make them more sympathetic to the police—or, at least, more critical of a press that questions whether the police are being impulsive and overzealous in the pursuit of their duties.

"We've found . . . the general public has stronger resentment against the media than we do," Pitchess says. "The public tells us, 'Clobber those bastards.'"

Television is another new factor in the equation. Only in the last two years or so has television begun to aggressively pursue stories involving charges of police misbehavior. Because television often has such immediacy, impact and high drama—and because some TV stories on the police have been irresponsible and inflammatory—police antagonism toward all the press has intensified.

The one story this year that has done the most to damage police-press relations has been the Eulia Love case.

Eulia Love was shot to death by two police officers early this year on the front lawn of her home. The officers had gone there because she had attacked a gas company serviceman with a shovel when he had tried to collect an overdue gas bill from her earlier in the day. When Mrs. Love started to throw an 11-inch boning knife at the two officers, they shot her. Eight times.

Investigations by both the Police Department and the district attorney found no evidence of wrongdoing by the officers. But the press covered the case aggressively, questioning whether the officers had acted properly and—in some instances—demanding that the officers be disciplined.

Ultimately the Police Commission itself said the two officers had made "serious errors" in the Love shooting.

When a *Times* reporter visited the Police Academy recently to speak to a class of new sergeants, their anger over the Love case was obvious.

"The press talked about how the police shot this woman because she didn't pay her gas bill," said Sgt. Wally Graves. "That's what people remember. But she was shot because she attacked one guy with a shovel and tried to throw a knife at two policemen."

Although the shovel attack and knife-throwing were featured prominently in most coverage of the case, the gas bill did become the major human-interest peg for the story. To the police that seems like careless, sensationalistic—even malevolent—journalistic shorthand.

This is not an uncommon criticism. Often, police say, stories on police-involved shootings are headlined "Police Shoot Youth." They are right. Recent *Times* stories have been headlined "Youth Shot by Off-Duty Officer" and "2 Policemen Slay Youth in Shootout" and "Teen-Ager Shot Fleeing Police."

Such headlines, police say, make it appear they are gunning down innocent kids when, in fact, these "youths" are often 18- and 19-year old criminal suspects, and the police are simply defending themselves.

Police are also upset that stories on police shootings often quote eyewitnesses critical of the police more prominently than they quote the police version of what happened. Even worse, they argue, the media often seem to give far more attention to the killing by a police officer than of the killing of a police officer.

But the most serious single complaint the police have about press coverage of police shootings involves a specific story broadcast last month by KABC, Channel 7.

KABC reporter Larry Carroll had said on the air that he had "solid information" that a man who would ultimately die of wounds suffered in a shootout with police had more gunshot wounds when he arrived at the hospital than he had when police took him from the shooting scene. Carroll also said witnesses told him an officer injured in the gunfight had been accidentally shot by another officer.

Police and doctors at the hospital vehemently denied both allegations; and it did turn out that the officer, who lost his left hand in the shooting, was shot by the suspect. The large number of wounds in the suspect's body resulted largely from the scattering pattern of the police shotgun blast.

KABC News Director Dennis Swanson acknowledged and apologized for the errors the next night in a carefully worded statement that Pitchess has called "a weak . . . half-assed . . . chickenshit apology."

The LAPD is, understandably, even angrier.

"In effect, he (Carroll) accused our officers of murder," says one police spokesman. "That's unconscionable."

Carroll says he relied for some of his information on sources in the hospital, and he realizes now he probably should have attributed that information more carefully. But if he were in the same situation today, he says, he probably "wouldn't do anything that much differently." Besides, he says, he remains convinced there are "discrepancies" in the shootout, and he's still looking into the story.

Gates says he finds that attitude "incredible" in a reporter he always thought was "very responsible." "It just gets back to the mental set at Channel 7," Gates says. "They have a predisposition to tear down this department."

Gates has been critical of Channel 7 ever since the station began investigating police shootings more than two years ago. "Unadulterated trash," he says of that coverage. Gates was angered again in September when the station interviewed an LAPD detective who charged that organized crime had corrupted the upper echelons of the department.

Swanson insists his station's coverage has been fair and responsible and — in the case of the officer-involved shootings — he has a prestigious Peabody Award (television's equivalent of the Pulitzer Prize) to back him up. But Gates seems convinced that personal and political bias — and a battle for ratings — have prompted the station's police coverage.

Similarly, he says, the *Herald Examiner* — which has published several stories critical of the LAPD — is "struggling . . . looking for sensationalism to get readers."

Gates' aide cite in particular a *Herald* story in October about a 63-year-old woman who claims to have been beaten by two teen-agers. The woman said a passing motorcycle police officer refused to help her as she lay in the street. "He said, 'You're drunk,'" she told the *Herald*.

But when the police investigated the case, they could find no one who had seen the incident, and people in the neighborhood coffee shop said the woman told them she had just fallen down in the street and hurt her arm. They said she mentioned no beating and no police neglect. (She refused medical treatment of a broken wrist until the next day.)

When police tried to question the woman after the *Herald* story was published, she refused to talk to them. When the police complained to the *Herald* about the story, editors sent a second reporter out to speak with the woman again. She stuck to her original story — as she did when she finally agreed to talk to the police earlier this month.

But the second Herald reporter said that if she had interviewed the woman originally, she would not have written the story because of inconsistencies in the woman's account and the absence of any witnesses or substantiating testimony. A *Times* reporter interviewed the woman recently and also found her story inconsistent and less than persuasive — especially her insistence that she told people in the coffee shop that she fell down because she didn't think they would believe the "truth."

LAPD officials think the *Herald* should have investigated the story more carefully; they see the story as "typical of the *Herald's* sensationalism." But *Herald* editors deny they are "out to get the LAPD to build circulation," and they cite several recent stories highly favorable to the department.

Nevertheless Gates has been so distressed by press coverage of his department — particularly by Channel 7 and the *Herald* — that he singled them out for public criticism and also videotaped a speech to all LAPD officers in October, suggesting that the "liberal media" was trying to destroy the police department.

When the *Herald* got a copy of the tape and wrote a story about Gates' remarks, the story contained misquotations and mistakes that enraged Gates anew.

But his criticism of the media is not limited to the *Herald* and Channel 7. He is critical of most of the media — including *The Times*. So are others in law enforcement. Their primary criticism is that the media gives prominent play to stories that make law enforcement look bad, but — in the words of one LAPD sergeant — "you ignore or bury on Page 68 anything that might make us look good."

Moreover, police point out, several civic groups periodically honor law enforcement, and stories about these tributes are rare. For example, a Watts woman has an annual open house to thank all law enforcement agencies, but the last time *The Times* covered it was in 1968. With a three-paragraph story. On page 30.

Last August, when the Justice Department filed a police abuse suit against Philadelphia Mayor Frank Rizzo and the city's Police Department, *The Times* put the story on Page 1.

"But when the judge threw (the major portion of) the case out of court," Gates says, "it was on Page 4."

The Sheriff's Department is equally critical of *The Times*.

Last May *The Times* gave prominent play to a story about the sheriff's substation in Malibu receiving preferential treatment that enabled its deputies to avoid long lines during the gasoline shortage.

But *Times* delivery trucks carried signs during that period, saying, "Any courtesy extended in providing gasoline to the driver of this vehicle will be appreciated. . . ."

Pitchess says:

"Why should you ask for preferential treatment and then complain when we do the same thing?"

Not that Pitchess defends what the commander of the Malibu substation did.

"I chewed his ass out to a fare-thee-well," the sheriff says. "We have a disciplinary process for our men."

But the press, he says, neither admits its mistakes nor reprimands or disciplines those responsible for them.

This is an often repeated complaint of those in law enforcement: A reporter can write or broadcast an erroneous—and damaging—story and he will not be punished or even censured. But when a police officer makes a mistake, the press howls for his scalp.

Editors deny such a double standard exists. They say reporters who make mistakes are reprimanded, disciplined and—if the mistakes are egregious or frequent—they are fired.

"We are the most public of all institutions," says *Times* Editor William F. Thomas. "Everything we do is hanging out there for everyone to see. To say that we escape the consequences of poor work is nonsense."

In particular, editors say, newspapers publish rebuttals to erroneous stories—in the form of corrections, follow-up stories and letters to the editor. It is the police, they say, who inevitably react defensively to charges of wrongdoing. They become hostile. Denials abound. Secrecy—stonewalling—is immediately invoked. As criminologist A. C. Germann puts it:

"To many police, THE mortal sin is for anyone . . . to question or criticize the police."

And yet police do make mistakes sometimes. They are guilty of racism, harassment and brutality. They beat people with nightsticks. They fire their guns impulsively and indiscriminately. They arrest innocent people. They kill innocent people. It is not common. But it happens. And it has been documented.

Still Pitchess insists that it is the media that has become "arrogant . . . oppressive. They think they should have total, unrestricted access to everything, to be able to do anything they want . . . be accountable to no one.

"There has to be some balance."

A *Times* story on the police-press confrontation at the Iranian demonstration in Beverly Hills last month is typical of that imbalance, Pitchess says. The story had a four-column headline and 27 paragraphs describing alleged police mistreatment of the media. Only in the 28th—and last—paragraph did the story quote two news media officials who said their crews had no problems with law enforcement.

Other members of the media since have told Pitchess the same thing.

"The media hasn't printed that," Pitchess says. Capt. Lee Tracy, acting chief of police in Beverly Hills, agrees with Pitchess on the "unbalanced" press coverage of the demonstration.

"If we can help the media, we want to do it," Tracy says. "When there's no emergency, we try to accommodate them. But when there is an emergency, we'd like them to try to accommodate us.

"At that demonstration, they caused a security problem when they wouldn't disperse . . . and our feeling was that it is more important to secure an area in an emergency than to help TV people get photos."

Reporters and photographers who covered the demonstration say they did not want police help so much as they wanted the police to leave them alone. But there were so many media people there—police estimate as many as 200 in a crowd that also included about 150 Iranians and 500 American demonstrators—that police say the press became part of the crowd-control problem.

Pitchess wonders why so many reporters and photographers were assigned to the demonstration. Some TV stations had three, three-person crews there. *The Times* sent five reporters and nine photographers.

Couldn't a pool arrangement be worked out so the media does not itself become a large, unruly crowd? Perhaps.

But a demonstration is "not like a presidential news conference . . . where you know you'll get exactly the same story and pictures as the person standing next to you," says Jay Feldman, news director at KNXT. "At a demonstration, the action is all over the place, and the crews that are the most aggressive and the most imaginative get the best stories."

There were other problems than heavy media concentration at the Beverly Hills demonstration, though. One is that Beverly Hills police are not accustomed to dealing with violent demonstrations.

"Christmas shoppers on Rodeo Drive is their idea of a riot," says one attorney.

Moreover, unlike the LAPD and the Sheriff's Department—which give their personnel training in media relations—Beverly Hills police receive no formal guidance in dealing with the press.

Worse, the action that day was so spread out—three major fronts, a few minor skirmishes—that many media people said they did not even see any of the sheriff's press representatives until long after their confrontations with deputies.

Another explanation for these confrontations may lie in Pitchess' charge to his men the night before.

"I told them . . . I didn't want to see one of our cars overturned," Pitchess says. "I told them I didn't want to see any deputies with their heads bleeding. If there's any bleeding, I don't want it to be us."

Thus, the deputies were told to expect trouble—violence—and to be prepared to deal with it . . . forcefully. One reporter says, and several others agree, that the deputies seemed "so pumped up, adrenalin racing, cars racing up and down the streets . . . so sure they were going to knock heads that they just overreacted."

There is some evidence that the media overreacted, too, though.

Some reporters and photographers say news people who were pushed and shoved by the police should not have protested so loudly.

"It just draws the crowd to you in an already tense situation," says one reporter who was there. "You could move away, come back from another angle, do your job and complain later."

A few news people who covered the demonstration acknowledge that their presence did make law enforcement's job more difficult—and that police treatment of the press was not sufficiently different enough from other demonstrations to warrant the media's subsequent protests.

"I hope we're not making mountains out of molehills," says the news director at KABC.

Three weeks ago representatives of four press organizations met with Pitchess to discuss the confrontation in Beverly Hills and to explore ways of preventing a recurrence. Among the avenues then considered and now being developed further:

— Meetings between media and law enforcement representatives immediately before major demonstrations take place.
— The use of media representatives as instructors in press relations at the Sheriff's Academy. (This was done once before, Pitchess says, but the media ultimately lost interest.)

Ironically press coverage of the very meeting at which these cooperative ventures were discussed only served to further damage police-press relations. Most stories—including one published in *The Times*—said Pitchess "acknowledged that some of his men had acted improperly" at the Beverly Hills demonstration.

But Pitchess angrily denies having made any such admission.

"I have personally investigated all the charges against my men," he says now, "and I haven't found a single complaint justified."

All he conceded at the meeting with newsmen, Pitchess says, was that " . . . maybe we could have handled it better."

"You can always say that," he says. "That doesn't mean you're admitting you were wrong."

Two *Times* reporters who attended the meeting support Pitchess's version of what he said. But a third *Times* reporter—assigned because he was not a participant in the meeting—wrote the story, relying largely on an interview with a television newsman who did attend.

Pitchess cited the erroneous reports of his comments as "typical" of the way the press treats law enforcement. But Pitchess himself refused to talk to reporters after the meeting, and it seems clear that the erroneous account of his remarks is less indicative of deliberate misrepresentation than of the unfortunate limitations intrinsic to daily journalism:

- The pressures of time and competition.
- The restraints on direct and immediate access.
- The shortcomings of individual reporters and editors.

All these make occasional errors inevitable, whether the subject is the police, the President or a plane crash.

British playwright Tom Stoppard exaggerates this problem when he has a character in his new play describe a journalist "doll" (Wind it up and it gets it wrong"), but—like the police—journalists do make mistakes.

Modern technology has compounded this difficulty. Mini-cameras now enable television crews to broadcast live from virtually any location, often with little time for reflection or careful investigation.

Print reporters sometimes act precipitously, too, demanding answers before the police have them. Police also complain that some impatient reporters blunder through interviews with witnesses to crimes before the police can apply proper interrogation techniques. That may compromise any subsequent investigation.

Journalists say police sometimes make their work more difficult, too—by being unnecessarily secretive and uncooperative, resentful of any questions or criticism, abusive of their statutory powers.

Some disagreement between the press and the police is, of course, inevitable. They have different—often conflicting—jobs. But what emerges from three weeks of interviews with people in the media and law enforcement is the inescapable conclusion that these ever-present tensions are escalating—and that neither side knows how to reverse that pattern.

THE PRESS AT THE EMERGENCY SCENE: ISSUES AND ANSWERS

RONALD B. JONES

CONFLICT between media representatives and police/public safety officials at the scenes of emergencies or other incidents is not a new problem. In fact, it is probably less of a problem today than it was 25 years ago. But the progress, the impetus to change, has not come overnight, and it has not come without significant impact to both sectors.

In 1950 the foremost authority on police administration allocated a scant 10 pages of some 700 pages to the issue of "media relations." Today there are entire texts written about that topic and there are even special training programs available to teach techniques and skills. Yet it would be false to contend that the concept of police-media relations is new. Relations between the two have always existed. The sad fact is that those relations have not always been very productive. What is new is the recognition of the poor state of relations and the efforts to improve them.

Reporters as Nuisances

Not very many years ago, the prevailing police attitude toward reporters was, to say the least, not very positive. Reporters were considered pushy, arrogant, and totally unnecessary (if not a hindrance) to the accomplishment of the police mission. And those were probably the nice things. The source of some of that discontent was no doubt the practice

---

Lt. Ronald B. Jones is research unit supervisor in the office of the superintendent, Louisiana State Police. He formerly served as supervisor of that agency's Public Affairs Unit. He teaches at the Louisiana State Police Academy, Southeastern Louisiana University and is an adjunct faculty member at University of North Florida.

of the media to report all events of interest, good or bad. Such events might have been reports of police brutality, political favoritism, bad arrests or investigations and the like. Is it any doubt that reporters were not thought much of by police?

Police as Hacks

Reporters, on the other hand, did not have a very positive view of police officers either. They considered the "men in blue" to be uneducated, political hacks who were officious and corruptible. Part of this attitude can be attributed to the focus of reporters' stories when the police were the headlines. How unfortunate for American society that it has taken some 125 years to realize that police and the media can cooperate with each other and still accomplish their respective objectives.

Scene Clashes

The management of the media at the scene of incidents or emergencies is a good model for studying and understanding the origins of friction between the two disciplines. It is at the scenes of such incidents and emergencies that conflict occurs and can be observed. The police are present in their official capacity to resolve the situation. The media are present to report the situation to a curious public. The police likely object to the presence of the media for a variety of reasons. Let's look at some of them and determine their validity.

Serious Problems Present

A number of problems are caused by the uncoordinated presence of media representatives at the scenes of breaking stories. They are uncoordinated to the extent that they have not been provided with a liaison officer or the slightest factual briefing on the situation. Worse still, they may find public safety officials "stonewalling" and uncooperative. Thus, left no other recourse, media personnel set out about the task of gathering information as best they can. Problems encountered as a result of such activity should be obvious.

Law enforcement officials are quick to point out that there can be actual danger to the operation at hand if reporters are less than cooperative. Hostage situations provide the most realistic example of what damage can be done. Technological and electronic state-of-the-art capabilities can compromise the tactical deployment of personnel in the area of the siege.

It is not unreasonable to presume that the hostage-taker has access to AM or FM radio reception or even to a television. How damaging then, to the attempted mediation effort, is the live broadcast of the scene from a helicopter or the roof of a building several hundred feet away? The description of the scene by a reporter or witnesses may be perhaps more damaging than TV shots. Witnesses, and in some cases reporters, tend to overemphasize the presence and size of weapons and armaments. They sometimes describe in lurid detail the number and position of SWAT personnel, and other tactical strategy better left unreported at the time.

Any trained hostage negotiator will confirm that the arduous task of negotiation is very fragile. It is built on trust and development of a relationship between negotiator and hostage taker which may consume hours or even days in the process. Inevitably, one significant principle is the reassurance to the hostage-taker than no immediate harm will come to him. That reassurance may be negated if response personnel are televised in live feeds from the scene.

Thus the hostage-taker, who has been lulled into a psychological state of well-being, sees that the bond of trust with the negotiator has been violated. It is likely that a feeling of futility in the situation—or, "I'll never make it out alive,"—may come over him. Thus the operation has been seriously compromised, and indeed the very lives of the hostages may well hang in the balance. At the very minimum it seriously erodes the negotiation process.

Moreover, presence of media personnel at incidents or emergencies may endanger not only innocent lives, but the safety of reporters as well. It is not all unusual for reporters to proclaim that they will assume all responsibility when requesting to enter a restricted area. Unfortunately, public safety officials cannot abdicate their responsibility for the safety of others. But it is probably the over-reaction to this safety issue by authorities throughout the years that has made the media suspicious of the intent of restricting access. That suspicion coupled with the gung ho perspective of an aggressive, competitive reporter can result in significant on-scene problems.

The SLA Shootout

The SLA shootout in California several years ago is a good example. Police had responded to the suspected location of members of the Symbionese Liberation Army in metropolitan Los Angeles. They believed that the "kidnapped" heiress, Patty Hearst, was there. Gunfire erupted and a firefight ensued. Because of problems caused by the location of the home in a heavily populated neighborhood, authorities were not able to maintain a secure perimeter. Reporters were wandering about the scene almost immediately. Raw television footage confirms that left to move about aimlessly, reporters will take unnecessary risks, either innocently or by design. At the shootout, reporters were in some cases in the direct line of fire and several were heavily exposed to tear gas.

Public safety officials must be cautious to provide a proper balance of accessibility and safety. They should also be cognizant of the effects that the mere presence of media representatives might have. A number of sociological studies have pointed out the changes in crowd behavior brought about by the presence and use of television cameras. When the crowd is potentially hostile, as in a civil disturbance, the exposure of participants to the glaring lights of cameras precipitates aggressive and disruptive behavior which may not have occurred otherwise. Gradually there has been recognition of this fact by newsrooms throughout the country. Coverage of the disturbances which struck Metro Dade County, Florida, in the early 80's was managed far better than coverage of civil disruptions in the 60's and 70's, largely through a cooperative media.

Reporters are usually not "the story" at the scenes of incidents, but, rather, they are there to provide coverage and insight into a particular situation. However, problems do occur when media representatives themselves become part of the unfolding drama. The Hanafi Muslim incident in Washington several years ago found the media acting as a party in the negotiations process. Rather than passively reporting the situation as it developed, reporters made direct contact with the hostage-takers and interacted with them. Their roles as reporters were expanded in an effort to provide exclusive interviews and coverage and, in the process, the media became a part of the story.

Media Terrorism Impact

While there are a number of lesser but similar incidents of intervention and participation by the media, it seems that such activity has decreased. Coverage will likely become more focused and less participative in view of increased terrorist activity. It is axiomatic that extensive media attention is an essential ingredient in staging political terrorism.

Without that attention, terrorists see their respective acts as having less intended impact. It is recognition of that fact that has resulted in some introspective examination by the media of policies regarding coverage. On the whole they resent being one of the players. They concede more readily now that their role is not participation, but coverage.

Complicating the Conflict

Competition is the root of all evil, at least insofar as news coverage is concerned. Let's face it. Few newspapers operate on a non-profit basis. Excepting governmental operations, still fewer television or radio stations operate in such a fashion. And that's fine, at least in terms of earning a profit. But when that market mentality dictates policy in the news-gathering function, problems are imminent. Canons of ethics notwithstanding, competition among news reporters forces them to resort to sometimes less than professional methods.

Reporters, not unlike other professionals, are in a constant state of upward mobility. They strive to be the best at what they do: to provide the most detailed and accurate story, before anyone else. And the same goes for television camera-persons and newspaper photographers. For it is through providing insightful news coverage that their skills and talents are recognized and rewarded. When successful, they move on to bigger and better markets. They can command higher salaries and benefits. So too can stations or newspapers with the best overall coverage command the highest advertising rates. When that quest for coverage becomes so all-consuming, reporters are sometimes reluctant to adhere to police officials' directives to remain within a certain area during an incident. After all, there is no competitive edge if you simply have the same facts and video as everyone else at the scene.

Hot Scenes, Cold Scenes

The nature of an incident, too, can have an impact on how reporters and public safety personnel interact. The incident can vary by what we might call hot scenes and cold scenes. The hot scene would be an incident which continues to evolve, such as a hostage situation. In those cases, as has been discussed, there is the possibility that coverage could well impact the resolution of the incident. A train derailment, where hazardous materials continue to burn and there remains a potential for further explosions is an example of a hot scene.

Cold scenes, on the other hand, would involve incidents where there is no safety threat to operations personnel, reporters or others. Such incidents might involve the site of an airplane accident where rescue operations have been discontinued, or the scene of a double homicide. The hotter the scene the greater the likelihood that officials will attempt to maintain a perimeter and perhaps even embargo certain information. And obviously the hotter the scene the greater the public interest and greater the coverage sought by media representatives.

It is in early stages of a hot incident that information is most critical. Ironically, it is also during this period of time that information is most unreliable and sketchy. An examination of tapes of hot incidents reveals that much information initially reported is in fact wrong. In the rush to get the story and get it first, the accuracy is often understandably compromised.

If public safety officials are hesitant to provide information, even the briefest of facts, then reporters will go elsewhere. Bystanders, witnesses, relatives of victims, anybody who will speak into a microphone often become unwitting (and often uninformed/misinformed) information sources. The fallacy of this practice is obvious. While good reporters should interview a variety of subjects in order to get a comprehensive look at an incident, it is essential that official statements corroborate, correct, or expand on the other versions.

A Shared Blame

We cannot, of course, fault the media for all the problems of false or incorrect initial reports. Police departments which have not yet adapted an enlightened public information/public affairs philosophy remain major principals in the media/police conflict at scenes of incidents. By not providing the most basic of information as soon as possible, by not providing a staging area, by not providing a spokesperson or updates, police officials send a signal to the news corps—get the information as best you can because we aren't in the news business.

Admittedly, the presence of reporters within hot areas can cause problems, and in such justified cases officials have reason to restrict their access. But technological capabilities present in the news gathering business have diluted the impact of separation from the scene by distance. The use of sophisticated lenses and listening devices has minimized, to some degree, the deleterious effects of perimeter enforcement. The fact is, that given the choice, reporters will tell an official that they must be present at the scene, in the immediate area, and that any physical separation, however slight, interferes with their ability to report. How much of that is true depends on the "heat" of the situation, distance and other circumstances.

It is suspected that some of the discomfort associated with reporting from a predesignated location, as established by the police, is that it is offensive simply because it places a restriction on the news gathering function. Yet the Supreme Court has recognized the importance of the public safety function in comparison to the First Amendment right of free press. As part of his opinion in Branzburg v. Hayes, Justice Byron White essentially said that the press have no right of special access to scenes of crime or disaster not afforded the public in general. That is, if public safety officials have articulable, reasonable and justifiable grounds for excluding the public from such scenes, then they might concurrently exclude the press. The issue obviously turns on the reasonableness of that decision and the degree or extent to which that prerogative is carried out.

What may be reasonable to a police officer may not be at all reasonable to a reporter. After all, their jobs, goals and responsibilities are decidedly different. Let us consider the two main parties, the on-scene commander of an incident and the reporter seeking to cover the incident. The responsibility of the commander might be to do one or more of the following: resolve the situation or incident as quickly as possible, keep it from getting worse, prevent further death or injury, protect innocent persons and their property, restore calm, or any number of other activities. The reporter, on the other hand, is there to gather accurate information as soon as possible and report it. The on-scene commander is not really concerned about the reporter's responsibilities or whether the incident gets reported properly. The commander is, however, quite concerned if the reporter interferes with the operation or places someone's life in jeopardy.

The reporter, on the other hand, must not always be cast as cold-blooded, ruthless and uncaring. He certainly does not want to be responsible for compromising the on-scene management of an incident where lives are at stake. But there is usually philosophical disagreement between the press and the police as to what constitutes jeopardizing the situation's management. It is difficult for a reporter to imagine what harm might be caused by flying a news helicopter over the scene of a hostage incident. But from a tactical standpoint, as we have seen, such a fly-over causes very serious problems.

Remedial Strategies

By far the single greatest remedy which can be suggested is training for moderating on-scene conflict. Police/public safety officials from top administrative officers to field personnel must be trained in the methods of media management at emergency scenes and incidents. They must develop an appreciation of the goals of reporters. Training must be directed at changing attitudes as much as teaching skills. In any agency one will find some longstanding ill feelings that exist between some officers and reporters. These were likely developed over a long period of time and usually result from some field confrontation. Overcoming mutual suspicion will be a difficult task and will not be accomplished overnight. But it is, nonetheless, an essential and fundamental first step.

Media management skills should also be included in any training effort. There should be a discussion of how, where and why a media command post/staging area should be established. There should be serious evaluation of what types of information can be immediately released. Who shall release the information and how often? How do we determine what is a reasonable perimeter? And finally, to what extent can the media actually be beneficial or helpful to us at the scene? By searching for the answers to these difficult questions, officers will begin to formulate a plan for media management, a necessary and essential part of the management effort.

But such training addresses only a part of the total at-scene problem. What of the media? It is the responsibility of the police agency to acquaint reporters with the potential problems caused by uncoordinated response and reporting of hot scenes. Reporters should have the opportunity to familiarize themselves with the agency's command structure and operational aspects. Reporters should have the chance to discuss the necessity of at-scene perimeters and why helicopters might compromise an incident's management. Most importantly, a dialogue must develop between the police and the media and an orientation session such as this presents an opportune time. There must be an open exchange of information, goals, and needs. Police should not view this as an occasion to "PR" the media, but rather, they should present a nuts and bolts approach to the entire issue of on-scene management.

Establishing and maintaining this liaison are at the very heart of a mutually beneficial police/media relationship. It is unacceptable that the police chief or his information officer do not know, on a first name basis, the news directors, assignment editors, or city editors for the local market outlets. There should be no reluctance on their part to pick up the phone and make a call when a problem is encountered. Police and media may not always agree, but they must seize the opportunity to discuss, mediate and compromise.

Police/public safety agencies have a further responsibility to promulgate policies regarding media relations. The policy should address the rights of the media to access information and scenes of incidents within certain limitations. It should communicate to all personnel a candid and forthright posture in dealing with the media and must require the cooperation of all officers with media representatives. The policy should outline those tasks which should be accomplished on the hot scenes which permit and facilitate the newsgathering function while at the same time preserving the autonomy of the police department to resolve the incident.

Insofar as is possible, a person (or persons) should be designated as a media liaision officer. Whether these duties require fulltime assignment must be determined by the size of the department, the activities of the agency, and the number and type of information requests generated by the media. Nevertheless, some predesignated person must act as the go-between, the coordinator between an on-scene commander and the media. (Recall the discussion of role responsibilities.) The police have a responsibility to provide a contact person at incidents, a link to the operation. Through that person, timely and accurate information may be furnished.

Unfortunately, there are no easy solutions to the problems of on-scene coverage. It has been suggested that perhaps the relationship between media and police should be strained to some extent. Is it practical to expect an even and harmonious working relationship in such situations? Rather than a marriage we should work for detente. From that condition may come order and if order does, in time come, then the effectiveness of both media and police might be enhanced. To that extent, the public benefits.

BOSTON: NO WINNERS IN CHINATOWN CASE

Detective Kelly's Suspension for Punching Huang Leaves No One Fully Satisfied

KEVIN CULLEN

FRANK Kelly and Long Guang Huang saw each other last Tuesday for the first time in more than nine months, and almost 13 months to the day since their star-crossed paths first crossed on a Chinatown street.

They sat 12 feet away from each other inside a small hearing room in a state office building, unwitting participants in what began as two punches on a sidewalk and has evolved into a major political, social and legal debate.

It all began May 1, 1985, at about 10:40 A.M., when Kelly, a Boston police vice squad detective, said he saw Huang and a woman Kelly knew was a prostitute in conversation. Kelly said he followed the pair down Kneeland Street in his unmarked police car. When he was convinced they were heading for a house of prostitution, where without a search warrant he could not enter, Kelly decided to place them under arrest.

When Kelly called her, the prostitute got into the police car, Huang kept walking, Kelly followed him on foot and grabbed him by the collar and led him to the car. Huang pushed away from the car, and a struggle ensued.

Kelly held Huang against the wall and threw a closed fist three times. Two of the punches landed.

Kevin W. Cullen, police reporter for *The Boston Globe*, Boston, Massachusetts also covered that beat for the *Boston Herald* and the *Transcript-Telegram* in Holyoke, Massachusetts.
†Reprinted courtesy of *The Boston Globe* from its June 8, 1986 edition.

Kelly says Huang struck him several times in the struggle and felt the use of his fist was necessary to subdue him.

Huang, an illiterate restaurant worker who came to the United States from China in April 1984, does not speak English. He says he had not agreed to go with the prostitute and was frightened when a stranger he did not know was a police officer tried to put him into a car. Last August, a judge acquitted Huang of soliciting a prostitute and assault and battery on Kelly.

Kelly Suspended For a Year

Testimony from witnesses has been conflicting, but two elements seem irrefutable; Huang resisted Kelly's advances, and Kelly punched Huang in the face twice. For those punches, and for filing a report that stated he struck Huang only once, Kelly was suspended from the Boston Police Department for one year last September 6 by Police Commissioner Francis M. Roache after a departmental administrative hearing.

Last week, Kelly appeared before the state Civil Service Commission, asking that his suspension be reduced or lifted entirely. Testimony in the appeal is expected to continue through next week, and a decision will follow.

The incident involving Huang and Kelly had never been debated nor judged simply on the facts involved. It was, actually, an ordinary situation that became extraordinary because of a multitude of outside factors—the media, the mayor, the neighborhood and the police commissioner.

Every day in this city, police officers struggle with, and sometimes punch, civilians who resist arrest. The public seldom sees this and even more rarely reports it.

Huang was arrested in broad daylight, on a crowded sidewalk. Some of the civilians who witnessed the incident considered the treatment of Huang barbarous. Fewer witnesses have testified they thought it was a minor scuffle, what one construction worker called "a Mickey Mouse situation."

Those who support Kelly, like Daniel Mahoney, president of the Boston Police Detectives Benevolent Association, say those who damn Kelly have no idea the amount of force needed to subdue someone who does not want to be taken into custody.

Those who support Huang, like Suzanne Lee, a Chinatown activist who befriended him, say because Huang was much smaller, he posed no real threat to Kelly; that Huang's eye, which was swollen shut, testifies that excessive force was used; and that Huang's acquittal on charges filed by Kelly vindicates Huang.

Impact of Eyewitnesses

Besides the punches themselves, the single factor probably most responsible for Kelly's predicament was his response to several in the crowd who closed in on him and angrily questioned his authority and treatment of Huang.

"Mind your own business!" Kelly yelled at them.

If some witnesses hadn't made up their minds to come forward after seeing the punches, that response cemented some convictions and reinforced others.

Some witnesses felt strongly enough about seeing what they considered an injustice to call a newspaper. When they did, *The Boston Globe* played an important role in transforming the incident into a major media event.

Margot O'Toole, a witness who had challenged Kelly face to face and was angered by Kelly's response, called the *Globe* hours after the incident. The next day, the first story about the incident appeared on the front of the Metro/Region section. The day after, an interview with Huang appeared on page 1, as did a story about the incident the day after that.

More than 50 articles about the incident or referring to it specifically have appeared in the *Globe*.

Other media soon did their own stories. Television showed Huang lying on a couch in his South End apartment, his eye badly bruised and swollen shut—a powerful image that was replayed during newscasts up to five months after the incident.

Media accounts varied. Most called it a beating. Some called it a "vicious beating." Some referred to Huang—who, at 56, was 18 years older than Kelly at the time—as an elderly man. Some compared Kelly's size with Huang's. At the time of the incident, Kelly was 5 feet 10 inches tall and weighed 180 pounds, while Huang was 5 feet 2 inches tall and weighed about 111 pounds.

Kelly feels the media attention prejudged him and made it impossible for him to receive a fair hearing.

"It made me look like an ogre, like me I was down there looking for someone to beat up," he said last week, during a break in his appeal hearing. Kelly also feels the attention attracted some of the outside factors that made his case extraordinary.

Five days after the incident, Mayor Raymond Flynn visited Huang's home with a bag of groceries and drove Huang to the hospital. Flynn's chief spokesman, Francis Costello, said the visit "was not to prejudice any case, it was a matter of expressing concern."

Nonetheless, Flynn's involvement not only increased media attention, it embittered many of the city's 1,800 police officers. Even some of the department's highest ranking officers have privately criticized the visit, especially because Flynn allowed the media to record it.

The publicity was heightened by citizen involvement. Chinatown, a community which has endured the encroachment of the seedy Combat Zone as well as commercial and residential development that has seldom benefited its citizens, had been waiting for an issue it could bring before the city as symbolic of past grievances. The treatment of Long Guang Huang became the issue, and Huang, unwittingly, became their symbol.

A small group of activists organized marches and rallies. Sometimes the crowds were small, but sometimes as many as 300 people showed up. Organizers called the television stations and newspapers, and very often media representatives showed up.

So, too, sometimes did Flynn and his new appointee, Mickey Roache. Often, they faced a hostile crowd, and often, they soothed that crowd, promising a "swift" investigation and action.

At the same time, Roache, who had been appointed police commissioner by Flynn only three months before and who took office promising to treat police misconduct with a firmer hand than his predecessors, faced his most controversial issue.

Roache had said one of his goals was to show that the department could police itself when it came to misconduct and did not need a civilian review board.

After the wide publicity surrounding the case, Roache knew his disciplining of Kelly would be closely scrutinized and widely reported. In that respect, Kelly became a test case.

There's little doubt the publicity surrounding the case resulted in its being treated differently. Kelly's departmental hearing was a full-blown trial, lasting 11 days, by far the department's longest administrative hearing. It was covered daily by the city's two newspapers and three major television stations.

What Frank Kelly deserved for punching Long Guang Huang is difficult to quantify. Discipline meted out to other officers over the years, and even today, would suggest he deserved less than what he got.

Some observers suggest those in City Hall and police headquarters fully expect the Civil Service Commission to reduce the suspension and that it was given out with that expectation.

No One Fully Satisfied

Would Kelly have received as long a suspension if the case was not publicized? Most likely not.

Would the media have played the story as prominently if witnesses and the mayor would not as willing to get involved? Probably not.

Was the length of suspension influenced by past grievances in Chinatown and used as an example for a department where internal discipline has become more emphasized? Most likely.

More than a year after Kelly punched Huang on Kneeland Street, satisfaction escapes all those involved.

Kelly still feels betrayed.

Huang still complains of headaches and dizziness and is seeking $700,000 in damages from the city.

Chinatown activists still feel their neighborhood takes a back seat to others.

Mickey Roache still has a group of detectives who feel Frank Kelly was a scapegoat.

And Ray Flynn still has police officers who are forever alienated from him and a neighborhood where people mistrust government.

The real irony is that in the weeks preceding the incident, Kelly and other vice squad detectives were instructed to step up their prostitution arrests in and around Chinatown.

Thus, the names of Frank Kelly and Long Guang Huang became, at the very least, synonymous with being at the wrong place at the wrong time.

THE POLICE/PRESS PUBLISH OR NOT TO PUBLISH, BROADCAST, OR NOT TO BROADCAST ISSUES

Police, Media and the Courts, a Balancing Act: Protecting the Rights of Victims and Defendants, While Preserving the Public's Right to Know

NAGLE'S GAG ORDER MANIPULATES NEWS

POLICE Chief Richard Nagle's lack of cooperation with the media is bad for the community and the department.

Since coming to town several years [ago], Nagle has imposed a gag rule on those who work under him. In addition, he has taken it upon himself to determine what information in the police log is available to the public. State law requires that the police log be public.

---

*The cartoon, by Paul Donelan, and the editorial which appeared in the June 7, 1984 edition of the *Old Colony Memorial* (Plymouth, Massachusetts) are reprinted with permission of *Old Colony Memorial*, MPG Communications.

†(EDITOR'S NOTE: In 1980 the Massachusetts Legislature passed what is informally referred to as the "log law," mandating that "each police department shall make, keep and maintain a daily log, written in a form that can be easily understood, recording in chronological order all responses to valid complaints received, crime reported, the names, addresses of persons arrested and the charges against such persons arrested. All entries in said daily logs shall, unless otherwise provided by law, be public records available without charge during regular business hours and at all other reasonable times." It was amended to also mandate inclusion of the ages of arrested persons.)

‡In this series, reprinted with permission of the *Daily Evening Item*, (Lynn, Massachusetts) the reporter interviews editors and police administrators in the Greater Boston area, as well as the advocates and a major political force behind the bill itself, to examine the police/media informational access issues the law's passage brought sharply into focus: release and publication of juveniles' names and the names of victims of crime, decisions from the law enforcement community regarding deletions of data it still deemed sensitive, and the whys behind the initial campaign to make police more accountable to the public in daily reporting procedures. The stories appeared in the May 20, 1982 edition of the *Item*.

Nagle's restriction of news is in fact manipulation of news. He orders the sergeants to "sanitize" public police logs by blacking out certain entries, including on some occasions, reported crimes.

By prohibiting his officers from talking to media representatives, Nagle prohibits a free flow of information. Such manipulation was recently evident when Nagle issued a news release after a suspect was arrested on an alleged scam. However, Nagle neglected to let the media—and the public—know that one particular officer headed that investigation and was credited by some with breaking the case.

By withholding those details, Nagle failed to give due credit to the officer and only added to the poor morale in the department.

The pure nature of the police department sets the scene for stories of crime and wrongdoing. However, this newspaper is always anxious to publish news from the police department, including feature stories of the officers themselves.

This is not generally possible, because Nagle doesn't share that information.

Nagle's gag rule is not one that is routinely practiced in police departments. Surely, the state police and departments in large cities throughout the state allow the officers to deal with the media.

Certainly, there are many competent people in the Plymouth Police Department, people who would effectively communicate details of accidents, crimes and other information. Such a policy works well at the local fire department.

It is unfortunate that Nagle expresses such a negative attitude. It is more unfortunate that he carries this attitude over to those who work under him and to the public.

NAMING NAMES: IDENTIFYING PERPETRATORS AND VICTIMS – THE POLICE AND PRESS PERSPECTIVES

Does the Public Have the Right to Know the Names of Juvenile Offenders?

Patricia A. Kelly

Twenty-three percent of violent crimes against the person in this country are committed by juveniles, boys and girls under 17 years of age.

And local statistics do not belie the national figures.

In Revere recently, a juvenile was arrested three times in one week and charged with committing a series of housebreaks.

Earlier this months two 14-year-old Swampscott boys were charged with arson in connection with two house fires in that town.

In Sudbury a newspaper publisher is being taken to court as a consequence of a decision he made last March: to back local police efforts to discourage young teens from making that municipality a "party town." The "partying" turned "nightmare," when youths, some of them reportedly spurred by drink or drugs or a combination of the two, split into groups, one lighting a bonfire, another beating up a teenager, and still another knocking a squad car out of commission.

Two summers ago police chiefs in some South Shore communities, having reached the limit of their tolerance with teenage vandals, public drinkers, and drug users, decided to strike back with a new weapon — disclosure of identity of the youthful offenders.

When they, contrary to custom, began to give the press the names and addresses of juvenile arrestees, and certain newspapers, also contrary to custom, began publishing those names, it was the articulation of a new get-tough policy. And that policy was directed at a segment of society that some feel has too long been molly-coddled by the courts and by paternalistic, small-town police departments.

On the North Shore, the reaction to spiraling juvenile crime rates has been more conservative, ironically, on the part of law enforcement arms themselves. But the aggressive stand of newspaper publishers in altering their own policy on disclosure and public outrage against protecting committers of felonies, no matter what their age, is prompting some measured mulling on the part of area police chiefs.

Revelation of juvenile identities as an option was brought into sharp focus with the passage of the 1980 legislature act mandating the keeping and publication of a daily log by Massachusetts police departments. The amendment said the log must contain the names of those arrested. It did not specifically exclude juveniles. Nor, to the surprise of some journalists and police officers, did the clause "unless otherwise provided by law" specifically include an exemption for youthful offenders.

There is no statute that provides for the confidentiality of juvenile records that are kept by police departments, although there is one that applies to court and probation records.

However, in an advisory opinion rendered by the acting state Supervisor of Public Records to South Dennis Police Chief Pasquale Santamauro in August, 1980, that office essentially recommended a safe course of action as being the discretionary one. That ruling read that names of arrested juveniles "may be withheld from disclosure at the discretion of the record custodian," and referred to, as a precedent, the statute regarding sealing of juvenile court records, and the statute prohibiting "unwarranted invasion of personal privacy." The acting supervisor, then Renee M. Landers, applied the litmus paper test of whether the "public interest served by disclosure" outweighs the privacy invasion that would be suffered by revealing of juvenile identity.

But, this opinion notwithstanding, there are police departments that include the names of juvenile arrestees on their logs; there are others that are rethinking their positions; and there are editors who are adamant about the public good to be served by such disclosure.

In Revere, however, there was no need to review policy.

"Our arrest book contains the names of everyone arrested, including juveniles, and the press can leave or take the names at their own discretion," said Revere Police Chief John A. DeLeire.

"It is no problem as far as I am concerned; it is public record."

Marblehead police are more protective when it comes to those under 17 years of age arrested in their town.

"I hate to see a young kid get such a black mark," commented acting Marblehead Police Chief John R. Russell.

Marblehead Police Lt. Delbert J. (Jack) Percy agrees, and also contended that perhaps disclosure of identity could be a negative factor of encouragement, making the youth a kind of anti-hero among his friends.

"I would like us to continue the status quo here as far as juvenile identification is concerned," said Percy. "I would not be in favor of releasing the names. I also would hate like hell to see a youngster have to carry around that mark the rest of his life. I also think that among his peer group the kid could be actually looked up to as a kind of toughie if he were identified."

Lynnfield Police Chief Paul N. Romano believes the decision of disclosure has to be made in the context of the severity of the offense. "Just because a youngster takes one bite of the apple, it does not necessarily mean a pattern. But I definitely would not have any objection to disclosing juvenile names, no compunction, if a felony was committed. I would, however, for example, not reveal the name of a teenage runaway.

The Massachusetts State Police have a policy, graven in written directive, against the publication of arrested juveniles' names on their logs.

The name, age, address, and sex of a person arrested is included only if they are not under 17 years of age.

"We also have a rule that, in the case of a juvenile arrest, a parental contact must be made," explained Staff Sgt. Maurice M. Carroll, Lynnfield barracks.

Lynn Police Chief Thomas F. Fay feels a blanket disposition to publish the names would disproportionately punish "the innocent, basically good kid that got caught hanging around with the wrong group." But he might consider being far less lenient about disclosure when it came to "the habitual offender."

"It has been this department's policy not to release the name of juvenile offenders," said Peabody Police Sgt. Robert Champagne." We really have not had any problems with it."

Although Nahant Police Chief Peter R. Bradbury is sympathetic with the sentiment that would differentiate between the first and the repeat offender and the gradation of the charge, he feels that the policy articulated should be a uniform one.

"I think you have to do for one what you would do for all. Otherwise you could be charged with discrimination, I am sure."

Bradbury, who is "contemplating" changing his department's traditional ban on the release of arrested juveniles' names, has some residual uneasiness about declaring a sweeping change that would not make a distinction between "the first offender or the juvenile with a minor offense" and the committer of serious crimes.

Swampscott Police Chief Peter J. Cassidy agrees with Bradbury's instincts concerning possible negative reaction to a set of guidelines that would create special cases.

"You either do it or you don't," maintained Cassidy, and he is currently weighing the pros and cons of Swampscott's police prohibition against disclosure.

There are many newspaper editors in Massachusetts, however, who are not equivocating any longer on their publication's policies concerning the inclusion of the identify of those under 17 years of age in their crime reporting.

John S. Moran, managing editor of *The Daily Evening Item,* Lynn says *The Item's* stand on the issue has "just been reviewed."

"If a juvenile commits a crime that is serious, we will use the name," said Moran. "If the deed affects many people, if it causes a public fanfare," the paper will identify the suspect.

"Our readers have the right to know, and for their own protection, we will not hesitate." Moran added that police departments who refuse to furnish the information "make us feel they are not being honest on a day-to-day basis about reporting crime. We will not tolerate a police department dictating to us about our right to know. We cooperate with them in many areas, protecting identities of witnesses and so forth."

"Juvenile offenders have hidden behind a mask of anonymity for too long a time," asserted James R. Stommen, editor of the *Salem Evening News.* "If they are old enough to commit what they are charged with, they are old enough to shoulder the consequences."

But the *News'* policy, too, is not a uniform one.

"We make a judgment case-by-case, like the judgments we have to make every day in this news business," he added.

The editor of *The Lawrence Eagle-Tribune* wants to make it clear that his paper's "fairly inclusive general philosophy" on the subject in no way seeks to punish in print. "Breaking and entering, auto theft, vandalism, particularly with high damage costs are some of the crimes we consider serious," said Daniel J. Warner.

The public safety is also uppermost in the minds of management at the *Quincy Patriot-Ledger* when decisions are made on how to report juvenile crime.

"Our policy is simple," said William B. Ketter, editor. Generally we do not use the names at time of the arrest or in connection with any of the judicial proceedings unless we feel that the offense, the alleged criminal act, is so serious, so important to public safety and information, to warrant doing so."

A case that was keynote in solidifying the sentiment on the subject among editors of the publication was the arrest by Rockland police of two juveniles who were charged with stoning motorists of the Southeast Expressway.

"Commuters were terrorized for two months," recalled Ketter. "We felt this was so serious the community should be notified."

Ketter referred to a study produced by the Norfolk County district attorney which recently criticized, in Ketter's paraphrase, "the overwhelming secrecy that surrounds the juvenile justice system."

"Under its guidelines, many a hardened criminal has been able to start out his adult life with a clean record," he said.

WHAT WAS A CUSTOM IS NOW LAW

PATRICIA A. KELLY

LYNN Police Chief Thomas F. Fay says the custom dates back "about as long as I can remember here."

What the veteran Lynn officer referred to as "custom" in his department was hardened into Massachusetts law in 1980.

It legislates the maintaining of a daily log that must be made available to the public, recording responses to valid complaints, crimes reported, and the identities of those arrested.

For most law enforcement officials on the North Shore, the implementation of the amendment to the General Laws simply made a hard-and-fast rule out of what had heretofore been local option. As Fay explained, "The press has always had access to our radio logs, incident reports, written log. Our relationship with reporters has always been a good one. They know we're not in the business of journalism, just as we know they are not in the business of handing out free publicity. They have always been able to get the information they wanted by looking at the logs."

But for a few police chiefs, the passage of the bill meant a dramatic change in procedures and an end to the practice of keeping arrests and complaint information under a figurative lock and key. Until only a few months ago, reporters who covered Swampscott police were limited to the oral transmission of information and had the right to question whether they were receiving the whole story and, more importantly, whether their readers were apprised of the same. If you asked the desk man "Anything happen last night?" and he said, "no," then you were forced to accept that response.

Now you have a written log to review.

Swampscott Police Chief Peter J. Cassidy says his department has just instituted the keeping of a log that is open to press and public, and that it contains "the minimum of the information required by the law."

"We will give out what is required by the law," he stated. "Up to this time, (two months ago) there had never been a log kept as such. Everything was in-house."

In Lynnfield, the compliance with the log law appears to be a selective one.

Although Lynnfield Police Chief Paul N. Romano maintains he has an "open and good" working relationship with the press, he also points out that, unlike other chiefs on the North Shore, he refuses to release the addresses of housebreak victims.

"I am not hiding any arrests in doing so," he claimed. "I am protecting the person. What if we reported that half of a hundred thousand dollar silver collection was stolen?/What we would be doing is telling everyone that the other half remained to be taken."

But the state Supervisor of Public Records, who gives advisory opinions of the law, disagrees with Romano, if a 1980 decision is to establish precedent.

That opinion, rendered to a police chief in another municipality, reads, "You (the police chief) have suggested that victims of armed robbery and burglary might be deterred from reporting the crime to the police by the prospect of having their names and addresses made public. I find this possibility highly unlikely in view of the victims' inherent-interest in recovering the stolen goods and arresting the criminals. This interest will not be overriden by the possibility that they will be identified as hapless victims of crime."

Marblehead Police Chief John R. Russell, believes that the disclosure of the location of incidents of housebreaks is an important measure for the benefit of the general public.

"People have the right to know if there are breaks in their neighborhood and that knowledge helps their protection," he said.

Of the north shore area municipalities sampled, Marblehead was one of the highest scorers on ease of access to legally-sanctioned crime-reporting information and on consistency and completeness of its police log.

"We have always kept one, and it has been public record for as long as I can recall," said Chief Russell.

Sgt. Robert Champagne and Inspector John Colella, Peabody police, talk daily with reporters "and know what they are looking for." They leave, from the shifts photocopies for the area press to pick up, a compilation of "all felonies, complaints, incidents, accidents, etcetera."

"We have had no complaints and no problems," said Colella.

"We even get a few requests from the public to see the log," said Police Chief Peter R. Bradury of Nahant. He was the only chief interviewed who actually had enough requests for access from citizens to remember such instances.

"People came in a few times to look up calls of complaints against a local establishment when a hearing was being held involving the business," he remembered. "Otherwise, we deal with requests mainly from the press."

John D. McDonough, superintendent of Metropolitan District Commission police, candidly admits that although the MDC "always kept a log, it was accessible neither to press nor the public." But now the record-keeping complies, although "We never, in any circumstance, covered up an arrest, and we always gave out the information, with the exception—an exception we are still hung up on—of the names of arrested juveniles."

In Saugus, citizens did not have the same access to the log that the press traditionally enjoyed until the passage of the law.

"We usually did not make public one neighbor's complaint against another because of obvious reasons," explained Saugus Police Chief Donald M. Peters. "But now the log is open to everyone."

State Police keep a log, in conformity with the law, and Staff Sgt. Maurice Carroll of the Lynnfield barracks said officers are informed in detail and in writing of procedures for maintaining the record, along with descriptions of information it should and should not contain.

When asked if his department had any reservations about the publication of data contained on its log, Revere Police Chief John DeLeire emphatically responded. "Why wouldn't we want to release the information? The public record law is the law, and I think it's fair and equitable. If we did not want to release it, it would be a cover-up. And a cover-up will never serve the public interest."

What Things Shouldn't We Know?

The word is "sanitizing."

In its special context of application to police logs, the term, to quote the state Supervisor of Public Records office, "refers to the process of deleting or covering over non-public information so as to preserve the confidentiality of investigatory materials or to protect the legitimate privacy interests of individuals named in the log."

Since the passage of the log law, police chiefs have been grappling with the gray areas of interpretation. Specific questions have been raised by law enforcement officials and in some cases they have been referred for interpretation to the state's Public Records office. Advisory decisions made by the legal staff there determine whether, in its opinion, the public good served by disclosure would outweigh the degree of need, in each case, to protect the individual's privacy.

The following survey is based on public record laws, written advisories furnished by the Supervisor of Public Records office, and the prevailing practices of area departments.

The "sanitizing" of this data is generally viewed as discretionary — that is, up to the judgment of the individual police department:

- citizens' requests to check homes while on vacation.
- domestic incidents not resulting in the institution of criminal charges.
- incidents relating to mental illness.
- identification of juveniles.

Although some Massachusetts police chiefs, like John V. Polio of Braintree, have issued directives to their departments ordering deletion of reports involving drug overdoses, protective custody, and suicide cases, other police chiefs still include that information on the log. There has, in fact, been a decision from a Supervisor of Public Records counsel regarding protective custody, defining those incidents as rightfully subject to public disclosure. In a 1978 decision directed to the Falmouth Police Department, antedating the log law, then-acting Supervisor John J. McGlynn maintained that "the public nature of the offense is a factor that might limit the privacy interest of the person taken into protective custody."

McGlynn continued that "the protective custody statute essentially reformed the law relating to public drunkenness. The privacy rights of someone who has been intoxicated in public are not as great as those of a person whose intoxication takes place in the privacy of his/her home."

What information is strictly prohibited by law, from disclosure?

The inclusive answer to that question would be any categories already exempted by statute. That includes:

- the identity of a rape victim (but the identity of anyone arrested for a rape must be disclosed); also reports of rape or sexual assault and conversations between police officers and the victims.

- investigatory materials necessarily compiled out of the public view by law enforcement or other investigatory officials, the disclosure of which would probably prejudice the possibility of effective law enforcement and consequently not serve the public interest. (Reporters historically feel this exemption is the one which has been most often abused by police officers refusing to disclose information; that is, some law enforcement officials claimed that to release data would be to "prejudice an ongoing investigation," when that kind of jeopardy did not, in reality, exist.) Revere Police Chief John A. DeLeire says he makes it a point, when this provision must be applied, to "cite reasons why it must be confidential, why it is essential to the investigation."
- information prohibited from release by the Criminal Offender Record Information Act (CORI), a statute governing records and data primarily relating to the prior criminal record of an individual.

In addition to the items mandated for inclusion in the log, what materials will police officers willingly furnish to the press, who in turn, furnish them to the reading public?

Guidelines, generated by the International Chiefs of Police Association, have been widely applauded and applied. They provide furnishing:

- Identity of a dead victim, after notification of next of kin.
- Name, age, address, occupation, and family status of accused.
- Information necessary to aid in apprehension of a criminal or to warn public of danger the accused may represent.
- Facts and circumstances of an arrest, including time and place, any pursuit, any resistance made, weapons used.
- Identity of investigating and arresting officers.
- Brief description of the offense charged.
- Time and place of any court hearing.
- Whether arrested person was bailed and amount thereof.

"Police personnel really want to cooperate in the matter of access to records," said Massachusetts State Police Staff Sgt. Maurice Carroll, Lynnfield Barracks. "I think maybe what some press people sometime forget is that we are here to serve the public first and foremost. If there's one man on the desk and we're trying to book someone and the phone's ringing off the hook with media calls, we have to do our job first. But we do our best to be cooperative and my feeling is that the relationship here and in general between police and press is a good working one."

NEWSPAPERS FOUGHT
FOR LEGISLATION

THE EXECUTIVE director of the Massachusetts Newspaper Publishers Association (MNPA) says his group lobbied for the log law's passage because its constituency, the working press, "was definitely one hundred percent opposed to the concept of secret arrests."

The Winchester legislator and lawyer who sponsored the measure and waged a dignified-but-persistent campaign against his "quiet opposition" says his aim was to insure that police departments across the state would conduct their business in the open.

The statute, signed in May, 1980 with an effective date of August, 1980, amended Chapter 41, the public records law, by adding the following section (98F): "Each police department shall make, keep and maintain a daily log, written in a form that can be easily understood, recording, in chronological order, all responses to valid complaints received, crimes reported, the names, addresses of persons arrested and the charges against such persons arrested. All entries in said daily logs shall, unless otherwise provided by law, be public records available without charge to the public during regular business hours and at all other reasonable times." (The law was later amended to include "ages" of arrested person.)

"Prior to the Seventies there was no law compelling any police department to keep a log," explained Joseph L. Doherty of Medford, executive director of MNPA. "Some did, some did not, and there was no penalty for not doing so.

"The Press is committed to keeping things in the open, and was disturbed about the possibility of secret arrests," he continued. "In addition, we were also concerned about a pattern in some towns where you had a very weak police chief, a system under which the chief was essentially a flunky and the selectmen operated as the real chief."

In municipalities such as these, feared Doherty, the town fathers were primarily dedicated to preserving the image of "spotlessness," and preferred to "sweep crime under the rug" as part of the charade.

"Sam Rotondi fought for this law. He did one hell of a job, with it passing 32-6 in the Senate with one person absent," he said in praise of the Winchester Democrat who has been a visible champion of right-to-know and access-to-public records issues.

Senator Rotondi says he responded to overtures from journalists by sponsoring and attracting support for the bill, but was careful to remind us that its provisions involve close-to-the-heart issues.

"I am totally opposed to any form of restrictions on access. I do not believe censure in this area is justified," he said. "You just cannot believe in a free and open society and at the same time deny right of access to or dissemination of information."

It was the Winchester legislator who made a personal appeal to "each and every senator."

I asked them if they wanted to vote against the public's right to know, and they did not. There were a few police chiefs who made attempts to kill the bill, but there really was no lobbying force against it. The opposition to it could be termed quiet opposition."

Although Rotondi refused to identify specific editors who funneled the complaints to him which resulted in the drafting of the measure, he did contend that "only, maybe, two percent of the newspaper editors and publishers in this state were having problems with their police departments."

But he felt any efforts from law enforcement officials to suppress information was "a violation of the spirit, if not the letter, of the law" and constituted an abuse potentially adverse to the general public good.

It is through the press that the public most frequently, immediately, and directly learns of police operations. And it was the press as conduit and the public in general whose interests he wished to represent.

"I received reports that reporters in certain areas were being denied access to a police log, and reports that even in some cases when they had access, they found nothing substantive in the log. As an attorney, I read the existing law, and I decided that this statute need only to amend the public information law, so police logs would definitely be under the category. Certain police chiefs were arguing and attempting to find a loophole, whereby they were saying that the log they were keeping did not have to be made public."

"I truly believe that in a free society, you cannot, under any circumstances, allow your police arm to keep secret and private all information pertaining to their operation. It is not only the public's right, but its need to know that is at stake. They must know that the police arm they support through tax dollars in indeed functioning properly and serving the purpose for which it is intended."

"I'M VERY AFRAID OF A POLICE STATE"

SAMUEL ROTONDI

"WHY DID I get involved with police law? Because I am very, very aware of the nature of a police state. Very, very aware of it. I'm very afraid of a police state getting to exaggerated power. That always concerns me.

"There was a group of kids on the Cape (reference here to Cape Cod, Massachusetts). "One of them was a constituent who called me. They were arrested by police and were beaten up. And when they went, these kids, to redress the situation by court action, there was no record, no police log of the incident. Because they were never formally arrested.

"I pursued it personally, "I was so upset about it. The police told me there was no need for them to record it. It wasn't an arrest. I said, 'What is this? Isn't there a law that deals with the right of the public to know about any incident dealing with procedures that cause individuals to be retained and, indeed, in this case, battered by police officers?' "No law, sir." "Oh, no, there's no law like that, sir.' I did my own research. There was a law. The law dealt with the issue of public information. The only time police logs were ever mentioned was in the strange context of the so-called public information law, amended in 1974. What it said was that police logs are public records if kept chronologically. That's all it said. So what did law enforcement personnel do about keeping it, pursuant to that statute? Those who always kept it as a matter of course, continued. Those who never wanted to keep it, just didn't keep it chronologically any longer.

(EDITOR'S NOTE: Following the publication of this series of articles, Senator Rotondi addressed students at Northeastern University, Boston, Massachusetts, on the subject of public access to police records, providing additional details concerning his role in the log law passage. This is an excerpted version of his remarks.)

"I was very upset that there was a police department telling me that by some quirk of a law, by the use of certain language, they were avoiding not only their responsibility, but their obligation under the law as a police arm supported by taxpayers and a system of free government. Seems to me that the public should always have access to information dealing with everyday activities of a police force.

"That's why I wrote the bill that I hope for the first time has clarified the following fact: police departments throughout this Commonwealth from now on have the absolute obligation by law to provide to the public in accessible form, a form that is easily understood, not in code, in English or a language easily understood by the person seeking the information, a police log that details the activities of the police station.

A Hard Fight

"Now that bill took a very long time to pass. Perhaps you should all know as students how difficult it was to pass. Then if you realize what was involved, perhaps you will realize how important it was to those who wanted it. They came at this bill—they being certain police chiefs and certain law enforcement types who saw this as a direct threat to their ability to work under their own procedures: not in effect to go out and harm the public, but to have a little more leeway in their everyday activity, for example, to keep the son of the mayor out of the paper. It was cool to do that politically, protect that good relationship, or to protect a police officer, that was most often the case, a police officer who just didn't know what to do in a certain situation.

"Like in that situation on the Cape—five of them (police officers) teamed up on five kids, five young kids, with bats and everything else, to protect a police officer.

They came out in waves that only a legislator who has been there six years like I have can really understand. "You go to the president of the Senate and you get a commitment for the bill, and the next day, the bill doesn't come out of committee.

What Happened?

"You wonder what happened. It wasn't the president of the Senate. It was somebody in the committee who had a tie to the police and it went on for six months. Every day something new happened to that bill.

Finally it got up to the Governor's desk. He wasn't going to sign it, because the current public safety chief was very close to chiefs, and he didn't want any part of the bill. And almost convinced the Governor not to sign.

A Public Appeal

"We had to go to the public at the end. Bring in the publishers. That's one thing politicians are very sensitive about—newspapers and the media. I brought in every major publisher in this Commonwealth right to that Governor's office. We started talking about parts of that bill. Now, you'd like to think that the public as a whole could have caused that to happen, but it wouldn't have. The public didn't care. The public didn't know. The whole issue was letting the public have the right to know. So it really did matter. There was top lobbying effort, trying to kill it any way you could have imagined.

It's a Law

"It is now law, and what has it meant since it has been law? Well, no law is that effective unless enforced. We haven't really seen yet how willing the public as a whole, publishers specifically, reporters, whoever, are going to be to enforce the letter of this law. Ninety-five percent of police departments in this state are complying with the law. Tell me about the five percent factor that's really frustrating this law and are doing it today, even with the change. Court action is going to become necessary perhaps even in the next couple of years to be able to fully implement it.

"It doesn't matter where the police force is in this country. It's still the same—no police force should have the unilateral right to withhold from the public it serves, access to its activities."

CRIME REPORTING:
FROM DELIRIUM TO DIALOGUE

DONALD M. GILLMOR

CRIME REPORTING in America has put 100 years of freebooting and extravaganza behind it and come into a period of self-doubt and introspective dialogue with the courts. Jazz journalism may have been fun for a reporter, but it was often horror for a defendant. And some of the most acclaimed journalists of their day got in on the fun.

In 1907, Irwin S. Cobb wrote 600,000 words on the sensational Harry K. Thaw murder trial for the New York *Evening World.* Thaw had shot Stanford White in a restaurant atop Madison Square Garden because White, a successful architect, had dared to shower favors on Thaw's beautiful wife before her marriage. William Bolitho, correspondent for the *Manchester Guardian* and the New York *World* and a renowned stylist, shocked the nation in 1919 with accounts of the Paris trial of Henri Landru, better known as Bluebeard, who was accused of murdering an indeterminate number of paramours, fiances and wives.

With a susceptible mass audience at his disposal, Ben Hecht covered Chicago in the roaring 1920's. In the first year of that decade a war hero named Carl Wanderer was executed for murdering his wife after a celebrated trial which Hecht and the Chicago *Daily News* had helped bring

---

*Donald M. Gillmor is professor of journalism and mass communication at the University of Minnesota and director of the Silha Center for the Study of Media Ethics and Law. He is the author of numerous books and articles including *Free Press and Fair Trial* (1969), *Mass Communication Law: Cases and Comment* (4th ed. 1984), *Justice Hugo Black and the First Amendment* (1978), and *Enduring Issues in Mass Communication* (1978). His articles have appeared in journals in Japan, France, Great Britain, Canada and Australia.

†Reprinted with permission of the author and *Current History.* This article appeared in the July, 1971 issue.

about. Wanderer, who had displayed bravado and scorn during the trial, sang a popular song as the noose was being adjusted over his head. This moved Alexander Woolcott to whimsy and he wrote, "From one of the crowd of reporters watching the execution came the audible comment that Wanderer deserved hanging for his voice alone."[1]

With similar levity Hazel MacDonald of the Chicago *Evening American* began a shocking story about an Owensboro, Kentucky, open air hanging with the paragraph:

> Rainey Bethea, Negro, 22 years old and skinny, dropped to his death here at sunrise today as 20,000 cheering fans packed every available spot of space to see the hangman, attired in a white seersucker suit, spring the trap.[2]

"A big murder trial," wrote Damon Runyon, that great improvisator of language, "possesses some of the elements of a sporting event." He continued:

> I find the same popular interest in the murder trial that I find . . . on the eve of a big football game, or a pugilistic encounter, or a baseball series. There is the same conversational speculation on the probable result, only more of it. . . . The trial is a sort of game, the players on the one side the attorneys for the defense, and on the other side the attorneys for the State. The defendant figures in it merely as the prize.[3]

Runyon may have been at his best in covering the trial of Al Capone for income tax evasion in 1931, and one of those stories began, "Capone was quietly dressed this morning, bar a hat of pearly white, emblematic, no doubt, of purity."[4]

In an April, 1927, International News Service report, Runyon said of the Ruth Snyder-Judd Gray murder case, a case celebrated for its sheer banality, "It was stupid beyond imagination, and so brutal that the thought of it probably makes many a peaceful, homeloving Long Islander shiver in his pajamas as he prepares for bed."[5] (Mrs. Snyder and Gray had conspired successfully to kill Mr. Snyder.)

Journalistic history was made when a New York *Daily News* photographer strapped a tiny camera to his leg, smuggled it into Sing Sing's execution chamber, and took a picture of the same Ruth Snyder straining at the thongs of the electric chair moments after the current had been turned on. The picture was a front-page sensation, which sold 250,000 extra copies; but there were doubts about its ethical attributes. Stanley Walker, then city editor of the *New York Herald Tribune*, contended, "The Ruth Snyder picture is regarded by men who take news pictures as perhaps the most damaging blot upon their professional history. There is a strong sense of honor, an undefined code which forbids shyster practices, even among this group of hard-boiled buccaneers." This concern may have been more in the spirit of lost competition than outraged morality. But even *Editor & Publisher,* more protective than critical of journalistic behavior, regarded this breach of faith with the prison warden as a deceit casting reproach on all American journalism.

Bernarr Macfadden's *Graphic,* nicknamed the "pornographic," promoted the execution in typical fashion:

> "Don't fail to read tomorrow's *Graphic.* An installment that thrills and stuns. A story that fairly pierces the heart and reveals Ruth Snyder's last thoughts on earth; that pulses the blood as it discloses her final letters. Think of it! A woman's final thoughts just before she is clutched in the deadly snare that sears and burns and FRIES AND KILLS! Her very last words! Exclusively in tomorrow's *Graphic.*[6]

Tradition of Crime Reporting

This tradition of crime reporting probably began with the Bow Street police reporters in London who by 1820 had discovered that this kind of news, if presented flashily, had mass appeal. Benjamin Day's *New York Sun,* the first successful penny press, specialized in news of crime and violence. Day hired George Wisner, a Bow Street veteran, to cover the courts, and within a year Wisner was co-owner of the paper.[7] That was in 1833.

Charles Dickens was a Bow Street reporter par excellence. When he was not editing his own newspaper, the *Daily News,* he was covering the courts and their abuses. In March, 1846, his newspaper carried a series of articles by Dickens himself attacking the death penalty and its brutalizing effects on the masses.

Crime news contributed to the success of Pulitzer's *World* and its notion of the new journalism and gave momentum to Hearst's *Journal* and its concept of yellow journalism. James Gordon Bennett's *Herald* had no equal in sensational, aggressive, and even fictional crime coverage. So the tabloids of the Jazz Age had a notable genealogy, and prohibition was to become their patron.

Yet even when the sporting theory of justice was at its zenith in the 1920's, crime news seldom occupied more than about five percent of the total news space. In 1928, Eric W. Allen studied 100 newspapers over a 75-year time span and found a crime news average of 1.4 percent of total editorial material, this in the face of estimates as high as 50 percent made by bankers, lawyers, dentists, engineers and college professors he had surveyed.[8] The inflated estimates may suggest a high intensity of readership for flamboyantly displayed news of this kind. A little bit of crime news has always been able to energize large crime-wave impressions.

More recently, a Midwestern community of 100,000 was studied for a two-month period during which 234 persons were arrested and formally charged with criminal offenses. Of these 234 only 39, or 17 percent, received publicity in at least one of the community's two local newspapers. Over a three-year period, 29 criminal cases were tried before a jury and of these 12, or 41 percent, were covered by at least one of the newspapers. In both situations, the more serious the crime, the broader the coverage. Five murder trials were reported by both newspapers.

Clifton Daniel, executive editor of *The New York Times,* has noted that in January, 1965, 11,724 felonies were committed in New York City; yet only 41 of these were mentioned in the New York *Daily News,* the most crime-conscious newspaper in the city. Other estimates of the proportion of trials covered have been as low as 2 percent; but, of course, we need to know more about the extent and type of publicity given to the reported cases.[9] A single case as bizarre as the Charles Manson case can push innumerable less deadly felonies off the front pages of all of the nation's newspapers.

A Watershed For Crime Reporting

As the tragic Sacco-Vanzetti case, best reported by Louis Stark of *The New York Times,* may have sounded the death knell of experimentation in America with genuinely radical politics, at least until the mid-1960's, so the grotesque newspaper and radio coverage of the Lindbergh kidnapping trial may have been a watershed for court reporting in America. Never again would the press descend like vultures upon a defendant without risking the wrath of peers, readers and the court system itself.

As many as 800 newsmen and photographers, among them Edna Ferber, Fannie Hurst, Kathleen Norris, Adela Rogers St. John, Winchell, Runyon and Woolcott, helped turn the tiny town of Flemington, New Jersey, into a midsummer Mardi Gras. They were joined by the great figures of stage and screen, United States senators, crooners and social celebrities, and as many as 20,000 curious nobodies on a single day. One report had it that the jury was seriously considering an offer to go into vaudeville. The small courtroom became a 24-hour news and propaganda bureau spawning headlines such as "Bruno Guilty, But Has Aids, Verdict of Man in Street," and news story references to Bruno Hauptmann as "a thing lacking human characteristics." Robert Benchley's famous February 23, 1935, *New Yorker* report, "Apres la Guerre Finie," best caught the magic of the scene:

> They are the correspondents who supplied us with the news that Mr. Wilentz was rivaling Mr. Reilly for the title of "best-dressed lawyer," that Flemington stores were having a run on cameras, that local bars had fixed up a drink of applejack known as The Hauptmann, that a dog named Nellie had become the mascot of the trial, and that the sale of "kidnap ladders" and miniature sleeping suits was progressing nicely. The world is always full of a number of things for these lighthearted reporters, and the metropolitan district is their oyster.

Legal attitudes toward press coverage and publicity-seeking lawyers were forever hardened by the case, and an era of free-wheeling court coverage may have ended with the Lindbergh case in 1937.

The constancy of human nature has assured lawyer-public official-journalist alliances bent on thwarting justice since the Lindbergh case, but such conspiracies have been unable to function with impunity. In the past 35 years there has been an explosion of renewed interest in the possibility of "trial by newspaper," a problem of democracy at least as old as our judicial system. (Chief Justice Marshall took note of extra-legal newspaper comment in a reference to the Alexandria, Virginia, *Expositor* in the treason trial of Aaron Burr.)[10]

Case after sensational case has led to soul-searching on the part of press and bar and to the pursuit of constitutional remedies for relieving the stress between the right to a fair trial and the right of a free press. It was not until 1961 that the United States Supreme Court took similar action when it reversed a state criminal conviction solely on the grounds that prejudicial pretrial publicity had made a fair trial before an impartial jury impossible.[11] In 1963, the Supreme Court reversed the conviction of a murder suspect because he had been interviewed in jail by a sheriff, and the filmed interview had been broadcast over a television station. Thousands in the community heard the suspect confess to murder, bank robbery and kidnapping.[12]

The Oswald epic and the subsequent Warren Report kept the fair trial-free press issue on the agenda, although by no means everyone was prepared to accept the commission's conclusions critical of the press. A presidential assassination is an atypical crime and the commission may not have appreciated the depth of public interest in the event. Bradley S. Greenberg and Edwin B. Parker, in their collection of essays and research reports on the assassination, find evidence to support the hypothesis that public fear during the dreadful hours following the President's death was minimized by quick, reassuring news reports. They conclude that "fear and anxiety might have been magnified to the point of hysteria" if news reports had not quickly informed the people that "the functions of government were being carried out smoothly, that there was no conspiracy, and that there was no further threat."[13]

The trial of Jack Ruby was an anticlimax. If the news media were florid and irresponsible, so were Melvin Belli, Ruby's chief counsel for a time, and Judge Joe B. Brown, who presided over the trial. Belli initiated a publicity campaign focusing on a series of autobiographical magazine articles about his client and, while appeals were pending, wrote a book about the case. Judge Brown was working under contract on a Ruby book manuscript while he supervised the trial.

If somehow Oswald and, to a lesser extent, Ruby, were necessary sacrifices to the public interest, Dr. Sam Sheppard should not have been. Here there were no overriding social rights at stake. On trial for the murder of his wife, the young suburbanite was given the full treatment in proceedings reminiscent of the Lindbergh kidnapping trial. Massive and vindictive newspaper coverage and the infusion of sob-sisters and columnists—more typically the comic relief of American journalism—created an atmosphere so potentially prejudicial to the rights of the defendant that the United States Supreme Court had no hesitation in overturning the conviction.

In an opinion reviewing the misbehavior of the press, the presiding judge and attorney for both sides, Justice Tom Clark wrote:

> From the cases coming here we note that unfair and prejudicial news comment on pending trials has become increasingly prevalent. Due process requires that the accused receive a trial by an impartial jury free from outside influences. Given the pervasiveness of modern communications and the difficulty of effacing prejudicial publicity from the minds of the jurors, the trial courts must take strong measures to ensure that the balance is never weighed against the accused. . . . Of course, there is nothing that proscribes the press from reporting events that transpire in the courtroom. But where there is a reasonable likelihood that prejudicial news prior to trial will prevent a fair trial, the judge should continue the case until the threat abates or transfer it to another county not so permeated with publicity. In addition, sequestration of the jury was something the judge should have raised . . . with counsel. If publicity during the proceedings threatens the fairness of the trial, a new trial should be ordered. But we must remember that reversals are but palliatives; the cure lies in those remedial measures that

will prevent the prejudice at its inception. The courts must take such steps by rule and regulation that will protect their processes from prejudicial outside interferences. Neither prosecutors, counsel for defense, the accused, witnesses, court staff nor enforcement officers coming under the jurisdiction of the court should be permitted to frustrate its function. Collaboration between counsel and the press as to information affecting the fairness of a criminal trial is not only subject to regulation, but is highly censurable and worthy of disciplinary measures.[14]

The court has indicated in this and other cases that it will judge, using its own non-empirical standards, the point beyond which prejudice must not go in a criminal trial, if a conviction is to remain valid. The fact that a relationship between news coverage and jury verdicts has not been demonstrated—except perhaps for the deleterious effect of a confession—[15] has not deterred the court from making its own subjective probability estimates, and it will no doubt continue to do so. The court has made the same "non-scientific" assumptions about the psychological effects of the camera in the courtroom, as we shall note.

Closely behind the landmark *Sheppard* decision came the report of the American Bar Association's Advisory Committee on Fair Trial and Free Press, better known as the Reardon Report, named for Committee Chairman Paul C. Reardon of the Massachusetts Supreme Court. Like the *Sheppard* opinion, the report spoke primarily to officers of the court, attorneys and police officials, directing that they restrict their communication with newsmen in the trial and pretrial periods. The only recommendation relating directly to the press was that the contempt power be exercised against any person who disseminated extrajudicial statements willfully designed to affect the outcome of a trial or who violated a valid order not to reveal information disclosed at a closed judicial hearing. And the report recommended that preliminary hearings generally be closed.

Fear of Contempt

Although press reaction to the report was generally negative, the most telling criticism of it focused on fear of a revival of the judicial power to hold reporters and editors in contempt for what they write in their news columns. After a long and tortuous legal and legislative history this authority was taken away from American judges as the result of a 1941 Supreme Court case involving labor leader Harry Bridges and the Los Angeles *Times,* both of whom had criticized the judicial process while a case was pending.[16] The court declared in this and subsequent cases that the contempt power could be used against out-of-court comment only when such comment created a clear and present danger that justice would be impaired, and the court seemed prepared to make a strong presumption in favor of a free press, as it has done since in cases of libel against public officials and public figures.[17] In other English-speaking countries, the contempt power is still a dreaded weapon against extra-judicial comment; and in those countries judges, police and prosecutors are not dependent upon the goodwill of newspapers for their continuance in office.

If the contempt power was an empty threat against crime and court reporters—except, of course for misbehavior in the courtroom itself—the way officers of the court reacted to the news media after the report's promulgation was not. Many sheriffs and country attorneys, most of whom had not read the report but were aware that lawyers and judges had spoken collectively on the free press-fair trial issue, simply refused to say anything about crime in their communities and for a time there were fears that a new kind of secret justice would be administered under a kind of "when in doubt say nothing" policy.

Free Press v. Fair Trial

Amid charges of overkill and over-reaction, the free press-fair trial dialogue has moved to the local and state levels. In lieu of secret trials, the contempt power, new laws, or repressive and unilateral court rules, bilateral press-bar councils have been developed in at least a dozen states. Problems of free press and fair trial are now being discussed by both sides and guidelines are being issued for the conduct of lawyers and newsmen. The criminal trial is not quite the game it used to be. One detects at least traces of restraint in the trials of Sirhan Sirhan and James Earl Ray. And Richard Speck, tried for the murder of eight Chicago nurses, was well insulated from potentially prejudicial coverage during the course of his trial in Peoria, Illinois.

In spite of the fact that there is a better understanding between press and bar than ever before on what kind of pretrial and trial information ought and ought not be disclosed, cases involving prominent people, the Chappaquiddick affair, for example, cases as bizarre and irrational as the Manson case, and cases with significant political implications such as the courts martial of Commander Lloyd Bucher and Lieutenant William Calley, and the "political" trials of the Chicago 8 and Angela Davis, lead to extravagances in reporting and to well-devised publicity campaigns that adversary attorneys believe may spell the difference between victory and defeat. The suspense element in such cases titillates the reader, and editors, propelled by long-standing professional norms, know it.

The right to publish inevitably includes the moral responsibility of deciding whether the public interest justifies placing private rights in jeopardy. As fundamental as freedom of the press is to the well-being of society, it was never meant to deny the high value that an open society places upon human life, as manifested in a civilizing system of law which presumes a man innocent until proven guilty beyond a reasonable doubt.

Where the public interest does seem to be overriding, responsible journalists will continue to expose crime and corruption in law enforcement, in government and in the courthouse itself. It would be scandalous if they did not. Pulitzer Prizes have been won for investigations which prosecuting attorneys were loathe to undertake. Herbert Bayard Swope, a gifted journalist and editor of the New York *Evening World*, made an expose of an alliance between police and the underworld in 1912 one of the great crime stories of all time.

Except for the occasional sensational criminal case, the judicial branch remains the least well covered branch of government. C. P. Corliss, a 20-year veteran police reporter for the Los Angeles *Times* and author of a guidebook for police reporters, says the job is more difficult than he or any of his associates dreamed it would be 20 years ago.

> With the increase of emphasis on civil rights, protest marches, and charges of overzealousness on the part of law enforcement officers, more and more space will be devoted by news media to spot news of this type. Also, there are going to be barriers placed in the way of gathering facts the public is entitled to know. There is a need for reporters who know how to surmount these barriers despite the trend on the part of some media to educate rather than inform.[18]

Inadequate Reporting

Other observers fear that the orthodox press has failed to deal with the underlying social conditions which produce crime and disorder, to examine white collar crime, to explain why the poor and the black often regard the judicial system with a blazing hatred, and to point out how the law is sometimes used as a bludgeon rather than a means for securing justice.[19] If journalists cannot probe as deeply as Feodor Dostoyevsky and Theodore Dreiser, they can at least tell us more about the social psychology of crime and the economic and cultural factors which provoke it. And yet the courts have made this difficult. Courtrooms are too small. Reporting facilities are far less adequate than those provided for newsmen by the legislative and executive branches. The standard courtroom is a journalistic closet.

David Grey, a student of the interaction patterns between the press and the United States Supreme Court, notes:

> In fact, it seems somewhat inconsistent for the Court to talk about such First Amendment rights as freedom of the press as an essential part of democratic dialogue and yet discourage efforts at improved public insight into the Court itself and the workings of law.[20]

The court could modify its procedures to effect a better comprehension of its momentous activities and courts down the line could follow those cues. The press itself could do much to make its coverage more interpretive, more systematic and less dependent upon news formulas suitable, perhaps, for covering the police beat but inadequate for a complex court of law.

Television Coverage?

Yet the courts are reluctant to open themselves to the public gaze. Chief Justice Warren Burger will not permit live television coverage of his public addresses, and this reflects the general unwillingness of the courts to recognize the broadcast media as part of the legitimate press.

This attitude goes back to the Lindbergh case, after which the American Bar Association adopted Canon 35 of its Judicial Ethics barring photography of any kind in the courtroom. All states, with the exception of Colorado, Oklahoma and Texas, have adopted Canon 35, or some modification of it, by statute or court rules. Rule 53 of the Federal Rules of Criminal Procedure keeps cameras out of federal courtrooms. The Supreme Court in the landmark Billie Sol Estes case certified Canon 35, arguing that prejudice is inherent in a televised trial, that the camera has immeasurable but certain psychological effects on jurors, witnesses, the trial judge and on the defendant himself. Television causes prejudice, Justice Clark said categorically in his opinion for the court, although "one cannot put his finger on its specific mischief."[21]

Aside from the empirical question of effects which has not yet been answered, does television coverage of a trial necessarily imply a morbid public interest, an interest former Chief Justice Earl Warren identified with Cuban Premier Fidel Castro's stadium trials and the Soviet Union's trial of U-2 pilot Francis Gary Powers in a huge auditorium? Could a wider public ever manifest a sincere interest in criminal procedures, or would the carnival atmosphere of Flemington, New Jersey, be re-created?

It is safe to say that we do not know and, furthermore, that news photographers have a fairly bad track record. Television, with its complex of sponsors, producers, directors, actors, makeup men, sets, special effects, time slots and ratings might very well turn a celebrated criminal case into a television spectacular. A courtroom is not a stage. Witnesses, lawyers, judges and juries are not players. A trial is not a drama for public entertainment. And yet the public business is being conducted.

In Denver, Colorado, last year an entire trial was televised with the permission of the defendant, a Black Panther leader who was charged with resisting arrest. An edited version of the film was shown over National Educational Television stations on four consecutive evenings with expert commentary by a Harvard Law School professor. The result was a rare view of how a criminal trial proceeds, with no apparent prejudice to the defendant who, upon being acquitted by a white jury, damned the court system generally for what he perceived to be its racism.

In the *Estes* case, Justices Potter Stewart, Hugo Black, William J. Brennan and Byron R. White dissented partly because they would give some latitude to television's future role and partly because they could find no demonstrable prejudice to Estes in the fragmentary television coverage of his trial and preliminary hearing. Speaking for the minority, Justice Stewart said that:

> It is important to remember that we moved in an area touching the realm of free communication, and for that reason, if for no other, I would be wary of imposing a *per se* rule which, in the light of future technology, might serve to stifle or abridge true First Amendment rights.

Justice John Harlan, although he voted with the majority, wrote a key opinion which kept the *Estes* case from becoming a blanket constitutional prohibition against televising state criminal trials. He argued that:

> We should not be deterred from making the constitutional judgment which this case demands by the prospect that the day may come when television will have become so commonplace an affair in the daily life of the average person as to dissipate all reasonable likelihood that its use in courtroom may disparage the judicial process.

One need not be a visionary to imagine the day when video tape will supplement the reporter's notes and provide appellate courts with "living" records of important trials. Unobtrusive camera and recording equipment will be built into the courtrooms of tomorrow as it has been built into the chambers of the United Nations building today. The new Criminal Courts Building in Los Angeles is already so equipped. And, in the long run, the camera may prove to be a more accurate recording instrument than the pencil and pad.

Another significant theme in the press-bar dialogue has been the newsman's privilege to protect his sources of information. In the absence of any common law right, at least 16 states have passed laws shielding newsmen from governmental inquisitions. Most of these laws are absolute or unconditional; a few qualify the privilege by extending to the courts the ultimate determination as to whether justice, and thereby the public interest, demand the information sought. Federal courts do not recognize the privilege and in recent years federal judges have been prone to issue subpoenas demanding tapes, notes, and other raw materials of the reporter's trade, especially where grand juries are investigating the activities of political groups like the Panthers and the Weathermen.

Some news media, among them the more prominent, have cooperated with the courts and with law enforcement agencies as well. Individual newsmen have admitted being on F.B.I. and C.I.A. payrolls for the primary purpose of political prying, a form of moonlighting not considered within the journalist's professional code. Either kind of cooperation may be destructive of the press' credibility as an honest broker between polarized elements of society.

There are also documented cases of police officers impersonating newsmen, suggesting that the two roles may be reversible more frequently than one would like to think, and shattering the validity of journalistic cries for protection against other forms of governmental intrusion and harassment. Underground newspapers have always assumed that the "straight" press prints only the police versions of crime news; and periodicals published by activist reporters are asking searching questions about the performance of the commercial press in some of our larger cities.

Not until Earl Caldwell, a black *New York Times* reporter, refused to honor a subpoena directing him to testify before a grand jury in San Francisco investigating the Black Panthers did the media begin to see their obligation to independence in a clearer light. A federal district court judge in California subsequently ruled that Caldwell, although he was required to respond to the subpoena, was under no compulsion to testify, under the rubric of the First Amendment, unless an overriding national interest, which could not be served by alternative means, could be established to the satisfaction of the court.[22] Legislation has been introduced in Congress which would prohibit governmental bodies from forcing newsmen to disclose their sources of confidential information except where foreign aggression, grand juries or the prevention of libel are involved.

Traditionally, responsible newsmen have been willing to accept contempt citations and thereby to risk fine and imprisonment rather than divulge their sources. A columnist for the New York *Herald Tribune* became a professional martyr in 1957 when she accepted a jail sentence rather than reveal the source of a statement that had provoked a million dollar libel suit by Judy Garland against the Columbia Broadcasting System.

The dialogue with the courts will continue; schools, young journalists and concerned segments of the public will be heard and, except for occasional lapses into the sensational forms of an earlier time and the kind of herd panic that sometimes afflicts newsmen, a more socially responsible level of performance will very likely emerge.

ENDNOTES

1. Louis L. Snyder and Richard B. Morris (eds.), *A Treasury of Great Reporting* (New York: Simon & Schuster, 1962, 2nd ed.), p. 377.
2. Quoted in Curtis D. MacDougall, *Newsroom Problems and Policies* (New York: Dover, 1963), p. 385.
3. Jerome Frank, *Courts on Trial* (Princeton: Princeton University Press, 1949), p. 92.
4. *Ibid.*
5. Snyder and Morris, *op. cit.*, p. 439.
6. Helen M. Hughes, *News and the Human Interest Story* (Chicago: University of Chicago Press, 1940), p. 235.
7. Edwin Emery, *The Press and America* (New York: Prentice-Hall, 1962, 2nd ed.), p. 215.
8. MacDougall, *op. cit.*, p. 360.
9. Thomas E. Eimermann and Rita James Simon, "Newspaper Coverage of Crime and Trials: Another Empirical Look at the Free Press-Fair Trial Controversy," *Journalism Quarterly*, 47: 1 (Spring, 1970), p. 143.
10. *United States v. Aaron Burr*, 25 Fed. Cas. 49 (No. 14692g), 1807.

11. *Irvin v. Dowd*, 366 U.S. 717, 6 L.Ed. 2d 751, 81 S. Ct. 1639 (1961).
12. *Rideau v. Louisiana*, 373 U.S. 723, 10 L.Ed. 2d 663, 83 S. Ct. 1417 (1963).
13. *The Kennedy Assassination and the American Public: Social Communication* (Stanford: Stanford University Press, 1965).
14. *Sheppard v. Maxwell*, 384 U.S. 333, 16 L.Ed. 2d 600, 86 S. Ct. 1507 (1966).
15. See specifically Walter Wilcox and Maxwell McCombs, "Crime Story Elements and Fair Trial/Free Press," unpublished manuscript, U.C.L.A., Los Angeles, 1967; F. Gerald Kline and Paul Jess, "Prejudicial Publicity: Its Effect on Law School Mock Juries," *Journalism Quarterly* 43: 113 (1966); Mary Dee Tans and Steven H. Chaffee, "Pre-trial Publicity and Juror Prejudice," *Journalism Quarterly* 43: 647 (1966). For a general review see Walter Wilcox, *The Press, the Jury and the Behavioral Sciences*, Journalism Monographs, No. 9, October, 1968.
16. *Bridges v. California*, 314 U.S. 252, 88 L.Ed. 192, 62 S. Ct. 190 (1941).
17. New York Times, Co. v. Sullivan, 376 U.S. 245, 11 L.Ed. 2d 686, 84 S. Ct. 710 (1964), and subsequent cases. (See Donald M. Gillmor & Jerome A. Barron, *Mass Communication Law: Cases and Comment* (St. Paul: West Publishing Co., 1969), pp. 250-284.
18. Newton H. Fulbright, "Police Reporter Jots Down Some Guideposts," *Editor and Publisher*, 103: 15, p. 11, April 11, 1970.
19. Nathan Blumberg, "The Orthodox Media Under Fire: Chicago and the Press," *Montana Journalism Review*, 12: 1969, pp. 38-60. See also the *Report of the National Advisory Commission on Civil Disorders* (Kerner Report), Chapt. 15, "The News Media and the Disorders."
20. David, Grey, *The Supreme Court and the News Media* (Evanston: Northwestern University Press, 1968), p. 140.
21. *Estes v. State of Texas*, 381 U.S. 352, 14 L.Ed. 2d 543, 85 S. Ct. 1628 (1965).
22. *Application of Caldwell* (N.D. Cal. Misc. No. 10426, 1970).

REPORTING RAPE: LIVE TV COVERAGE GENERATES A DEBATE

BILL SEYMOUR

REPORTING on rape—a crime that forces some self-censoring among the media—left television breaking the traditional ground rules this year and forcing some newspapers to follow in pursuit.

Live televised testimony in a Fall River, Massachusetts gang-rape trial, stemming from an incident in Big Dan's bar in the old whaling port of New Bedford, prompted several newspapers to decide whether to reveal—when TV does—an alleged rape victim's name.

At issue: Should live television influence a newspaper to go against its policy.

The case: Television, during live reporting, broadcast the name and testimony of the alleged victim of the gang rape.

---

*(EDITOR'S NOTE: The so-termed Big Dan's rape trial serves as a provocative case study for the ethical dilemmas which surround the police/press/court issue of rape victim identification. National headlines were made in March, 1983 when a woman said several men raped her, while others cheered, in a tavern in New Bedford, Massachusetts called Big Dan's. The trial was held in February, 1984 in the neighboring Fall River, and because Massachusetts is one of the more than 40 states which permit cameras in the courtroom, broadcast media provided live coverage. Bill Seymour, formerly a reporter with *The News-Times* of Danbury, Conn. explores the controversy which swirled around the publication and broadcast of the then alleged victim in his article "Reporting Rape/Live TV Coverage Generates Debate." He interviews Charles McCorkle Hauser, executive editor of the *Journal-Bulletin*, Providence, R.I., which published the woman's name, and James Ragsdale, editor of *The Standard Times*, New Bedford, which did not identify her.)

Hauser's view is amplified in remarks he made during a seminar held in Boston and sponsored by the media for examination of rape coverage policies in the wake of Big Dan's. Ragsdale's elaborations were made during an interview I had with him in 1986. The comments of the rape victim (not Big Dan's) were made during that same seminar at which Hauser spoke and are included here on the condition that she remain anonymous. A lawyer's argument in defense of shielding rape victims' identities is made by S. W. Sweetser, an attorney practicing in Vermont.

†Seymour's article originally appeared in the *1984-85 Journalism Ethics Report* prepared by the National Ethics Committee, Society of Professional Journalists, Sigma Delta Chi and is reprinted with permission of Society of Professional Journalists, SDX.

Interviews with Charles McCorkle Hauser, executive director of the Providence, R.I., *Journal-Bulletin,* and James Ragsdale, editor of the New Bedford (Mass.) *Standard-Times,* offer contrasting views. *The Journal-Bulletin* papers published the woman's name, following a nationwide television broadcast of it, while the *Standard-Times* refused to break its long-standing policy to shield alleged rape victims' names.

Both said that in the same circumstances, they would make the same decision.

The question divides standard procedures from practicality. This question and other journalistic issues have prompted stories in *The Journal-Bulletin* papers, *The Standard-Times, The Boston Globe, Columbia Journalism Review, Editor and Publisher, The Bulletin,* a monthly magazine of the American Society of Newspaper Editors, and other publications.

The story surrounding this issue became the focus of national news reports in early March, 1983, after a woman said several men raped her, to the cheers of others, in Big Dan's. The trial, which started in late February, 1984, was held in nearby Fall River, where the courtroom could hold more spectators than New Bedford's. The trial drew national media attention.

Gavel-to-gavel live coverage came from a local cable television station in New Bedford and the Atlanta-based Cable News Network, which sent broadcasts around the country. These stations used the woman's name and her testimony in court. This pushed newspapers into deciding whether their self-imposed and traditional policies—which barred disclosure—remained valid because of the television broadcasts.

"It was foolish to suppress the name when broadcasts are going to put it out," said Hauser, whose morning and evening papers broke their policies and used the name.

Said Ragsdale, who did not budge from his policy, "I refused to allow television to influence my policies. TV didn't participate in making them and [it] won't dismantle them.

"We're serving notice to the readers on what we stand for," he said, explaining that his policy is firm, but he later conceded it's not absolute.

"We avoid it [naming the alleged victim]," he said, unless the editors face an "unforeseeable, undefinable and unpredictable" event that would force disclosure of the name.

Asked for an example, Ragsdale replied, "Chuck [Hauser] found his. We still haven't."

Hauser said the key element was television's live coverage.

If the name had been used in a six or 11 o'clock news report, "We probably wouldn't have used the name," he said. "The live broadcasts have changed the print reporter's procedures. . . . The way our readers see something live affects the way we report it," he said.

Neither Ragsdale nor Robert Kierstead, ombudsman for *The Globe,* agreed with Hauser. *The Globe* refused to use the woman's name.

"Hauser and *Journal-Bulletin* Executive Editor James Wyman had no obligation to run [the name]. It's a cop-out," Kierstead said of the Providence editor's reasoning.

The issue at heart is the strength of a policy regarding the publishing of alleged rape victim's names, he said, not competitive interests.

The issue could have a tough time in Massachusetts again, particularly in the courtroom of Superior Court Judge Williama G. Young, who presided over the trial. It ended with a guilty verdict for four of the six defendants charged.

In Kierstead's July 30 column in *The Globe.* Young explained his misunderstanding of television, and he vowed to stop the incident from repeating.

At the close of the trial in March, Young said publication and broadcast of the name was "an absymal error in judgment." "I regret intensely that you did not exercise your usual self-imposed embargo not to use her name. I can assure you that, in the future, I will take whatever measures I can to ensure that you don't use her name."

In his column, Kierstead quoted the 43-year-old judge as saying, "I never made any order with respect to the name being broadcast or published . . . I never conceived that any press organization was going to use it. I thought that the tradition was so strong that it wouldn't be used."

Young said that he supports having cameras in the courtroom, but in a similar situation he would impose guidelines at a pre-trial hearing. The rules would include forcing the broadcaster to censor the victim's name and picture from the screen. He said he would have the hearing far enough ahead of the trial, so that an individual or firm "could challenge it, because they have a right to challenge it formally, before I get the witness on the stand."

Both Hauser and Ragsdale said the judge shouldn't have been surprised when the broadcast media, allowed in the courtroom under Massachusetts law, used the woman's name.

"When I heard about the request for live TV coverage, I just shook my head. I figured the judge must have made arrangements to protect the woman's name," said Ragsdale.

Both journalists agreed that public attitudes should weigh heavily into any decision to change a policy about revealing an alleged rape victim's name, although journalistic philosophy contradicts this notion.

"No news should be suppressed," said Hauser, adding, "Get rid of the 'gentlemen's agreements' and you're better off."

But he qualifies that statement. In practice, this measure wouldn't work effectively. This is the reasoning behind the *Journal-Bulletin*'s decision to retain its policy for shielding the names of alleged rape victims, yet remain flexible to respond to special instances, he said.

With today's public mood, reader reaction against the newspaper may cause more problems than would disclosing the name, he said.

The lines of self-censorship are vague and sometimes difficult to see, said Ragsdale.

"We must draw from life's experiences. Not only as journalists, but from other points of view—from lawyers and judges," he said. "Editors who aren't asleep are always in search for refining our policies and what people think."

"Newspapers have done a poor job of letting people know what their standards are. We have policies, but don't communicate them to the public.

"Standards are in place [but] they're evolving all the time," he said.

THE LESSONS OF BIG DAN'S

JAMES M. RAGSDALE

"THE GENESIS of the policy not to publish the names of rape victims was late in coming, but it came in a set of guidelines from the work of a bench-bar-press committee. The first guidelines, which were completed in the mid 60's, grew out of a recognition that a free press is also a responsible press and that there were some policies in regard to the covering of criminal activities that we had not maintained in a uniform way.

"It was an era of great soul-searching for the media and a time of conflict with the courts. What we had to do was temper ourselves and see how that tempering would take place. We agreed we would avoid publishing confessions, avoid publishing the names of juveniles, and in the early 70's came the guidelines about rape victims, so when we came up against Big Dan's the decision was not difficult; the guidelines were in place. And if they weren't, I would have worked to put them there, because there is a specialness about a rape victim that sets that victim apart from most victims of crime.

Journalists Get Itchy

"I know that journalists get fleas every time you have a guideline to withhold information, as well they should. But there is a new awareness today about the victims of crime and whether newspapers unwittingly fall into a trap about encouraging crime, rather than discouraging it, by publishing the names and addresses of crime victims. A report that the burglars got all the paintings but missed $150,000 worth of fine china — from the victim's perspective it is just a signal for more intrusion.

"We will withhold a housebreak victim's name upon request, but mostly we do publish the names and addresses of victims.

"As far as rape victims are concerned, there is no reason to change our policy at any stage from police to court action [he refers here to publication of the victim's name during or after the trial.] Some newspapers say their policy not to publish ends with the verdict, especially if the defendants are found not guilty. I disagree with that completely. It is irrational and inconsistent. Why do you have a policy in the first place? We do not want to punish someone because someone else is found not guilty. They are treated equally in the courtroom. The defendants and the alleged victim are there both for the jury to see and hear.

Guideline Is Fair

"It is argued that the press is being unfair by not publishing the victim's name, but I do not see how that wrecks the defendant's ability to have a fair trial. We are trying to be as fair as we possibly can, and in the course of human events, fairness is uneven. The guidelines we have are based on the fact that society is uneven itself in the way it views certain crimes. A rape victim is different from the victim of a purse snatching or the woman who is a teller in a bank that has been held-up. Society's view of the crime of rape is uneven, and our policy addresses that.

Increased Awareness

"Since Big Dan's there has been a heightened consciousness about rape. I had been across the country after Big Dan's, talking to different groups, and rape has become the topic of discussion within media groups, in high schools, in colleges. Maybe those discussions took place before, but I don't think so.

I think also Big Dan's has helped to improve police investigatory techniques regarding rape. Early on, police learned some lessons about handling rape cases, and it sent a signal to police to sharpen procedures, to make sure there are rape squads, to make sure they are prepared to move in quickly and deal with the on-the-scene investigation. Same thing regarding the hospital caretakers, because those early moments are crucial.

How the Story Grew

"Alan Levin, who was our police reporter then, first learned about the rape in making a routine check of the police blotter on a Monday morning while he was also covering a fatality. He cleaned up the fatality story, and then filed a brief story on the rape. That first story carried no alarming details, but when he returned to the police station later that morning to do a follow-up, he discovered the number of persons alleged to have been involved.

"By the time the story made national headlines, we had pretty much cleaned up all the information we were going to get from the cops. The district attorney's investigation had begun and we are not privileged to have that information, so the national exposure did not close off any avenues which would not have been closed off anyway. But what the exposure did do was put a microscope on the details of the case, so that every word was inspected and reinspected much more carefully than it would have been in a so-called ordinary case. We doubletracked and checked on who told us what and when.

"The media have been criticized for the fact that the details of the trial did not match the early publicity on the case, but I disagree very strongly with that. What journalists did, and I will speak about my paper specifically—they were faithful and loyal to the best information they could get at the time. We were accused of relying only on police reports and passing on only police reports, but we did interview other people who had been in the bar, and those people's estimates, like how many persons had been in the bar at the time of the rape, those came very close to the police reports, to the interviews with the eye witnesses and with a person who later became a defendant.

"Most of the information came from the victim herself, and this is where the media critics lost focus. All journalists are victims of what people say. But the question is, are we faithful to the official report, or have we enhanced it, or generalized it, or what?

"We passed on what we were told by the victim, by police, by eyewitnesses, and I saw a lot of columns after the trial that said, 'my goodness, it wasn't the same case—referring to the estimates of the number of people in the bar and the cheering. But I think two very important, critical things have been overlooked here. If you reread the victim's testimony, you will see repeated references to numerous voices, to cheering, like at a baseball park, that's from the victim's point of view.

"But cheering was not on trial in that courtroom, and there is a reason for that. The d.a.'s star witness was the bartender, and the d.a. didn't want to start asking the bartender about the cheering because from all the information we got, the bartender was involved with it—the cheering, and the last thing the d.a. wanted was for cheering to go on trial, for that would damage his number one witness.

No Need to Defend

"So I don't have to get up and defend our early reporting, based on what went on in that trial.

The Victim's Ordeal

"Another thing: think about what that poor woman was going through. How could you hold her accountable for whether there were eight or twelve or thirteen men? If you buy onto her story, and the court did, and the jury did, allow for the emotional stress and the psychological impact. And her recounting of what happened may very well be fuzzy, whether there are eight or nine or thirteen—that's splitting the hair very, very thin. Also, there were two men who left midway, and add that to the count.

"I really bristle when a guy from *The New York Times* comes here and spends a day and a half and then a guy from the *Los Angeles Times* comes and spends eight hours and then handles the rest of the coverage by telephone from L.A. And they make grand pronouncements how the final results were not like the original report.

"There was cheering going on, there was a strange rapture that took over inside that bar that night, something very weird, where I think civilization broke down for a while, and I think everybody, espousing his own cause, is seeking to deny that happened. You play a tape of her testimony, you listen to her words, I don't think she was lying. The police were very protective of her; she has a relative on the police department, I believe. They were very concerned."

WHY WE USED HER NAME

CHARLES M. HAUSER

"I'D LIKE TO talk about rights of the press, rights of defendants, rights of the judges and the victims and accusers. Let me start by saying this: the press has no right to do anything in a court of law but be there. I repeat that. The press has no right to do anything in a court of law but be there.

"The right to be there derives not from the First Amendment which guarantees freedom of the press, but from the Sixth Amendment which gives defendants the right to a public trial. If the trial is public, I have a right to be there as a member of the public, not as a representative of the press. Once there, I have the right under the First Amendment to publish anything I see or hear. Anything I want to. No judge can take that right away from me.

Judge Is King

"But other than that, the judge is king in his courtroom. He has the authority to tell me to leave my equipment, my tape recorder, my camera, my typewriter at home. If he allows me to bring my camera into the courtroom, he can tell what I can and cannot aim it at. If he allows me to bring my tape recorder into the courtroom, he can tell me what to record and what not to record. If he allows me to set up live broadcast facilities in the courtroom, he can regulate what part of the proceedings can be carried live and what part cannot.

"In the Big Dan's case, Judge Young allowed still and live television cameras in his courtrooms. He allowed pictures and voices in the courtroom to be transmitted live to radio and television outlets. He has indicated that he assumed the radio and television outlets would censor the name of the victim in this rape case when they were on the air.

"In fact, I don't believe he really gave it any thought. If he had, he might have asked. In any event, I think he was wrong to criticize broadcasters after the fact for doing what he had given them permission to do.

"He also criticized certain newspapers, mine among them, that took the position that if the rape victim's name was being broadcast into homes throughout the area, there was no reason to observe the normal policy of suppressing that name in print. Censorship should be important to anyone who believes in the free, honest and fair press. It's important to me. Censorship of facts that are on the public record is particularly distasteful.

Why Withhold?

"If the accused has a constitutional right to publicly confront his accuser, why should the accuser's name be withheld from the public? The answer is, it shouldn't be. But I am ashamed to say that most of us in the newspaper business, rationalizing our actions on the grounds of some worthy motive that other speakers will belabor here today, deliberately withhold from the public certain facts which are a part of public record. So the question should not be, what special reason did we have for publishing the name of the victim in the Big Dan's case? We don't need a special reason to publish the name.

"We need a special reason to not publish the name. In this case, the special reason was removed and we decided to publish. Now, consider this question: Do you really want the editors of your newspapers—for whatever high motive they ascribe to themselves—to decide what items of pertinent information should be withheld from you? If we start down that road, who's to keep us from going too far and dreaming up what we think are worthy motives for suppressing other types of information? The problem is we've already started down that road.

> (EDITOR'S NOTE: In a letter dated July 30, 1986, Hauser said there has been no change in the *Journal-Bulletin*'s rape victim's name publication guidelines: . . . "Policy was and still is NOT to carry the names of rape victims. The Big Dan's case was an exception to the policy, for the reasons outlined in my remarks." He referred to sections of the newspaper's policy manual which deals with the withholding of names with a footnote: "We have no other policies or practices of withholding information that is newsworthy or legally obtained, except that we normally do not print what is said or done in a courtroom out of the presence of the jury, to avoid being responsible for a mistrial.")

Following is the *Journal-Bulletin's* crime coverage policy regarding specific types of crimes and specific types of accused and victims:

JUVENILES

A juvenile, for purposes of these policies, is anyone 17 or younger.

Since children cannot be charged with crimes — rather, the prosecution petitions Family Court to find them *delinquent* — we will **not** identify a juvenile implicated in a crime.

In *extraordinary* circumstances — e.g., juvenile allegedly implicated in a crime so heinous that the needs of public safety may be served by identifying the juvenile — exceptions may be authorized by the ranking editor on duty. Underline *extraordinary.*

If the child of a celebrity or prominent figure, such as a governor, is implicated, an exception may be authorized by a senior editor, but only if the crime itself is also of significant newsworthiness. Names will not be used merely because the parent is prominent if a child is implicated in a minor shoplifting incident, a minor act of vandalism, etc.

We will **not** identify juvenile victims of sexual assault or molestation by name or by inference.

Use caution in identifying juveniles involved in any situation which could embarrass or permanently scar them.

In non-sexual child-abuse cases, unless a death or severe injury is involved, we will avoid specifics about the child (name, age, sex) if possible, even though a child's identity may be inferred from the story reporting the charging of a parent.

SERIOUS MORALS CASES

Our general policies regarding serious morals cases, generally referred to as *abominable and detestable crimes against nature* (bestiality, incest, sodomy.)

1. We refer to *serious morals charge(s)*. We do not mention the specific aberrant behavior and we do **not** name the specific charge.

2. We will play such stories in routine, low-key formats.

3. We will avoid detailed, clinical descriptions of circumstances involving such offenses.

4. We will **not** identify victims at any stage of police or court action.

5. If a person is charged with *rape* and two offenses that fall under the category of *serious morals charges,* be sure to say the person was *charged with rape and two OTHER serious morals charges*. If the word other is omitted, it appears in context as if *rape* is something less than a *serious morals charge.*

RAPE, ATTEMPTED RAPE

The name of a victim in a rape or any other first-degree sexual offense will **not** be used in either a story about the incident or a subsequent trial.

A person who successfully beats off a rape attempt may be named in the newspaper.

A RAPE VICTIM TO THE MEDIA: "DON'T YOU KNOW YOU'RE DEALING WITH PEOPLE AND PEOPLE'S LIVES?"

"I WOULD JUST like to share with you what happened to me. I was raped in December, 1980, in _____. Most people know most other people [there]. It happened on a very bad night. It was freezing rain. When I got home to my house, after the attack, I had to make a decision. Number One—How was I going to tell my husband let alone tell the police or tell anyone else?

"First of all if I was going to tell my husband or if I was going to let anybody know and I also made the decision to call the police and to report it to them initially. They had taken me to the hospital. I was pregnant at the time I was assaulted. It took me two hours to get to the hospital, even though it was just 17 miles away, because of the weather. I had an awful lot of time to think in those two hours what I was going to say to the police.

"In fact one of the first things that crossed my mind, the first thing that crossed my mind, was am I going to tell them anything? Am I going to give them any facts? Am I going to try to identify this person because my name might become public?

"And I can assure you that was the foremost consideration in my mind. It was in fact the first thing I asked the state trooper after I had been examined in the emergency room at the hospital before I said anything. I asked him, Am I going to be identified to the media? And he told me at the time he really didn't know and he could not make any guarantees to me and at that point it was my decision whether I wanted to go forward to at least give him the facts, let alone going to the prosecution.

"And being the person who I am, I made the decision I wanted this person brought forth for justice. I wanted something done to him for what he had done to me. As already stated, rape is an awful crime. It is brutal. It is degrading. It is humiliating. It is the most awful thing that someone could go through.

"This event had been over three years and I still feel the effects of what happened to me. So I made the decision to go ahead and relay the facts to the police. ("Excuse me") [victim's voice breaks] And then I had to make the decision whether I really wanted to identify this person.

"He was of course free on the streets somewhere. No one knew who he was. It was my decision to go before a police artist and try to give a description, which I did. And based on that description, he was caught, or at least initially identified.

"I then identified him through a photo line-up. And this person had just been released from prison a month before after serving eight years for sexual assault, which was the sentence as the result of a plea bargaining. There had actually been three sexual assault charges brought — three separate victims involved. The state had been warned at the time when he was up for parole that he had not maxed out, that if he was let out he would rape again. It was interesting that was never brought up in the press.

"So after this person had been arraigned initially, (I had not been informed of) I found out through the media. My name was not brought out at that time.

"There were basically three major newspapers in _____. The _____ which has a policy of not printing rape victims names, The _____ and _____, which is basically the same newspaper. They had a policy of not printing the rape victim's name until she testifies at trial. As soon as she took the stand, she was considered fair game. Those were the words that were given to me after my name became public and I had demanded an explanation from the _____ [reference to a newspaper]. As soon as you take the stand you are fair game.

"The trial occurred approximately ten months after the assault. After I had had my baby, I graduated from college and I was going to go to graduate school in the fall and since the trial had been postponed, I didn't think I could cope going to graduate school and having to deal with this trial at the same time. So I put that off for a year.

"I'd like to show you an article that was printed after I had testified. My name is used twenty times throughout this article. The headlines describe me as the rape victim. The headlines described the defendant as a Vietnam Vet. With a name like _____ it is not too hard to figure out who I am. The newspapers prior to this had identified me as a 22 year old pregnant _____ woman. [refers to hometown] I can assure you that anybody in _____ who had read a newspaper figured out who it was because I was the only 22 year old pregnant woman in _____ at the time. In a town of 700 people.

"But that didn't really bother me too much. I could deal with that because most of those people were my friends and most of those people knew me and I didn't really have to worry about those people thinking that I might have been contributorily negligent that it might have been my fault that I might have asked for it. I didn't really believe all that. Because I know those people cared about me.

"But beyond living in a little town, I also had another life. I was fairly active in the _____ [refers to a political group affiliation] at the time. I had a business. I had to deal with people on a different level besides on a personal-friend level. And those were the people that I was worried about.

"I knew when I took the stand, I was told by the State's Attorney, that the press may use my name and I knew at that time that I could take the stand and I could say I'm not going to testify and go ahead and hold me in contempt and go ahead and put me in jail, but I'm not going to risk it. Damn it after what that man did to me. I wanted something done to him.

"And I took the stand. This is what happened to me. And just in case, just in case people didn't figure out who _____ was after being identified twenty times throughout this article, the reporter has in here _____ (in case you didn't already identify me) appeared on national television in the summer of _____. [refers here to coverage she received relating to her role in a national political convention] Bingo. Anybody who didn't know me personally all of a sudden could remember all the news stories about me prior to the summer of _____. And could note who it was, who had been raped. All right. So that was all well and good. What happened to me after the trial — in many respects I was ostracized, not brutally, perhaps, not intentionally.

"You cannot deny the fact that society looks at rape differently than it does any other crime. And you can talk about the fact that all other victims' names are printed. All other victims are not treated as rape victims are. All other victims are not looked down upon. All other victims are not blamed for possibly contributing to allowing the crime to occur, it's just a lot of garbage. Nobody else suffers from rape trauma syndrome. There could be other victims who do suffer trauma, but rape trauma syndrome is a specific reaction to rape.

"The fact that the media printed my name, I reacted immediately. I called them the next day. And at the time I was probably not very coherent. Because I was extremely upset. And for awhile I guess I kind of hibernated because I didn't want to deal with anybody else after this happened to me. It was bad enough that I had been raped but it was worse to see my name and every intricate detail you saw in this article.

"It's taken me basically three years to get back to where I was three years ago. To make the connections that I had three years ago, to get my act together to go to graduate school and to deal with the fact that I am a rape victim and to deal with the fact that there are always going to be people that once they find out are going to treat me differently.

"You're not dealing with constitutional rights out in space somewhere. You're dealing with people and you're dealing with people's lives. And when the media prints the victim's name, media is basically saying you no longer have a right to decide what your life is going to be like. I had made a decision not to tell my mother-in-law that I had been raped. She's an elderly woman. She's a very sickly woman. I wasn't sure how that would affect her. My mother-in-law doesn't read the newspapers but suddenly this came out and I had to deal with that because she found out from someone else who told her. It did a real number on her. [voice breaks, testimony ends]

> (EDITOR'S NOTE: I contacted this rape victim in 1986 and asked her how she was treated by the police officers who investigated her complaint. She clearly felt victimized by the press, and did she, as some rape victims contend, feel equally as victimized by law enforcement officials and the judicial system? Following is her response.)

"The law enforcement officials were so kind and thoughtful. When I was at the hospital, immediately following the rape, a state trooper wanted to interview me after I was examined in the emergency room. The first thing he told me was that he wanted to catch the perpetrator, but if I didn't want to talk to him, that was all right. He let me know that he felt it was important for me to tell him as much as I could, but, if I chose not to, he understood and would not pressure me.

"I spoke to him and told him as much as I could remember. He then told me that he would file a report and contact me in a few days so that I could review his report. True to his word, the following day he called, told me he wanted to go over the report and asked if I could be willing to meet with a state police artist to try to have a picture drawn of my attacker.

"I agreed and the state police dispatched another trooper and a police artist to my home. This second trooper was even more understanding than the first (if that's possible). He explained to me that if he was caught, I would have to testify at trial and, at that point, it was my decision whether I wanted to proceed any further. Again, I knew that he wanted me to, but I also knew that he wouldn't pressure me and would understand if I chose to stop the investigation.

"Throughout the whole investigation period, the police kept me up to date and let me know when they had a suspect. However, once the matter was no longer in their hands and was, instead in the hands of the prosecutor, I heard nothing.

"I didn't know that the perpetrator had been arraigned and that the judge set bail—for a man who had just been released from prison after serving a sentence as part of a plea bargain for three prior sexual assaults—at a mere $5,000. I had to read about it in the paper.

"The police had notified me when they had arrested this man and had him in jail. The newspaper notified me that he had been released on bail. To say that I was furious and incredibly scared would be a gross understatement. This type of treatment, that is, let's not bother letting the victim know what's going on, continued until a woman deputy state's attorney was assigned to the case. Thereafter, I was kept abreast of what was going on."

A LAWYER'S ARGUMENT: SPECIAL VICTIMS NEED SPECIAL REMEDIES

S. W. SWEETSER

IN 1975, the U.S. Supreme Court held that a Georgia statute imposing civil liability on the news media for reporting the name of a rape victim violated the First Amendment.[1] In that case, a Georgia television station broadcasted the name of a 16-year-old rape victim who died as a result of the attack. The victim's father sued the station, based on the Georgia statute, for an invasion of privacy. The plaintiff prevailed in the trial court and on appeal, the lower court's decision was upheld by the Georgia Supreme Court.[2]

The Georgia Supreme Court held that the right of privacy overrode the defendant's First Amendment right to free speech. The court was unable to find any "public interest or general concern about the identity of the victim of such a crime as to make the right to disclose the identity of the victim rise to the level of First Amendment protection.[3] The U.S. Supreme Court, however, disagreed.

Because the rape victim's name was a matter of public record in that it was recorded in court documents that were open to the public, the Court held that such information could not be restricted by the state and any statute imposing liability for the publication of public information was a violation of the First Amendment. In the Court's opinion, an individual's privacy was not invaded by the publication of already public information. Further, the Court stated that in publishing such information, "the function of the press serves to . . . bring to bear the beneficial

---

(EDITOR'S NOTE: This article is an excerpt from a paper titled "Rape Laws Today: The Still Mistreated Victim," prepared by the author in 1984 as part of a law school class assignment.)

effects of public scrutiny upon the administration of justice.[4] The Court, however, did not totally preclude the State from protecting a victim's name from disclosure. It stated that i[f] there are privacy interests to be protected in judicial proceedings, the State must respond by means which avoid public documentation or other exposure of private information."[5]

After Cox — Media Response

Since the Supreme Court's decision in Cox, the states have left the issue of publication of a rape victim's name to the discretion of the media. Most media sources have had the compassion to refrain from disclosing the identity of a rape victim, given society's treatment of rape victims. One such example of this is *The Washington Post*'s policy of not publishing a rape victim's name unless the victim identifies herself publicly.[6] The *Post* recognizes its right to publish a victim's name, but refrains from exercising that right because of the nature of the offense and its effects upon the victim.

The *Post*'s policy recognizes that society still does not accept the fact that rape is a violent crime and that rape victims are suspected by society as somehow having been at fault. An assistant prosecutor for Arlington County, Virginia stated that "[p]ublicity is one of the things that seems to disturb the victims most. Rape is, under the best of circumstances, very traumatic . . . let alone discovering all the gory details have been spread across the front page of the local newspaper."[7] In the *Post*'s opinion, a rape victim's right to privacy outweighs the public's right to know.

The Washington Post has even gone as far as to publicly criticize another newspaper for changing its policy from not printing a rape victim's name to printing it.[8] Herman J. Obermayer, editor of the *Sun*, stated that "[p]rotecting the accuser's anonymity, while fully identifying the accused is tantamount to a pre-trial presumption of guilt. A malicious woman could try to make the state take away a man's freedom for life without even risking public embarrassment."[9]

In an editorial attacking the *Northern Virginia Star* from changing its policy, *Post* editor Stacy R. Taylor pointed out that rape victims have not been treated the same by society as victims of other crimes. "Many people still think that women want to be raped and that the victim has lower morals than other women. . . . Because of society's unsympathetic reaction to rape victims, women who have been raped want to hide their victimization."[10] Ms. Taylor feared that by printing a rape victim's name, the media would discourage many women from reporting rape and law enforcement officials would be hampered in trying to rid the streets of rapists.

Vermont's two major newspapers until recently had competing policies concerning the publication of a rape victim's name. *The Burlington Free Press,* as a matter of course, will not print the victim's name at all in reporting the crime or in any subsequent criminal court proceedings.[11] The *Free Press* does not feel that there is any benefit to be gained by printing the victim's name; she has been through enough trauma already.

The Times Argus, on the other hand, did not formerly feel as compelled to protect the victim's identity.[12] They would not report a rape victim's name until the case had gone to trial. At that time, if the victim "chose" to testify, they felt free to use her name. Their feeling was that it was only fair to report the victim's name because she had reported the defendant's name and, by so doing, had maligned his character. Currently, *The Times-Argus* has instituted a pilot program wherein a rape victim's name will no longer be reported as a matter of course once she testifies at trial.

New Problem — Cameras in the Courtroom

The U.S. Supreme Court has ruled that the media has a presumptive First Amendment right to be present during a criminal trial.[13] The Court has not yet ruled, however, that the right to be present includes the right to have cameras in the courtroom and, given the wave of conservatism in the Court, it is unlikely that the Court will make such a ruling in the near future.

However, within recent years, many states have begun to allow media camera courtroom access. This additional access has created new problems for rape victims and the protection of their anonymity. First, throughout a typical rape trial, the attorneys and the judge refer to the victim by her name. Second, in all likelihood, the media will want to film the victim's testimony. What then can a victim do to protect her identity from public scrutiny?

An example of this problem was recently presented in the New Bedford gang rape trial. Massachusetts allows cameras in the courtroom and only the trial judge can restrict that access upon a strong showing by either the State or the defense that such access will prejudice their case in some way. In the New Bedford case, camera access was allowed with the exception that the trial judge forbid filming the victim during the course of her testimony. Audio recording, however, was allowed throughout the trial. A local Massachusetts television station covered the entire trial. Throughout its coverage, the victim was identified.[14]

Why Should a Rape Victim's Name be Protected From Media Disclosure?

As pointed out earlier, rape victims have been the most misunderstood victims of crime. Our culture as a whole subscribes to a variety of myths and misconceptions about rape. One of those myths is that women frequently fabricate rape and lodge false accusations or that women are somehow to blame for being raped. Given societal attitudes toward rape victims and the fact that one of the symptoms of rape trauma syndrome is a feeling of overwhelming guilt suffered by the rape victim for having been raped, a newspaper policy that provides for printing a rape victim's name only serves to further injure the victim. More people will further identify her as a rape victim and treat her differently, and she will suffer further humiliation.

Another fear of rape trauma syndrome is the fear of being attacked again. Printing the victim's name only serves to exacerbate this fear because now "potential" rapists know the victim's identity. Such publication also hampers the ability of therapists to treat rape trauma syndrome.

Because society has mistreated the rape victim for so long, the question ought not to be why should a rape victim's name be protected, but, instead, why would a newspaper want to print a rape victim's name? Printing a rape victim's name does not make a story more journalistically appealing or more readable. Readers would not feel that they got half the story if they read an account of a rape that excluded the victim's name. Again, that is because rape is a charge easy to be made and hard to defend against, and, based on old myths that still exist, society views women who cry rape with suspicion.

Some newspapers still reflect society's attitudes by being insensitive to the rape victim. Such newspapers fail to recognize that such publicity is an invasion of privacy. It is one of the reasons rape is so under-reported.[15]

If rape is to be treated as other criminal offenses, then media policies should refrain from permitting the printing of a rape victim's name. By so doing, one of the under-reporting factors will be removed and perhaps there will be some increase in the number of reported rapes. It will also serve to reduce the amount of adverse treatment a rape victim receives from society simply because she was unfortunate enough to be a rapist's victim. A media policy withholding a rape victim's name would

> deflect the special shame which is seen to attach only to victims of sexual crimes. Unlike the victims of any other crime, they are somehow suspected by society of being partially guilty; they are imagined to have contributed to the crime through some form of explicit or implicit seduction, or simply by not being as careful as they should have been. That these assumptions and suspicions are, in virtually all rape convictions, unwarranted, does not remove them from the conscious or subconscious minds of many. . . . [T]he media's special sensitivity [toward the rape victim would be] a necessary and welcome policy, considering the public perception of the rape victim.[16]

In states where the media still insists on reporting the rape victim's name even though society labels the victim as being partially guilty, some method ought to be devised whereby the victim's name is not used in public court documents and is therefore not protected by the First Amendment. All state court administrative agencies should enact a rule that provides for withholding a victim's full name in all public documents. For example, in all public court documents, the victim could be identified by using her initials, similar to the manner in which juveniles are identified. Through discovery, the defense would still, of course, be able to have access to the victim's name, would still be able to depose her, and during trial would still be able to exercise the right to confrontation by cross-examining her. The defendant's right to confrontation and right to a public trial would in no way be prejudiced because confrontation would still occur and the trial would still be public.

In states where cameras are allowed in the courtroom, the rape victim should have an automatic right to veto camera coverage of her testimony. A camera access rule similar to the proposed Vermont rule which allows the State, the defense, *any* witness (for their testimony) and the judge a right to veto would protect the victim from being visually identified. Further, throughout the trial, the victim should not be referred to by her name. Using a Jane Doe label (or Ms Doe) would solve the problem of the victim's identity being referred to throughout the trial and picked up by television cameras or microphones.

As stated earlier, these are only band-aid approaches to the ultimate change—redefining rape. However, the band-aid approach is necessary if the ultimate change is to be accomplished because, as has been demonstrated, society is not even ready to embrace the band-aid changes let alone a radical change. If what we want to accomplish immediately is better treatment of the rape victim and increased reporting of rape, the band-aid suggestions should be adopted. At the same time, a program of public education is needed if we want to bring about the ultimate change. Society as a whole must begin questioning why lack of consent must be proven by a rape victim, but is not required of the victim of any other crime. When such a public consciousness is aroused, the correlation between rape as a crime almost totally against women by men as compared to other crimes and the different standards of proof applied to rape will become much more obvious. A continuous effort must be made to redefine rape and turn societal attitudes around.

ENDNOTES

1. *Cox Broadcasting Corp. v. Cohn*, 420 U.S. 469 (1975).
2. *Cox Broadcasting Corp. v. Cohn*, 231 Ga. 60, 200 S.E. 2d 127 (1973).
3. *Id.* at 68, 200 S.E. 2d at 134.
4. *Cox Broadcasting Corp. v. Cohn*, supra n. 59.
5. *Id.* at 496.
6. *Washington Post*, February 15, 1978, p. 22.
7. *Id.*, quoting Helen F. Fahey.
8. *Washington Post*, February 9, 1978, p. A-25.
9. "Naming Names," *Time*, vol. 111, p. 61, Jan. 30, 1978.
10. *Washington Post*, supra n. 66.
11. Telephone conversation with Sam Hemingway, editor, *Burlington Free Press*, February, 1984.
12. Telephone conversation with William Porter, editor, *Times-Argus*, February, 1984.
13. In *Richmond Newspapers, Inc. v. Virginia*, 448, U.S. 555 (1980), the Supreme Court held that the right of media access to the courtroom was implicit in the First Amendment. However, the right was not absolute, but the Court failed to set forth standards to evaluate the right in future cases. In *Globe Newspaper Co. v. Superior Court of Norfolk*, 457 U.S. 596, 102 S. Ct. 2613 (1982), the Court struck down a Massachusetts statute requiring courtroom closure during rape trials involving victims who were minors as being too inclusive. The Court again recognized the right of media access to the courtroom and the fact that such a right was not absolute. The Court ruled that each case must be looked at individually and a balancing test applied before courtroom closure would be allowed. The balancing test requires a showing that denial of courtroom access in criminal trials is "necessitated by a compelling governmental interest, and is narrowly tailored to serve that interest." *Id.* at 607.

14. It is also interesting to note that while one local newspaper used the victim's name in its reporting of the New Bedford case, the New Bedford *Standard-Times* did not. The *Standard-Times* had an existing policy whereby it generally refrained from reporting rape victims' names and it saw no reason to deviate from that policy even though the victim's name in this notorious case had become public via the printed and the television media.
15. *Matter of Pittsburgh Action Against Rape,* supra n. 42, 139-140, quoting Judge Gafni of the Court of Common Please of Philadelphia County in *Commonwealth v. Gray,* February Term, 1980, Nos. 748-778.
16. *State v. Evjue,* 253 Wisc. 143 33 N.W. 2d 305, 312 (1948).

ON THE POLICE/PRESS CONNECTION

JAMES M. RAGSDALE

"THE CITY police is covered in person, but police in the other outlying areas are covered mainly by telephone, and that is not a good way. Understandably, we get more police news out of the city. We use seasoned people on the police beat, but with other newspapers, that is not always the case. Sometimes there is a high turnover on their beats, and they just do not hold the beat as important, but that is not the case here.

"But I do believe we can find better ways to cover police, and especially important is the eyeball to eyeball contact. Police need that, and that helps to develop a mutual respect, greater understanding, spirit of help, so there will not be distrust and fear. We just need to spend more time stopping by our police stations.

Good Relations

"Over the years, we have had a good relationship between this newspaper and police. They know our reporters are very savvy and they do not play games, but we need more of the old-fashioned milking of the beat. Sometimes with so much surface covering, there is very little time to mine stories on that beat. Over the years we have done some of that kind of work, but not enough.

James M. Ragsdale is editor of *The Standard-Times* in New Bedford, Massachusetts, a daily newspaper. He was Chief of Bureau of The Associated Press in Boston, was News Editor in charge of AP's news-gathering operations in Washington State and Alaska. His career with AP also included assignments in West Virginia, Eastern Washington, Northern Idaho, and Western Montana. While headquartered in Boston as bureau chief, he was responsible for AP's operations in five New England states.

(EDITOR'S NOTE: This interview with James M. Ragsdale, editor of *The Standard-Times,* New Bedford, Massachusetts, was conducted in 1986, and his remarks developed from an observation that the national headlines given the Big Dan's rape trial had actually originated in a daily visit by a police reporter to his local police station and his eyeing of a significant story in a police log entry.)

Many Changes

"There have been all kinds of changes, many of them through the United States Supreme Court, affecting the relationship between police and the public. It used to be more informal. You one time were able to walk in and sit down with a police chief, and he would say something like, 'look at this,' shoving a confession in front of you — 'this bird just said he was guilty of murdering a woman.'

"But there has been the Miranda decision, and the American Bar Association has evolved rules restricting lawyers' ability to talk with the media, and there are rules and regulations restricting our court officers and prosecutors from talking.

Casual, No More

"It used to be casual, you could chat with a prosecutor and lawyer at a coffeeshop, shoot the bull with a judge, talk to a d.a. about his strategy, with all of them knowing you were talking to all sides. They were acquaintances, they called you by your first name. It was easier, life was simpler, but now we are too structured, too inflexible to develop these kinds of contacts.

"And on the press' side, the rules have also changed. We have become meticulously clean-scrubbed. There is a threshold we can't cross, and cannot risk even an appearance of being unethical. We have become superclean and have put those people now on the other side, those people who are now not to be trusted, and they have done the same to us. We have become unfamiliar with one another, suspect of mutual intentions and roles, and a degree of mistrust has developed, not just between politicians and reporters, but between reporters and judges, lawyers, department heads, governmental heads.

"But we got clean, and we can no longer be pals, and we became official not friendly, and natural human relationships are not allowed to exist. And we can start not being human and not having compassion. I think when journalists make the First Amendment their life, they have gone too far, and to an extent, in this post Watergate era, such has been responsible for a great credibility crisis. I am not advocating a return to the Old Chicago reporting days, but reporters are not completely special, they are part of a system, and we have disassociated ourselves with our superclean codes of conduct.

"We have invited police chiefs in our area to come in and sit down with us and discuss issues, and it is clear there is misunderstanding. They begin by saying that the most important thing to us is selling papers. But by these types of meetings we can begin flaking away at the barriers and at stereotypes and begin to see one another as professionals whose goals in many instances are the same."

SECTION III

ETHICS, RULES AND REGULATIONS

CODE OF ETHICS OF THE SOCIETY OF PROFESSIONAL JOURNALISTS, SIGMA DELTA CHI

THE SOCIETY of Professional Journalists, Sigma Delta Chi believes the duty of journalists is to serve the truth.

We BELIEVE the agencies of mass communication are carriers of public discussion and information, acting on their Constitutional mandate and freedom to learn and report the facts.

WE BELIEVE in public enlightenment as the forerunner of justice, and in our Constitutional role to seek the truth as part of the public's right to know the truth.

WE BELIEVE those responsibilities carry obligations that require journalists to perform with intelligence, objectivity, accuracy and fairness.

To these ends, we declare acceptance of the standards of practice here set forth:

Responsibility

The public's right to know of events of public importance and interest is the overriding mission of the mass media. The purpose of distributing news and enlightened opinion is to serve the general welfare. Journalists who use their professional status as representatives of the public for selfish or other unworthy motives violate a high trust.

(EDITOR'S NOTE: The codes of conduct, the rules and guidelines which Editor Ragsdale referred to in the previous article as responsible for making polite strangers of police and press have been generated by both groups. Selected for inclusion in this collection are an ethical code promoted among journalists, reprinted with permission of Society of Professional Journalists, Sigma Delta Chi (SDX); and excerpts from *The Public Information Policy Manual* of the Delaware State Police, a thorough and detailed guide to dissemination of information and related police/media policy areas, reprinted with permission of that agency.)

Freedom of the Press

Freedom of the press is to be guarded as an inalienable right of people in a free society. It carries with it the freedom and the responsibility to discuss, question and challenge actions and utterances of our government and of our public and private institutions. Journalists uphold the right to speak unpopular opinions and the privilege to agree with the majority.

Ethics

Journalists must be free of obligation to any interest other than the public's right to know the truth.

1. Gifts, favors, free travel, special treatment or privileges can compromise the integrity of journalists and their employers. Nothing of value should be accepted.
2. Secondary employment, political involvement, holding public office and service in community organizations should be avoided if it compromises the integrity of journalists and their employers. Journalists and their employers should conduct their personal lives in a manner which protects them from conflict of interest, real or apparent. Their responsibilities to the public are paramount. That is the nature of their profession.
3. So called news communications from private sources should not be published or broadcast without substantiation of their claims to news value.
4. Journalists will seek news that serves the public interest, despite the obstacles. They will make constant efforts to assure that the public's business is conducted in public and that public records are open to public inspection.
5. Journalists acknowledge the newsman's ethic of protecting confidential sources of information.

Accuracy and Objectivity

Good faith with the public is the foundation of all worthy journalism.

1. Truth is our ultimate goal.
2. Objectivity in reporting the news is another goal, which serves as the mark of an experienced professional. It is a standard of performance toward which we strive. We honor those who achieve it.
3. There is no excuse for inaccuracies or lack of thoroughness.

4. Newspaper headlines should be fully warranted by the contents of the articles they accompany. Photographs and telecasts should give an accurate picture of an event and not highlight a minor incident out of context.
5. Sound practice makes clear distinction between news reports and expressions of opinion. News reports should be free of opinion or bias and represent all sides of an issue.
6. Partisanship in editorial comment which knowingly departs from the truth violates the spirit of American journalism.
7. Journalists recognize their responsibility for offering informed analysis, comment and editorial opinion on public events and issues. They accept the obligation to present such material by individuals whose competence, experience and judgment qualify them for it.
8. Special articles or presentations devoted to advocacy or the writer's own conclusions and interpretations should be labeled as such.

Fair Play

Journalists at all times will show respect for the dignity, privacy, rights and well-being of people encountered in the course of gathering and presenting the news.

1. The news media should not communicate unofficial charges affecting reputation or moral character without giving the accused a chance to reply.
2. The news media must guard against invading a person's right to privacy.
3. The media should not pander to morbid curiosity about details of vice and crime.
4. It is the duty of news media to make prompt and complete correction of their errors.
5. Journalists should be accountable to the public for their reports and the public should be encouraged to voice its grievances against the media. Open dialogue with our readers, viewers and listeners should be fostered.

Pledge

Journalists should actively censure and try to prevent violations of these standards, and they should encourage their observance by all newspeople. Adherence to this code of ethics is intended to preserve the bond of mutual trust and respect between American journalists and the American people.

NEWS MEDIA RELATIONS AND PUBLIC INFORMATION POLICY OF THE DELAWARE STATE POLICE

News Media Relations

NMR 1. GENERAL PROVISIONS: The Division's goal is a maximum flow of information to the public through press, radio and television services with a minimum disruption of police activity. The public is very much interested in police activities. A police department which fails to provide complete information will not achieve good public relations. The public depends on press, radio and television news service to provide information and the Delaware State Police cannot operate apart from the public view.

Every member of the Division must deal fairly with newsmen, operate openly and allow the reporter to be the judge of what represents news for the public. Members should have the necessary and proper liaison with press representatives in each troop installation area so that we may provide them with proper service and for them to understand our problems.

Most matters handled by the State Police are not secret and will become public eventually, so every effort should be made within the limits of these guidelines to cooperate with the news media to facilitate the prompt release of factual information. If a matter is such that publicity might be detrimental or defeat the ends of justice, the news inquiry should be directed to the Troop Commander and Public Information Officer.

NMR 2. ROLE OF THE NEWS MEDIA. A well-informed public is essential to the existence of a democratic nation. To effectively exercise his franchise, a citizen must be aware of current events and the state of government. A free press serves the public by supplying needed information by stimulating thought and by providing a medium for expression.

Crime, its results and the efforts to combat it are all matters of continuing public concern. The Division is regularly involved in events at which members of the news media are properly present and performing their task of gathering information.

NMR 3. ROLE OF THE STATE POLICE. The State Police actively seek to establish a cooperative climate in which the news media may obtain information on matters of public interest in a manner which does not hamper police operations. However, certain information must be withheld from the news media in order to protect the constitutional rights of an accused, to avoid interfering with a Department investigation, or because it is legally privileged.

NMR 3A. RELATIONSHIP BETWEEN GOVERNMENT AND THE NEWS MEDIA. Government agencies are largely dependent on the news media for the dissemination of information to the public regarding agency activities. These same agencies have a right to expect fair and objective reporting by the news media. The news media, in turn, has a right to expect that the information being offered by government agencies in news releases or by other means has not been compromised or knowingly intended to mislead the public.

In compliance with the foregoing and with the policy mutually agreed to by the Governor, the Secretary of the Department of Public Safety, and the Superintendent of the Delaware State Police, all members of the Delaware State Police will offer to the news media only true and accurate information to the best of their knowledge. False information will not be given to the news media under any circumstances except with the approval of the Superintendent and the Secretary will not give such approval unless concurrences are obtained from the Attorney General and the news media.

Due to the fact that most of our law enforcement and investigative activities are a prelude to possible prosecution of cases by the Attorney General, it is necessary that we coordinate our activities with the Attorney General. When such uncommon circumstances exist that the release of false information to the news media or other unusual technique is being considered, after obtaining the approval of the Superintendent and the Secretary, the proposed action should be submitted to the Attorney General for his review. If the Attorney General approves of such action, the complete circumstances will be described to the news media to seek their assistance and to justify the release of a false story. If the news media refuses to cooperate, the "false story" technique will not be used.

It is mutually beneficial to the Delaware State Police and the news media that they have trust and confidence in the statements and iterations of each other.

NMR 4. NEWS RELEASE POLICY. The Division recognizes the right of the public to be fully and accurately informed on all matters of public safety and that the news media is responsible for providing this information to the public. The policy of the Division therefore, shall be to maintain a relationship with the members of the news media that is built on trust, cooperation and mutual respect and one which will generate a free flow of information between the Department and the news media. To accomplish this, the Division, when requested, will provide complete and accurate information, within legal and investigatory limitations, as quickly as practicable, to all accredited media representatives. These representatives shall judge whether or not the information is newsworthy.

NMR 5. NEWS MEDIA IDENTIFICATION. To assure that the Delaware State Police is communicating with an authorized news media representative at the scene of a police incident, and to assure the representative that he will not be unnecessarily obstructed in the pursuit of his functions, the State Police issues and honors news media passes. These cards will identify the bearer as a representative of the news media and do not entitle the holder to special privileges. Members of the Division will extend, within the guidelines of this policy, all reasonable assistance and cooperation to holders of the News Media Identification, who are in pursuit of their news gathering duties.

1. Issuing credentials to news media representatives shall be the joint responsibility of the Superintendent of State Police and the Public Information Officer. News media credentials may be revoked for just cause, after consultation with the holder's employers.
2. State Police News Media Identification Cards shall be issued only after application is made, in writing, to the Public Information Officer on the official letterhead of the requesting press, radio or television media agency. The request should include the full name of the representative.
    A. Identification cards will be issued, upon proper application, any time during the year.
    B. All identification cards, regardless of when issued, however, will expire at midnight, December 31, of the year in which issued.

NMR 6. ALLOWING NEWSMEN TO ENTER AREA OF A SERIOUS POLICE INCIDENT OR CRIME. Police lines may be established to prevent persons from entering the area of a serious police incident or crime scene. Dependent upon the tactical situation and the likelihood of jeopardizing police operations, members of the news media may be allowed in such areas. Authorization for entry is normally dependent upon the possession of a State Police issued news media pass.

NMR 7. WHERE A NEWSMAN IS NOT AUTHORIZED. While a newsman may be permitted in the area of a crime scene or a serious police incident, he does not have the authority to be within a crime scene or area which has been secured to preserve evidence or at any location where his presence jeopardizes police operations.

NMR 8. NEWS MEDIA NOT EXEMPT FROM LAWS. A newsman's primary responsibility is to report the news by obtaining information and photographs at newsworthy incidents. His opportunity to do so is frequently momentary at an emergency scene, however, members of the news media are neither impliedly nor expressly exempt from any municipal, state or federal statute.

NMR 9. REQUESTING WITHHOLDING OF PUBLICATION. Newsmen may photograph or report anything they observe when legally present at an emergency scene. Where publication of such coverage would interfere with an official investigation or place a victim, suspect or others in jeopardy, the withholding of publication is dependent upon a cooperative press, not upon censorship by the Department. Upon such circumstances, officers should advise the newsmen or their superiors of the possible consequences of publication. However, officers may not interfere with newsmen's activities as long as that performance remains within the confines of the law.

NMR 10. RESPONSIBILITY FOR THE RELEASE OF INFORMATION.

1. *General.* All members will ensure that any information which may be released to the news media:
   A. Is accurate.
   B. Does not interfere with the successful conclusion of an investigation or pose a security threat upon a person involved.
   C. Is not prejudicial to the rights of the suspect or accused.
   D. Is in accordance with the provisions set forth in this Public Relations Manual and is not otherwise restrained by these guidelines or other Division or Departmental policy or General Orders.

2. *Information Office — Responsibilities*
   A. The release of information affecting the Division and any statements concerning Division policies which emanate from the Headquarters level or from the scene of major incidents in the field.
   B. Performing duties as outlined in the Delaware Emergency Operations Plan and/or State Police Civil Disturbance Manual.
   C. Assisting Headquarters Staff, Troop Commanders and Shift Commanders with any problem that may be encountered in dealing with the news media.
   D. Provide an official liaison relationship between representatives of the news media and the Division.
   E. Serve as coordinator for all Public Information activities of the Division.
3. *Troop Commander.* The responsibilities of the Troop Commander shall include:
   A. Serving as, or appointing a Commissioned Officer to serve as the Public Information Officer in the event a major incident occurs in troop area that is likely to generate more than routine news interest.
   B. Furnishing information to the Division's Public Information Officer regarding major incidents that are likely to generate more than routine news interest.
   C. Establishing and maintaining a good rapport and working relationship with members of the news media within his troop area.
4. *Troop Shift Commanders, Special Units and Section Chiefs.* Troop Commanders, Special Units and Section Chiefs shall be responsible for the release of routine news information from their respective troops and offices or request the Public Information Officer to prepare or assist in same.
   A. It shall be the Troop Shift Commander's responsibility to see that a News Release Form is prepared by the investigating officer or himself on all incidents occurring during his shift.
   B. The Shift Commander shall be responsible, in a courteous and prompt manner, to all requests for information from all members of the press, radio and television media.
   C. The Shift Commander shall be responsible for obtaining from investigative officers basic information to provide the following information to representatives of the news media.

(1). Nature of incident being investigated, i.e., personal injury accident, fatal accident, shooting, bomb threat, rape, etc.
(2). Time the incident was reported to police.
(3). Number of troopers and/or fire companies and ambulances dispatched to the scene.
(4). Location of incident (unless classified, i.e., drug raid).
(5). Number of injured and/or dead, their sex, if known, and name of hospital where injured and/or bodies were taken.
(6). Traffic conditions and/or detour instructions for public.
(7). Estimated time when detailed News Release is expected to be completed.
(8). The information outlined in sub-paragraphs (1) through (7) above, shall be reduced to writing on a News Release Form.
D. If a shift change occurs during the course of an investigation for which a detailed News Release has not been completed, the Shift Commander going off duty shall inform his relief Shift Commander of the basic information as stated in "C" above so that he may be responsive to inquiries from the news media.
E. It will be the responsibility of special unit and section chiefs to see that a detailed News Release is prepared on all incidents listed for whom primary investigative responsibility was of a special unit or section.
(1). If investigation is of such nature that it would draw the immediate attention of the news media, information for a News Release shall be relayed by the officer in charge of investigation to the Troop Shift Commander or Public Information Officer in whose area investigation is taking place so that he can be responsible to news media inquiries.
(2). The detailed News Release shall be prepared by investigating officers and delivered as soon as possible to the Troop Commander in whose area investigation took place.

5. *Investigating Officer.* The investigating officer of any accident, crime, or incident shall be responsible for relaying to the Shift Commander in whose area investigation is being conducted, the basic information required for a News Release as soon as possible after all injured and dead have been properly cared for and the scene of the incident properly secured.
A. News Release information should be relayed to the Shift Commander by public service phone whenever possible from the scene or upon arrival at the hospital.

B. Upon return to the troop, investigating officer shall, as soon as possible, prepare a detailed News Release and leave it with the Shift Commander before resuming routine patrol or going off duty.

C. The original copy of every news release shall be sent weekly to the Public Information Officer where it will be kept on file for one year.

NMR 11. SCOPE AND CONTENT OF NEWS RELEASES. Members will make every effort to cooperate with the press, radio, television or other public information media; however, sound judgment must be exercised. Information will not be released which would serve to weaken, or in any way hinder, or investigation being brought to a satisfactory conclusion, or endanger the lives of investigating officer and/or victims, suspects or the general public. All information released shall be based upon fact, not supposition or rumor. If any question, contact the Public Information Officer.

1. *General.* The following information shall not be disclosed unless authorized by the Superintendent of State Police or his designee:

    A. The identity of any deceased or seriously injured person prior to notification of the next of kin. Every effort must be made to notify the next of kin of the deceased before the news media is notified of the names. If notification cannot be given within a reasonable time, preferably six hours, but a maximum of twenty-four hours, the reason will be determined and the news media advised of the circumstances and the identification of the victims. The responsibility for disseminating names of the victims to the public will then be that of the news media.

    B. The specific cause of death until announced by the State Medical Examiner of his Deputy.

    C. The identity of any victim of a sex crime.

    D. The home address or telephone number of any member of the Division.

    E. Information or statements which may result in disproportionate favorable "publicity" (as opposed to legitimate news) for any member, unit, or section of the Division, or any other agency, including other non-police, local, city, county, state or federal government offices and agencies.

    F. Personal opinion not founded by fact.

    G. Unofficial statements concerning internal affairs, policy and/or personnel matters concerning the Division and/or Public Safety Department.

2. It is the practice of news media representatives to contact the various troops for the purpose of soliciting information upon which news stories might be predicated. Proper response shall be furnished by personnel answering such inquiries. If the member answering such a call does not have the pertinent information concerning an incident in question, then a check should be made with the Shift Commander and/or Traffic Lieutenant or Criminal Lieutenant to ascertain the information requested or an official explanation as to why such information is not available.
3. Information shall be disclosed without partiality to any particular news media representative or agency, and shall not be withheld or delayed to favor any person or agency.
   A. It is absolutely necessary that all accredited representatives of the news media be treated equally and that no favoritism or discrimination be shown to one media over another. If one newspaper, radio or television news bureau is furnished information initiated by the Division, then other news media representatives must be furnished the identical information in order to protect the Division from allegations of favoritism.
4. Good judgment, of course, must be utilized in furnishing information to the news media to ensure that the Division's official duties are not hindered. For example, in fatal accident cases, the fact that the victim is unidentified is no reason for withholding the fact that there has been a fatal accident.
5. In situations where inquiries are received by member other than the Shift Commander, who may be occupied on some other matter, and no news release is available, the member taking the call shall take the name and phone number of the news representative. The Shift Commander shall be advised immediately so that proper attention can be given to the inquiry and the news representative recontacted and furnished any information available.
6. Division personnel in their contacts with the news media must be constantly alert to utilize proper language to describe the Division's responsibilities without reference to cliches and terminology, which may be misleading or misrepresentative of the Division's functions.

NMR 12. RELEASE OF INFORMATION TO NEWS MEDIA, CONCERNING PRE-ARREST AND POST-ARREST SITUATIONS. Division policy on making releases of information to news media on pre-arrest and post-arrest situations is set out herein. There are limitations on what may be released. Adherence to these instructions will materially protect the Division in judicial review of cases and at the same time permit continuing cooperation with news media while fulfilling basic responsibilities.

1. **PRE-ARREST PROCEDURE — WHAT CAN BE GIVEN OUT.**
    A. Information relative to criminal investigations which shall be released, if it is not otherwise restrained by the effects of these guidelines, shall include:
    (1). The type of event or crime — when accurately known.
    (2). The location, time, items, or amount taken, injuries sustained or damages incurred.
    (3). The identity of the victim (except when release of identity would endanger life of victim).
    (4). Whether or not there are suspects, without further comment.
    (5). Numbers of officers or people involved in an event or investigation and the length of investigation, if such information is requested and would not hinder the investigation or performance of duty.
    (6). Requests for aid in locating a suspect or evidence.
    (7). The name, address, description, employment, and marital status of a person for whom a warrant has been issued.
    (8). The exact offense charged — brief description of the offense and method of complaint, i.e., officer, citizen, warrant, indictment, summons.
    B. Items of evidence, which if disclosed would be prejudicial to the solution of the case, should not be made public. Photographs of a person accused by indictment or warrant, without police identification on them, may be furnished. Where the identity of a suspect has not been established, it may be desirable to publicize descriptions, artists' sketches, or other information which could lead to the identification and arrest of the suspect.
    (1). Suspects who are interviewed but not charged should not be identified.
    (2). The finding of physical evidence, such as weapons or proceeds of the crime, the issuance and service of a search warrant, and the positive or negative results of the search, may be released. Information as to how a weapon or proceeds of the crime was located should be withheld if this involves information which is prejudicial.

(3). Fugitive cases may require wide publicity. Prior records of conviction should not be publicized. Common sense should dictate the manner in which fugitive cases are handled with a positive view toward the public interest and safety and the protection of other law enforcement agencies.

   (a). Fugitives, who have a past history of being armed or who have shown a propensity for violent acts, shall be characterized as being dangerous and why, so that an arresting officer will be well aware of dangerous aspects involved in the apprehension of such a subject. This normally is handled by teletype.

2. ***POST-ARREST PROCEDURE — WHAT NOT TO GIVE OUT.*** To avoid jeopardizing prosecution of a criminal matter by prejudicing the right of the defendant to a fair trial, members shall not make statements to the news media in the period between arrest and trial relating to the following: Pre-Trial, Prejudicial Publicity.

   A. Character or reputation of a suspect or the existence, if any, of a prior criminal record.
   B. Existence of a confession, admission, or statement by an accused person, or the absence or failure of an accused to make the same.
   C. Re-enactment of a crime, or the fact that a defendant may have shown investigators where a weapon, loot or other evidence was located.
   D. References to a defendant as (for example) "a sex-crazed maniac," a "depraved character," a "typical gangster," "professional burglar," "shakedown artist," etc.
   E. The existence or contents of any confession, admission, or statement given by the accused or his refusal or failure to make a statement; and/or the performance or results of any examinations or tests or the refusal or failure of the accused to submit to examinations or tests.

   (1). Information may be given out only if requested as to whether an individual arrested, refused or submitted to the normal test in DWI cases. No results of any such test shall be disclosed to the news media.
   (2). Information *may* be given out concerning the general facts that physical evidence is being examined. However, the description of such evidence and the results of such examinations shall not be disclosed without the concurrence of the Attorney General's office.

F. Guilt or innocence of a defendant, or the possibility of a guilty plea to the offense charged, or to a lesser offense (i.e., plea bargaining) or possibilities of other dispositions such as "nolle prosequi."
G. Identity, credibility, or testimony of any prospective witness.
H. Testimony, credibility, or character of any victim witness.
I. Information of a purely speculative nature.
J. The merits of the case, such as evidence and arguments, whether or not it is anticipated to be used in court.
K. Transcripts, reports, or summaries of occurrences taking place during the course of judicial proceedings from which the public and press have been excluded.

3. *POST-ARREST PROCEDURE — WHAT CAN BE GIVEN OUT.*
   A. Personnel authorized to deal with the news media should supply any relevant information on the arrest, provided it cannot be construed as prejudicial to a fair trial. Information which *may* be given out, but is not required to, includes the following:
   (1). Defendant's name, age, residence, employment, marital status, and similar background information.
   (2). Substance or text of the charge on which the arrest was made and the identity of the person preferring the charge (when such information does not constitute a danger to the complainant).
      (a). Members, dealing with the press, shall withhold identification of persons preferring charges when such persons are victims of a sex crime and publication of their identity would be a matter of serious embarrassment to them or jeopardize their security.
   (3). Identity of the investigating and arresting agency, the duration of the investigation.
   (4). The facts and circumstances immediately surrounding an arrest — time, place resistance, pursuit, possession or use of weapons, and a general description of contraband seized, if disclosure is not prejudicial.
   (5). Pre-trial release or detention arrangements, i.e., amount of bond, location of detention.
   (6). The scheduled dates or results of the various stages in the judicial process.

(7). Photographs of defendants (without police identification) may be furnished to the news media. Members shall not assist in posing defendants for news or television cameramen, but the efforts of such cameramen should not be hindered during the course of any normal movements of members or defendants which expose defendants to public view. The Public Information Office should be contacted prior to any of the above.

B. When there is a question as to whether an item should be released, the decision may be made by the Troop Commander or officer in charge of the investigation on the general principle that information should be made available unless it reasonably could be construed as prejudicial to the defendant, harmful to prosecution, or endanger the lives of persons involved in the case.

NMR 13. SPECIAL CONSIDERATIONS.

1. *Photographing or Television.*

    A. In public places, and places where the press may otherwise lawfully be, no member shall take any action to prevent or interfere with the news media in photographing or televising an event, a suspect, or an accused or any other person or thing except that the presence of cameramen and crews shall not be allowed to significantly interfere with the police mission at hand.

    (1). Troop Commanders may properly extend cooperation when departmental property is required for the recording of interviews, news releases, documentaries, or events of an unusual nature. In routine circumstances, public information programs and the press may be permitted by the Troop Commander to use their own equipment within police buildings or property.

    B. Members shall not deliberately pose a suspect or accused in custody to be photographed, televised or interviewed.

    C. Members shall not pose themselves with a suspect or accused, nor shall they enter into any agreement to have a suspect or accused in custody at a prearranged time or place to be photographed, televised, or interviewed.

    D. Police department photographs or films of the following shall not be released, except by the Superintendent of the State Police or his designee:

    (1). Crime scenes.
    (2). Suspects or accused persons prior to actual arrest.

(3). The victims of any crime, accident, or suicide.
(4). Juveniles (under 18 years).
(5). Members of the department.

2. *Names of Juveniles*
   A. In compliance with Rule 350, of Court Rules for Family Court of the State of Delaware, March 1, 1973, no child having been arrested shall be publicly named. Permission may be granted by a Judge of the Court for good cause as the interest of justice may require.
   B. The names of juveniles involved in motor vehicle accidents, who are not arrested, will continue to be released to the news media routinely, unless specifically ordered not to by an official of the Family Court. Release of juvenile names in other cases will be made only upon specific request by an accredited news media representative, unless ordered not to by the Family Court.
   C. The fact that the name of a juvenile is being withheld by order of the Family Court should be stated, if questioned by a representative of the news media.

3. *Sensitive and Confidential Operations.*
   A. Information, concerning the activities of the Vice and Intelligence Units, Inspection and Internal Affairs Units, Operations Branch or any special police operations necessarily deemed to be confidential by the officer in charge of the operations, shall not be disclosed, except by the express permission of the respective officers in charge, Section Chiefs, or the Superintendent.

4. *Suicide Notes.*
   A. The contents of a suicide note or electronically recorded message is to be considered personal and confidential. No member shall make such written or recorded statements public. The fact that a suicide note exists may be reported without further comment.

5. *Withholding Information.*
   A. At the time information is denied to the press in the face of a legitimate inquiry, the denial shall be supported by a courteous, logical, and adequate explanation, which can be justified upon further inquiry. Failure to do this can unnecessarily damage the positive efforts to build good police-press relations.

6. *Names of Armed Forced Personnel.*
   A. Requests for information directly concerning the military (such as names, ranks and missions of military personnel involved) should be referred to military authorities. Only accurate, factual information directly concerning the State Police investigation is to be given, and whenever possible that information should be coordinated with the proper military authorities.
      (1). Information concerning military personnel involved in a civilian automobile, train, or plane crashes will be released in the same manner as though the serviceman were a civilian.
      (2). Cooperation of the news media photographers should be requested, but no force should be used by State Police personnel to prevent their taking photographs at military crash scenes. Military authorities should, however, be advised that photographs have been taken, and, if possible, they should be supplied with the name of the photographer and the agency for which he works.
7. *Weather and Road Conditions.*
   A. Members on patrol, observing changes in highway or weather conditions which would endanger or interrupt traffic, will immediately notify their Shift Commanders. Such information shall be made available to the public and the news media. Requests from a television or radio station for the services of a member to broadcast live or recorded routine weather or highway conditions will be complied with, whenever possible.
8. *Recognition of Department Members.*
   A. Names of members should be incorporated into news releases, if the Troop Commander or officer in charge determines that the members are deserving of special attention, due to their actions relating to the incident.
9. *Publication by Division Personnel.*
   A. Members are prohibited from releasing stories or statements concerning the policies and/or operations of the Division of Public Safety Department to magazines, periodicals or other similar publications without the written approval of the Superintendent of State Police.

Public Information

PI1. GENERAL PROVISIONS FOR REQUESTS OF INFORMATION. The public has an abiding interest in law enforcement and in the activities of the Division. The news media and members of the public frequently direct inquiries to the Division seeking information on a variety of subjects. While it is the aim of the Division to fulfill such requests, it is not always possible to do so. Whether to release information or to grant interviews will be determined according to the facts of each case.

PI2. PERMISSION FOR USE OF DIVISION FACILITIES. Normally, the Division will not grant permission for its equipment or the interior of its facilities to be used for television, motion pictures, or other entertainment productions. However, when coverage is required for recording interviews, news documentaries, news releases, or events of an unusual nature, representatives from the news media or public information programs may be allowed to use their equipment inside police facilities under supervision.

PI3. COOPERATION FOR FEATURE ARTICLES OR PROGRAMS. Requests for Department cooperation in the preparation of articles for newspapers, magazines, and other publications will be individually considered, and, if approved by the Superintendent, permission for the interviewing of Division personnel and the photographing of police facilities will be limited to the scope of approval. Officers, participating in the preparation of such articles, should ascertain the scope of approval and should be cautious not to exceed those limits. In any event, officers should exercise care and discretion so as not to make statements or convey information which, if later quoted, may create a misunderstanding or compromise the effectiveness of the police service.

PI4. RESPONSIBILITY OF OFFICERS TO SUPPLY INFORMATION. When a request is made for information about a police matter, an officer should decide if he is in possession of sufficient facts and is qualified to respond and whether the person making the request is a proper person to receive the information. Generally, an officer should be open in his dealings with the public and unless there is reason to the contrary, he should supply requested information. He should, however, be cautious to avoid representing as fact that which is his opinion.

PI5. PUBLIC INFORMATION PROGRAMS AND EDUCATION. The Division conducts various public information and crime prevention programs to educate the public and to eliminate specific crime problems.

PI6. TOURS OF STATE POLICE FACILITIES. To acquaint the public with the law enforcement task, the Division will hold "open house" and, upon request, conduct tours of police facilities. The scope of such tours will be dependent upon security requirements and personnel availability.

APPENDIX A

It shall be the Shift Commander's responsibility to have the investigating officer complete a News Release for each of the following incidents as soon as possible:

I. A Traffic News Release shall be completed for each of the following types of traffic accidents or incidents:
   1. All Fatal Accidents
   2. All serious Personal Injury Accidents (requiring admission to a hospital)
   3. All unusual Property Damage Accidents (causing extensive damage to public buildings and/or property, or causing detour of traffic over a long period of time
   4. All PI and/or PD Accidents involving railroad trains (including derailments)
   5. All high speed chases resulting in arrests and/or personal injury
   6. Major traffic detours

II. A Criminal News Release shall be completed for each of the following crimes that are investigated and found to actually have occurred:
   1. Homicide
   2. Kidnapping
   3. Rape
   4. Robbery
   5. Assault on a Police Officer
   6. Aggravated Assault resulting in injury requiring medical attention
   7. Sexual Assault
   8. Arson
   9. Hijacking
   10. Burglary (Papers normally not interested unless there is $200 loss, or more)
   11. Grand Larceny
   12. Counterfeit Money
   13. Escape
   14. Bomb Threat (Only if bomb is found)
   15. Riot
   16. Public Disorder or Disturbance involving a group of individuals and resulting in arrests

17. Suicides
18. Forgery (arrest only)
19. Embezzlement (arrest only)
20. Drug violation (arrest only)
21. Obscene Material (arrest only)
22. Prostitution (arrest only)
23. Gambling (arrest only)
24. Smuggling (arrest only)
25. Liquor violation (arrest only)
26. Bribery (arrest only)
27. Weapons and/or explosive offense (arrest only)

III. An Incident News Release shall be completed for each of the following incidents that are investigated and found actually to have occurred.
1. Search and rescues involving State Police helicopter and/or State Police personnel
2. Lost persons for whom a search has been initiated
3. Drownings
4. Explosions
5. Aircraft crashes and forced landings
6. Storm and/or flood damage
7. Accidental shooting
8. Sudden death (accidental)

IV. These guidelines in no way prohibit the members of the Delaware State Police from responding to direct inquiries regarding arrests that are not routinely covered by a news release.
1. Public Information Officers are to be contacted immediately upon verification of any one of the following incidents:
   a. Natural Disaster
   b. Aircraft Crash
   c. Bank Robbery
   d. Prison Disturbance
   e. Shipwreck
   f. Homicides
   g. Racial Disturbance, Riots, Violent Pickets, etc.
   h. Injury to divisional personnel
   i. Fatal accidents or serious personal injury accidents involving popular or well-known personalities

j. Major criminal investigations and clearances involving felonies
   k. Incidents involving important personages
   l. Any situation which is likely to arouse special media interest
2. a. The Public Information Officer will be notified at the initiation of any investigation so information can be collected and disseminated to the media at the scene and immediately thereafter to relieve the investigating officer or the shift commander.
   b. In investigations which may not require the Public Information Officer to respond to the scene, notification in the above manner should still take place to allow the Public Information Officer to make a determination as to the proper immediate action.
3. After the arrival of the Public Information Officer at the scene, if the investigating officer is approached by a media representative, for reasons of safety and to prevent impedence of the investigation, the officer will direct the reporter or photographer to the Public Information Officer, who will coordinate the movement of media personnel at the scene.
4. In such cases as those listed, where a Public Information Officer has been contacted, when questioned concerning the case, the officer will tactfully inform the reporter that the Public Information Officer is working on his behalf and will contact him as soon as information is available. Upon receiving such a call at the troop, the officer will take the caller's name and telephone number so his call can be returned before his deadline.
5. No interviews or stories will be granted to any member of the media, by any member of the Delaware State Police, without the Public Information Officer being contacted prior to same.

CREDIBILITY AND ETHICS AND THEIR IMPACT ON OUR PROFESSION

PHIL J. RECORD

IN 1974, the late Arizona publisher, Eugene C. Pulliam, made his last formal address to our Society, which he helped found 75 years ago.
He closed that speech in Phoenix with these words:
"If you forget everything else I've said, remember this:
America is great only because America is free."

And one of the reasons America is free today is because there was and is a free press.

Not necessarily a fair press, or an objective press, or a responsible press, but a press which has guaranteed its freedom by the First Amendment to the Constitution.

When our forefathers added the First Amendment to our Constitution they did not do so with the understanding that the press would be responsible, fair and objective.

The fact is, the press in those days—and there were only 8 daily newspapers in the United States at that time—was anything but responsible, fair and objective.

They were snarling, partisan publications which asked for and gave no quarter. More often than not they attacked the very people who found them to be so necessary to liberty that they preserved their independence and freedom from government control with the First Amendment.

---

*Phil J. Record is associate executive editor of the *Fort Worth Star-Telegram,* Fort Worth, Texas. He is also past president of Society of Professional Journalists, Sigma Delta Chi. During his tenure in that national office he presented portions of the speech included here to audiences across the country.

†Portions reprinted from the *1984-85 Journalism Ethics Report* prepared by the National Ethics Committee, Society of Professional Journalists, Sigma Delta Chi, with permission of Society of Professional Journalists, SDX. The entire speech is included with permission of its author.

I think it appropriate to recall some of the words of James Madison, the principal author of The Bill of Rights.

Listen to the words of the man who was to become the fourth president of the United States:

> Some degree of abuse is inseparable from the proper use of everything, and in no instance is this more true than in that of the press. It has accordingly been decided by the practice of the States, that it is better to leave a few of its noxious branches to their luxuriant growth, than, by pruning them away, to injure the vigour of those yielding the proper fruits. And can the wisdom of this policy be doubted by any who reflect that to the press alone, chequered as it is with abuses, the world is indebted for all the triumphs which have been gained by reason and humanity over error and oppression; who reflect that to the same beneficent source the United States owe much of the lights which conducted them to the ranks of a free and independent nation, and which have improved their political system.

Today, Madison and his fellow patriots would probably be stunned to find how responsible and fair the press has become.

But this fairness and responsibility was not imposed by governmental fiat.

Journalists imposed these standards on themselves. And we should not retreat from these standards.

With the growth of the penny press in the mid-19th century, the nation's newspapers decided to make their pitch to attract a mass audience. They began to abandon their historic partisan roles and adopted a more neutral posture.

With these changes came attempts at fairness, responsibility and that ideal we call objectivity. The press began to boast about these ideals — ideals that are difficult — sometimes impossible — to reach.

Today we are still reaching, as reach we must.

And the public came to expect us to live up to these ideas, as expect they should.

But reaching has not been enough.

Look at what has happened to our credibility. It has declined.

Our diminished credibility has hurt our fight for the free flow of information because too often the public for whom we are fighting fails to rally to our support.

Look what happened when the current administration put the press on a slow boat to Barbados instead of on the beaches of Grenada. Where were the outraged howls from the public? Instead of howls we too often heard folks cheering because those arrogant journalists finally got what they had coming.

And many of us reacted like wounded elephants. We thundered with outrage instead of really listening to what our critics were saying and why they were saying it.

Because of the decibel level, many of us immediately concluded that the majority in this country had turned on us.

One of the top network anchor men addressed a large meeting in Chicago and ranted about how shabbily the press had been treated by the Reagan Administration and how wrong the public was in cheering about that treatment.

He waved the First Amendment banner. Not once did he concede that we of the press do indeed have our warts.

But he did further polarize that audience into an us vs. them position. He did our cause no good.

And, now it appears that we jumped to some hasty conclusions.

In a more calm atmosphere, it has been determined that there remains in this country a silent majority that does indeed underwrite freedom of the press. A Harris Survey made in December disclosed that 83 percent of the respondents agreed that "A basic freedom is the right to know."

That is not to say there is little hostility toward the press out there.

There is. It is vocal. And it can incite others to hostility.

The question is why is there such ill feeling toward the press?

And we need to ask ourselves a couple of more questions.

Are we journalists to blame? Is there something we can do about it?

The reasons, I believe, are varied and often complex.

We must share part of the blame.

And there is something we can do about it.

Today we are all inundated with news. It is available 24 hours a day. It is available everywhere we turn.

People say there is so much more bad news today. I really don't buy that. But try to sell that notion to the public.

Perhaps Wes Gallagher, former General Manager of the Associated Press, is on the right track. Gallagher's "Law" says that criticism of the press by the public "rises in direct proportion to the amount of news read or heard that does not fit the reader's or listener's preconceived ideas of what the news should be."

Well, with all the news available to today's reader or listener, there is plenty available that will not fit his or her preconceived ideas.

And we must not forget that there is a lot of inaccurate and biased listening and reading going on out there.

In addition, there is no question that the news has greater impact.

Newspapers splash their pages with color photos . . . photos which have greater impact.

There is the instancy of radio.

Television is a super hot medium. It stirs the emotions.

Once our people read about wars. Now they experience it in their living room in living color.

No, I don't think there is more bad news today. That bad news is just more intense these days.

But the public's perceptions can be just as damaging as reality.

We of the press are prone to get down right timid when it comes to telling our story.

We say it is too self-serving.

Well, that story is too damn important not to be told. It is important to us, but it is also important to the public.

The public needs to understand this institution which is so vital to our freedoms.

And if we don't tell the story, I don't know who will.

Tell it on our editorial pages. Tell it on our op-ed pages. Tell it to the Rotary Clubs and to the Lions Clubs.

Explain the First Amendment.

Tell of our constitutional mission.

Tell why we behave as we do.

Tell of the difficulties we face.

And admit we are humans who try, but sometimes fail because we are humans just like our readers and our listeners.

We can help educate — inform if you prefer — our readers and our listeners.

Let me quote from an editorial which appeared on the editorial page of the *Dallas Times Herald* on March 16, National Freedom of Information Day:

> A recent Gallup poll, however, found that three of every four Americans don't even know what the First Amendment provides. Many citizens mistakenly believe that it gives special privileges to journalists; they do not realize that the First Amendment belongs to each and every American.
> The fiercest foes of the First Amendment are fear and ignorance. As much as some Americans may be appalled by what the amendment occasionally allows, they must remind themselves that the alternative to a free flow of ideas would be much worse. For all of its abuses, the First Amendment is far superior to anything found in societies that repress expression.

And television, especially the 60 Minute variety, has exposed some of our sins, our weaknesses, our wants.

And there has been a wave of mistrust of authority, of power, sweeping over the land for some time. And whether we like it or not, people view the media as part of the power structure.

Undoubtedly this has a negative impact on our credibility.

We have done a poor job of telling our story to the people.

We have not convinced the public that the First Amendment is in the Constitution to benefit them. . . . That it also belongs to them and is there to protect their liberties, their right and their need to know.

Recently the officers of our Society met with Glenn English, the Democratic Congressman from Oklahoma. He frequently has championed our cause in Congress, but he took us to task for doing a lousy job of telling our story, especially of the benefits of the Freedom of Information Act.

And he is right!

A couple of years ago, a lawyer in Austin, Texas, introduced a resolution at a precinct meeting that read:

> "Congress shall make no law respecting an establishment of religion or prohibiting the free exercise thereof: or abridging the freedom of speech, or of the press; the right of the people peaceably to assemble, and to petition the government for a redress of grievance."

We recognize those words as the First Amendment to the Constitution.

But those people in Austin, Texas, apparently did not for they quickly tabled this resolution as being too controversial.

Yes, Congressman English was right.

We have a lot of educating to do.

Let us capture the fervor of Bob Packwood, the Republican Senator from Oregon, who says of the First Amendment:

> "It is without question the most single, important sentence in the world guaranteeing the protection of human liberties."

Today, journalists attempt to do more things than ever before. We are more aggressive. We do take more risks.

And that is as it should be.

Without these traits we would not be the finest press the world has ever known. And in my heart I do think we are the best ever.

Even Spiro Agnew once conceded as much in a 1970 speech in Honolulu.

But we must get better!

We must reduce our errors, our sins, our shortcomings.

I don't believe them to be as great as the public perceives them to be.

But they are still there, and they will always be there.

In this day, when the air is charged with a negative view of the press, our shortcomings, our sins, our errors are magnified in the eyes of the public.

So our task is to minimize them.

There is much work to be done.

It is an uncomfortable feeling for a journalist to be the interviewee instead of the interviewer.

I have been on the receiving end of questions as I have criss-crossed this nation since being installed in November as the national president of the Society of Professional Journalists, Sigma Delta Chi.

And my discomfort has turned to genuine concern after having found myself to be the victim of some sloppy, lousy reporting. I expected better.

Perhaps it would do all of us a lot of good if, from time to time, we were put on the other side of the fence. It is indeed an eye-opening experience.

It has caused me to see too many things about our noble profession that tire me, too many things that worry me.

I'm tired of our failures.

I'm tired of seeing us ignore the rights of others. Too often we make one look guilty when he is merely exercising his right to remain silent, to not speak to us.

I'm tired of seeing us invade their privacy. Too often we make a perfectly legal private meeting look like a surreptitious gathering of rascals. We needlessly intrude during a family's hour of grief.

I'm tired of seeing instances of arrogance. Too often we print or broadcast because it is our right, not because it is right.

I'm tired of signs of our paranoia, of our knee-jerk reaction. Too often we try to cloak our errors by hiding behind the First Amendment. Such acts are a clear and present danger to that cherished amendment.

I'm tired of journalists who tend to start every assignment by assuming the worst. This makes for narrow-mindness, not open-mindness.

I'm tired of just plain sloppy reporting and failure to double check things.

I'm tired of seeing too much reluctance to correct errors. Too often we try to disguise our corrections . . . or hide them . . . or to outright ignore our errors.

I'm tired of the journalists who still take freebies . . . handouts . . . gifts for doing their jobs.

I'm tired of those journalists who shy away from codes of ethics.

I'm tired of seeing too many defensive reactions to criticism. We can dish it out, but too often we can't take it.

And, I'm worried!

I'm worried about herd journalism, pack journalism. Instead of just covering a problem, we too often tend to compound it, or become part of it.

I'm worried about the too frequent use of the good old reliable source. For some journalists, this has become a way of life. They are too prone to take the lazy way, the easy way out.

I'm worried about those reporters who are quick to say, "Don't worry, we will win in court." They forget it may cost us $20,000 or $30,000 or more to win in court.

I'm worried about journalists who are more interested in seeking glory than they are in seeking the truth. They are the ones who will put out 110 percent for a by-line or a credit-line, but will take little care with a three-graph story. Yet the errors in three-graph stories are killing our credibility.

I'm worried about coverage which gives more sympathy to the criminal than to the victim.

I'm worried when journalists forget about our responsibilities and our awesome power . . . power that can destroy a man's reputation or business or family-life with one written or spoken sentence.

I'm worried about journalists who lack sensitivity and concern for their listeners or readers . . . who think it is corny to wave the flag or support a worthy cause . . . who are quick to label all religions as superstition.

I'm worried about reporters who begin an assignment by deciding what they think the thrust of a story should be, then seeking out quotes and data to support that thrust. Can't you just hear the door slamming shut on an open mind?

I'm worried about journalists who are so isolated from their community that they cannot grasp its needs, its concerns and its values.

I'm worried about editors who neglect to question, to challenge, to demand, to teach, to admonish, to inspire, to console.

I'm worried about editors who get so burdened with administrative detail they don't have time to know what is happening in their news rooms.

And I am outraged when anyone in this profession will stoop to bending the truth—however slightly—to enhance a story. Banish them from our midst for they are corrupting.

They corrupt the one thing we hold most holy—the truth.

Fortunately, they are few. Let's make them fewer.

Is it any wonder that at least once a week I say this prayer:

"Lord, lead us to the truth;
"Let us always be fair in our quest for it;
"Give us the wisdom to recognize the truth;
"And the courage to proclaim it as we find it to be, not as
"I wish it to be."

Yes, we are far from perfection.

But the good we do still far outweighs our faults. And I repeat my belief that we are doing a better job today than journalists have ever done before.

We will never reach perfection, but we must strive for it.

We must keep reminding ourselves, that we are servants of the public, servants of the truth—and don't expect the public to always be ready to receive the truth.

We should emblazon that word "servant" in our own minds and in the minds of our staffs.

We must act like servants. We must abandon our too frequent isolation from our readers and listeners. And we must banish all thoughts of elitism.

We must keep reminding ourselves that we are guests when we enter a reader's or a listener's home, and that as guests, we must not needlessly—repeat needlessly—offend our hosts.

Surely it is a tiring battle, an often discouraging battle to keep our own house in order.

But we must continue, weary though we be, to do so in order to win the respect, the support, the trust, the understanding and the tolerance of the public we serve.

Note I did not include the word "love." We shouldn't expect to be loved. The love affairs we have had with the public have usually been short-lived.

The very nature of our job—that of being servants of the truth—almost precludes love affairs with the public.

Servants of the truth have frequently faced an unloving public throughout the history of mankind.

Just turn to your Old Testament and see what happened to the prophets God sent to preach the truth to the Israelites. Listen to the words of poor old Jeremiah as he begged the Lord to free him from his mission:

"For the word of the Lord has become for me
"A reproach and derision all day long. . . .
"For I hear many whispering.
"Terror is on every side.
" 'Denounce Him.' Let us denounce Him.'
"Say all my familiar friends, watching for my fall."

But the Lord would not extinguish that "burning fire" in Jeremiah's heart which motivated him to proclaim the truth.

So, like the prophet of old, we too have been called to proclaim the truth. And we must not extinguish the fire in our hearts.

Let us not make love our goal. Let us not try to win popularity contests.

Such action would be contrary to our mission of the only American private enterprise that has a constitutional guarantee of its right to exist.

But without the respect, the support, the trust, the understanding and the tolerance of the public, it will be much more difficult to meet the challenges to the free flow of information.

Most certainly we have tasted some victories. But the challenges remain, and grow.

The F.O.I. Act remains under attack in Congress . . . the federal bureaucrats still wield the "classified" stamp with abandon . . . attempts are made to silence the sources of news . . . our broadcast journalists are still restricted by the shackles of the federal government . . . too many agencies at all levels of government still try to charge outrageous sums for copies of public documents . . . there are still too many secret — and here I use that word deliberately — secret meetings in our city halls, our courthouses, our school administration offices . . . some juries in libel cases base their verdicts on their negative feelings about the press instead of on the facts of the case.

Frightening, isn't it!

We all should be frightened that President Reagan declined to meet with the leaders of our major journalism organizations in the wake of the Grenada invasion, but will host the board of the National Interfraternity Conference at a White House luncheon.

We should be frightened when Laurence Gold, special counsel to the AFL-CIO, testifies before a senate committee that his organization not only favors the continuation of the equal time regulation on broadcasters but would like to see an equal space regulation imposed on the print media. This is mainstream America testifying. Senator Packwood described the testimony as "discouraging . . . unbelievable . . . shocking."

Earlier this year, I was one of two journalists who presented to Congressman English and Senator Patrick Leahy petitions signed by some 6,000 journalists in support of the F.O.I. Act.

During his brief talk, Senator Leahy warned those present not to let the Fight for the Freedom of Information become a Conservative-Liberal issue.

How right he was. We do have many allies on both sides of the political spectrum. We need to keep them as allies.

In Congress, for instance, First Amendment champions include Republican Senators Dan Durenberger of Minnesota, Dan Quayle of Indiana and Packwood, and Democratic Senator Leahy of Vermont and Democratic Representatives English of Oklahoma and Jack Brooks of Texas.

And there are many more such friends in our legislatures, our city halls and our courthouses.

After that Washington ceremony, Senator Leahy pulled me aside and stated more emphatically:

"Don't let up the fight."

"Let up" we cannot. We should not retreat to the path of low-risk, or no-risk journalism.

We must continue on our constitutional mission to serve the public and the truth.

We must continue to be available to serve those treated unjustly; to be willing to side with the minority and the oppressed when their cause is just; to be willing to express unpopular opinions on our editorial pages; to be willing to present controversial ideas in order to stir public debate, and to have the courage to present the truth even though it may disturb a valued advertiser or cost us subscribers.

We must continue to be responsible if we are to demand responsibility of others.

And we must continue our essential role of the watchdog.

These are the reasons we can never be an elected press, an appointed press which champions only that which is popular. These are the reasons our founding fathers protected the press in the First Amendment.

Most certainly our mission is difficult.

Just trying to keep our own houses in order, educating the public and supporting our friends will not do the job.

We must work together. Print journalists, broadcasters and journalism educators must support each other. Our major journalism organizations must work together and avoid duplication of efforts.

It has been demonstrated that we can do so.

Look at the very solid "Statement of Principle on Press Access to Military Operations" ten of the leading journalism organizations managed to produce once they agreed to sit down and reason together.

On February 1, 1984, the Society of Professional Journalists was host to a journalism summit in Washington, D.C. Participating in this meeting was the American Newspaper Publishers Association, the American Society of Newspaper Editors, the Associated Press Managing Editors, the National Newspaper Association, the Radio-Television News Directors Association and SPJ, SDX.

We discussed our plans and programs, discovered areas where we could work together, and determined where we could avoid some duplication of efforts. So successful was this meeting, that the participants decided to hold the journalism summit annually.

In closing, let me return to our role as watchdog. Perhaps it is this service which stirs much of the public's annoyance with the press.

But the role is vital, and we need to explain it to the public.

Alan Barth, the late editorial writer for *The Washington Post*, explained it well in a 1977 speech:

> If you want a watchdog to warn you of intruders, you must put up with a certain amount of mistaken barking. Now and then he will sound off because a stray dog seems to be invading his territory or because he sees a cat or a squirrel or is outraged by a postman. And that kind of barking can, of course, be a nuisance. But if you muzzle him and leash him and teach him to be decorous, you will find that he doesn't do the job for which you got him in the first place. Some extraneous barking is the price you must pay for his service as a watchdog. A free press is the watchdog of society.

SECTION IV
SUMMATION

CONFESSIONS OF A PRAGMATIST: THE P.I.O. AS TRUTH SAYER

PATRICIA A. KELLY

THE ADAGE that guides Lt. Michael T. Wright in his interactions with the media as director of public information for New York State Police is both a pithy and practical one: "You don't argue with people who have ink delivered by the carload."

Time was, says Lt. Wright, (in the days before the drafting of a formal media relations policy), when there were lessons graphically learned about the consequences of a confrontal posture of police toward press.

"Our people, our troop commanders, our superintendent, our commanding officers were always taking the media on," he recalls. "It seemed to be the thing to do. We responded with letters to the editor, we demanded rebuttals, and what we learned is the more you kick crap around, the more it gets on you.

"It's an interesting phenomenon. The media really loves this type of thing. They love the controversy. If you are going to do battle with them in any way, you'd better be right. Because they are going to respond. You'd better be one hundred percent right, and not ninety-two percent right or ninety-five percent right."

A "no-comment" was a frequent police reaction of the past in response to media personnel probings, he maintains, sometimes resulting in compromising and misleading images of agency-orchestrated coverups.

Lt. Michael T. Wright is director of public information for the New York State Police. He is a 19-year veteran of that agency. When he was appointed to his current position in 1984, he was assigned the task of revamping the Division Headquarters Public Information Office and setting up a statewide network. That office coordinates the activities of public information and crime prevention officers in each of the ten troops and Manhattan.

He offers two incidents as cases in point, one exemplifying the negative spin-offs of police silence, the other the benefits of up-front dissemination of information. The first involved the tempest surrounding alleged misconduct by troopers assigned to policing the state fair in Syracuse.

"A few years back, all our troopers were housed in one motel, and we had allegations of alcohol abuse by them, drug abuse, and brutality while taking prisoners," he recounts. "Everything was blown completely out of context. This was before we had a public information office really intact. I was not there, we did not have public information officers. Our organization decided to say 'no comment.' And we really got burned. We really did not get our side of the story in. And the media went to the other people who wanted to talk. We really learned a lesson from that. We were backtracking, looking like we were covering up, and we were not. And that hurt us."

All allegations were false, says Lt. Wright, and no indictments were handed down against troopers, but the management mistake which fanned adverse publicity was "not getting our side of the story out first."

Ironically, a recent incident which had a facts-based potential for righteous public backlash "worked out well," because, says Wright, the information flowed freely.

Two on-duty troopers were killed in a head-on collision.

"There was the problem of the troopers being off post," he says. "They were about 22 miles south of where they should have been. When we found out, we gave it out. We were up-front about it."

Autopsies on the officers revealed that one "was in fact legally drunk," he continues, "and we came out with that immediately. And then the other shoe dropped and cocaine was found in the autopsy of the other trooper. We decided to go with everything at the end, we told everything."

The result was, "it was a big story for about two or three days." Satisfied they had received a truthful and full disclosure from the reliable sources, the media gave the story what they judged proper coverage, and the police did not feel "burned" by distorted perspectives.

New York State Police, like law enforcement agencies of all sizes across the country, have come to acknowledge, through experiences such as these, that the media's presence in the daily worlds of policing cannot be denied. It will not disappear under imposition of information blackouts which, in fact, often only feed the fervor of watchdogging tactics. So the position chosen by many departments has been to assume the assertive, rather than the defensive stance and to deal with the media in ways that can actually help police in their central objective to function for the common weal.

The establishment of the New York State Police Public Information Office in 1983 under Superintendent Donald O. Chesler was an official recognition on that agency's part that police/media relations are complex and changing, with elements of major importance for the goals of both groups.

In its budgetary allocations, in its public service and its public relations functions, the office has been, contends Wright, "an overwhelming success, thanks to a progressive superintendent who really believes, as I do, that in the 1980's, if you don't exist in the media, you don't exist. It's unfortunate, but true.

"What the New York State Police do, and how they do it should be publicized, so it can be done in even more efficient ways for the benefit of even more citizens. If you are doing good work, and it is not properly publicized, you are not really achieving your objective, because your objective is to do even more good work."

Education in such areas as child abuse, drug abuse, hazardous materials handling, traffic safety, crime prevention are among the community services performed by his agency which, Wright feels, needs and deserves as much day-to-day coverage as hard-news law enforcement activities.

And, in a way, he sees that hard news as good for barter.

He believes a way to get maximum exposure for events which television, radio and print reporters may feel are less timely, less riveting and generally less newsworthy is to consistently and conscientiously "provide them with the hard news."

"We always try to help the media as much as possible," he says. "But we can also realize that because we have hard news to give out, we can get the media to respond when we have soft news to give out.

"When we want to publicize a fingerprinting program or Photo-Identi-Kid, sometimes the media is a little reluctant to come out, but we can sort of call in our chips at that time. If we are there when they need us, we try to tell them we would like you to be at a certain place at a certain time to cover this event, something important to us, and the media understands this. We keep a healthy balance, and they do respond and help us."

For the police organization, according to Wright, such mutual aid can have pragmatic, as well as altruistic benefits.

"Image, very honestly," he concedes, "is important for police, and I feel strongly that we are getting a bigger slice of the criminal justice pie because of our public relations efforts. Our budget has gone up 40 percent in the last two years, and I believe that legislators and people who vote on our budget read the papers, and their perceptions of us come mostly from the media."

In detailing the development and layered functioning of the New York State Police public information central and satellite offices, Lt. Wright refers to a philosophy on his agency's part that is essentially non-offending and strategically offensive. Guided by sound management principles, he and his central office staff and the troop representatives attempt, when interacting with the media to: be prepared, be well-organized, be informed, know their audiences' needs, periodically evaluate their performances, stay in charge, emphasize the personal approach and learn from the professionals in the communications fields.

The division of New York State Police is divided into 10 separate troops, outlines Wright, with a contingent in Manhattan. Each troop has a fulltime public information officer and a crime prevention officer who acts as an alternate public information officer. Lt. Wright heads the unit. Statewide news releases emanate from division headquarters and cover such topics as holiday safety messages, policy statements, or arrests where the investigations might cross state lines. These releases are teletyped to the troops' officers, who maintain media contact lists and call down those lists, generally reading the information over the telephone.

"We really blanket the state in a matter of hours," says Wright.

The troop information officers are freed from having to go through the normal chain of command, and they report directly to the troop commander. Those officers' duty is "to establish and maintain a rapport with the local press to ensure a constant flow of information to the media.

"They are expected to issue press releases as necessary," he adds. "We are in the news continuously because of arrests we make and our general activities, but before the program was put into place, these press releases were helter-skelter, sometimes made up by an arresting officer, sometimes not made up at all. Now the troop public information officer coordinates all of these."

Lt. Wright says he stresses with those officers the importance of daily contact with the media, and he checks on that activity level in monthly reports which come to him.

He advocates at least weekly face-to-face contacts between the troop public information personnel and reporters in their respective coverage areas.

Troop public information officers are generally sergeants, with the director holding the rank of lieutenant or above. The New York State Police have also drawn from a civilian pool of talent in their efforts to assemble a competent public relations staff. Reporting directly to Lt. Wright is a man with a journalism background who edits state police publications, including the magazine and functions as public information officer for the academy.

A key function of the individual troop officers is to prevent the press in its information-gathering tasks from distracting police personnel from the proper performance of their duties.

"They are to continually brief the press so that our police officers are able to do their jobs without interference," says Wright. "He or she is to assist the troop commander in all dealings with the media and community relations. This is very important."

Such became important, he explains, because of prior poor relations between the commanders and the media:

"Some of our troop commanders have been alienated, but we try to get the public information officer to make them more visible. And hopefully they will become more accustomed to dealing with the media and seeing their names in the paper and, hopefully, liking it. We are not trying to make media stars out of our troop commanders, but we are trying to present them in a positive light."

According to optimum qualifications drafted for the position of troop public information officers, the New York State Police are not looking for the glib-tongued or the glad-handed among their ranks. They need, says Wright, to be "well-versed" in just about everything—knowledge of the manuals, in preparation of work schedules, in the intricacies of station administration and operation.

"They have to know how scheduling affects troopers responding to the press," he points out. "They have to be experienced in acting with authority to direct troopers at major crime scenes and incidents. And the public information officer is expected to move from the trooper right up through the troop commander or even higher with minimum amount of conflict."

And Wright works at determining just how well or how poorly police-media relations are progressing in each sphere. Each station throughout the state is required to clip the local papers of "anything referring to New York State Police, good or bad," and these are ultimately reviewed by Lt. Wright and his staff.

Police-media statistics are compiled. Wright says that 3,000 media contacts were made through the officers during a recent three-month period; 200 "major news releases" were disseminated within the same period, and more than 100 original radio and television public service announcements were aired.

In addition, the troop representatives are expected to maintain a speakers' bureau, function as a services coordinator and liaison with other police agencies and generally direct the troop's involvement in community activities. The troop public information officer also coordinates stories for *Trooper* magazine, the bi-monthly publication with a circulation of 14,000, sent to all law enforcement personnel in the state.

Public information officers are involved in training sessions at least twice a year, during which media representatives from across the country are invited to address them, and panel discussions are encouraged for the airing and ironing out of "problems."

"Now it seems like we are hearing the same old things," maintains Lt. Wright. "We do know what the problems are. What we need to do is work on them."

The officers receive instruction, specific and targeted to protect the integrity of the police function and avoid at all costs "hostility or the appearance of hostility" with the media.

His men and women are told to be "organized when you're dealing with the press, hopefully try to be in charge, let them know they are dealing with a professional. Have the facts at hand, if not, get back to them."

"Never give a reporter your personal opinion, only the consensus opinion of the New York State Police," advises Wright. "Avoid off-the-record comments.

"Sometimes, personal friendships do develop between police public information officers and reporters, but the officers can be misled by off-the-record promises. We have been burned in the past and I feel it is better to be safe than sorry. Although there are gray areas here, I have given off-the-record comments myself, but I do not advise it."

Be careful, he cautions, about what you say, how you say it, and when you say it.

"We have been burned by television crews that have taken footage when we thought the interview was over," he recalls. "Early in the game we talked on camera when we shouldn't have. Now we do not assume an interview is over until the interviewer or TV camera or radio crew is gone."

Again, he emphasizes to trainees and in-service personnel that the no-comment response is never appropriate: "If you can't answer the question, explain why."

He reminds them not to make "light, flip comments" that could "appear out of context."

If troop commanders are involved in a "particularly sensitive interview," he recommends that the interview be tape-recorded.

He feels it is especially important that public information officers be aware of and responsive to media deadlines:

"We understand they have a job to do, we try to help them meet deadlines."

And Lt. Wright's final snippet of advice is, by his admission "rather funny, but true," and a tacit acknowledgement that police are human and err, and the press has its foibles, too:

"Be careful of slow news days, slow news days are killers. If you are going to screw up, in some way, don't do it on a slow news day. If there is not much going on, the media builds a story on the smallest incident. If there is a lot going on, you can get away with it."

POLICE ADMINISTRATORS SHOULD FACE PRESS WITH FACTS, NOT FEAR

JOSEPH E. SCURO, JR.

"PROBABLY the first basic area of concern in creating effective police and media relations is the problem faced by many police administrators — fear — fear of both the published word by the print medium and video representation by the electronic medium, that is, television and radio.

"This fear is something that is picked up and understood very quickly by a trained reporter. In fact, even an inexperienced reporter will pick up on this apprehension, triggering an instinct that there is a story somewhere.

"So the first thing a police administrator needs to realize is that the media is there, is going to be there, and he or she better learn how to deal with them effectively, or there will be all sorts of difficulties for the individual administrator or the department in general.

"Police management has to understand that the press has a job to do. And the media need to respect the department's right to conduct an investigation in an uninhibited manner, to protect informants and to, generally, keep a premature news leak from causing a law enforcement problem. I think the media must learn to respect these kinds of prerogatives regarding withholding incomplete information or confidential information that may damage the lives or safety of police officers and police operations.

Joseph E. Scuro, Jr., a practicing attorney in San Antonio, Texas, is counsel for the San Antonio Police Officers' Association and is no stranger to police/media conflicts and issues. In March, 1986 he and the SAPOA were embroiled in a legal contest to prevent the release to the news media of an officer's photo from personnel records. He is also counsel to the Combined Law Enforcement Associations of Texas, the San Antonio Firefighters Association and several other police officer associations throughout Texas.

"The press does have interests, and the only way a police administrator can hope to survive — assuming that a reporter is fair and objective — is to accept the reality he must work with the media, develop some trust and an interaction in which both interests can be balanced. Frequent misunderstandings and conflicts occur because neither side tries to understand the other's duties and responsibilities. Lack of understanding breeds lack of communication, which breeds mistrust, which, in turn breeds the fear and becomes a catalyst for conflict.

Nonsense and No Comment

"Mutual trust deteriorates when police administrators engage in nonsensical, noncomittal conversations with the media. For example, an officer-involved shooting occurs, and the department, rather than simply making an honest statement that the matter is under investigation and identifying, if proper, the participants involved with a promise that a detailed report will follow, instead says, no comment." Such behavior leads a reporter to speculate, to seek out sources that may not be as informed, and it puts a great deal of pressure on a reporter to compile a story subject to deadlines without any real knowledge or pertinent facts.

"With a few exceptions — and you are going to find good and bad individuals on both sides of the police and media issue — you learn that most reporters will try to present a fair representation of a particular incident. But you will find reporters who are going to use their job, particularly in a smaller circulation area (for newspapers) or a smaller market (for electronic media) as a stepping stone to personal gain.

Media Mean Business

"I think also that a police administrator has to be aware of the economics involved and that in many instances a reporter he or she talks to does not have the final says as to what makes it on the air or into print. A goal of a newspaper and of a television station is to sell advertising, through circulation for the print medium and ratings for the electronic. The media are involved in a business; business is translated into advertising dollars predicated on circulation and ratings. And a police administrator should never lose sight of the fact that such interests may well influence the type of focus a police story gets. The top-rated television station can charge the highest advertising dollar for its time, and the second-rated, a little less, and the third, even less. And you find in a lot of cases that it is the third in-the-cellar station that harps on police.

The Reactionary Interview

"The manner in which a law enforcement agency most often finds itself dealing with the media can be described as the reactionary interview. That interview occurs when the reporter makes the initial contact. If an incident occurs—let's say a crime, a shooting, or, perhaps an investigation has been concluded and criminal charges are about to be filed— the media is anxious for information from law enforcement officials. And many such officials make the mistake of saying 'no comment,' instead of issuing a carefully-prepared statement of fact. The reporter's curiosity is stimulated; he or she has deadlines, too, and therefore may react to half-fact.

The Public Information Function

"Some departments have a public information officer, and such an office is a good means of bridging the gap between police and media. But you have to have a public information officer who is well-respected and appears to be and is giving out legitimate information, not suppositions. This is the positive approach in dealing with the press as a police administrator because it gives the media access to accurate information in an atmosphere they trust, rather than having to root it out themselves from sources which may not prove reliable.

"What I am saying is don't take a reactive approach. When an incident occurs, don't wait for the press to contact you. Be proactive and affirmative in providing the media with information as that information develops. One gets the impression that sometimes police administrators feel that if they don't talk to the press, or if they ignore the incident, it is going to go away. That's not the case. The press is going to be there as long as the First Amendment exists and as long as there is revenue generated in print and electronic advertising.

Don't Be the Ostrich

"And the police administrator who takes the ostrich approach is just exercising self-deception. The facts of a particular incident are known to the department, and the department is in the best position of performing the function of providing information to the press.

A Bonus By-Product

"A healthy by-product of establishing an on-going working relationship is that the media can sometimes be called upon by the department in more difficult situations where there is a need for a certain degree of discretion in how a reporter reports a story or if they do.

"A department that issues orders to its personnel saying they cannot talk to the media is generating a policy that probably will cause them legal problems. The right of the public to know, the duty of the press to report it, the obligation of the department to the public to run its affairs in a proper manner—these are interests that need balancing. And the media must understand that it is not the sole judge of what is public information and what is not.

A Summary

"We are dealing with the following elements in creating an effective police/press relationship: mutual respect and understanding of one another's rights and responsibilities, a need for a police department to provide information in an affirmative and proactive mode whenever possible, the need of each side to understand the operations of the other, and the need of a department to provide information on a regular basis whenever possible.

"A police administrator who cannot handle the press, who cannot deal with the press is doing a disservice to his or her department, as well to his or her own personal careers. Unfortunately, what happens when the press turns on a department is that it affects the men and women who are out on the street doing the job that police officers are hired and trained to do. And their job is difficult enough without having a perception presented to the public through the press that is less than complimentary, as well as less than accurate."

WHAT'S AHEAD FOR POLICE/PRESS RELATIONS? P.I.O.s PAVE THE WAYS

DAVID M. MOZEE

I AM OFTEN distressed when I hear police administrators speak of "training" their P.I.O.s when they should really be speaking about "educating" their P.I.O.s. There is a vast difference between education and training, especially when reference is made to specialty courses such as "supervision," "administration," "internal affairs" and "police/media relations," just to name a very few. Training, in my opinion, deals with how, what and when to do things (programmed responses). Education, on the other hand, should deal with the above plus why things are done and then how best to complete the particular task under differing sets of circumstances (in other words—non programmed responses). Through application of the proper stimulus, almost any living creature can be trained, given enough time and effort, to perform routine and repetitive

---

*(AUTHOR'S NOTE: Most of what I say in the following pages is based on the assumption that the Public Information Officer will be appointed from within the existing department structure. I do not mean that those P.I.O.s from "outside" cannot be effective—they certainly can. The controversy about whether or not it is better to hire a P.I.O. from the media or appoint a P.I.O. from the agency has been going on for some time and will go on for some time to come, and I do not think anyone will ever be able to say conclusively which hiring policy is in fact better. P.I.O.s from both the outside and the inside have a very difficult learning process, but I believe the task of the P.I.O. drawn from a media background is a little more difficult because of the reluctance on the part of some police personnel to deal openly with other than their own people, and that could be the topic of a future work. I will deal here mainly with the "internal" appointee because with the learning of job skills of a P.I.O., there must also come a change in perception regarding the value of good media relations to effective law enforcement and an awareness of the need for the transmittal of this perception to other members of the agency. The P.I.O. from the media is already committed to the concept of a free press and will not have to have his/her perception altered in any great degree.)

†(EDITOR'S NOTE: Part of David M. Mozee's duties as management specialist for Institute of Police Technology and Management, University of North Florida, is the training of police public information officers to perform their function.)

tasks on command, but it takes education to understand why we do certain things and why we do not do certain other things. It takes education for the P.I.O. to choose the best course of action when faced with an unusual situation and apart from the requirement for routine annual press releases, almost all situations faced will be unusual.

The Whys Have It

Before a police/media relations program can be effective and efficient, the top police administrator and his/her designated public information officer should be committed to learning why their media relations are important (if not absolutely vital) to citizen support and cooperation, why the free media process is necessary to our democratic form of government, why different media operate in different ways, why police and media must both exist to preserve domestic tranquility, and why the public does in fact have a right to know what employees of the public are doing and how they are doing it — whatever "it" may be.

After truly understanding these whys, the P.I.O. can go about the task of being educated in the skills of how best to do the job to the mutual benefit of the police and the public of the particular jurisdiction.

Who Benefits?

There seems to be a misconception among some police officials that their media relations efforts will be for the exclusive benefit (profit) of the media. While it is true that media organizations are, in the main, businesses and do gain from the information they receive from the police, the police can also gain if they have a positive media policy and their efforts influence the public. The general public has no way to see for itself what the police do and must depend heavily on media reporting for its opinion-forming information. It is a wise administrator and a wise P.I.O. who will recognize that we live in an information age and will do all in their power to ensure that there is some "good news" to report. Even if there are "bad news" episodes within the department, the skill with which the P.I.O. gives the facts can give the public the honest impression that its police department is making all the right moves to clear up the episodes and prevent or reduce the probability of similar situations in the future.

Hands-On Education

The state of the art in P.I.O. education now seems to consist of proactive, hands-on, fast-paced courses of short duration, taught by experienced professionals. This I believe is far better than the sink or swim method used by some administrators when they appoint an inexperienced employee to act as P.I.O. There is too much chance of not only failure, but also agency image destruction when the P.I.O. doesn't have the confidence and/or expertise to cope with some of the major problems he/she could be immediately thrust into. Or if the P.I.O. is lucky enough to get a few undramatic episodes under his/her belt before the "big one" hits, the belief that he/she "knows" what to do can sometimes be more damaging than being unsure.

An Inside View

I was fortunate enough to serve under Chicago's Superintendent of Police James Rochford and had the further good fortune of being selected to be his director of news affairs. Prior to being given the job, Jim sent me to intern at WGN TV for several months. I was also encouraged to take some journalism classes. At WGN I learned media from the inside as a member of a camera crew. I was helped along the way by media professionals who knew I was a police officer and were gratified to see that Chicago's top police official was so interested in bettering his relations with the media that he was willing to take the time necessary to give his intended P.I.O. some on-the-job education.

Once the crews and management from other TV channels and media outlets found out who I was and what the purpose of my internship program was, they too began to help by giving me tips about media conferences, interviews, releases, strategy, and innumerable things that helped "educate" me as to why media does some of the things they do and why they thought their profession was important. I always appreciated the fact that they did not attempt to "convert" me—they just gave me information and let me decide what to do with it. I have told this to you for the same reason.

Superintendent Rochford thought that it was vital to his success to have in the important post of director of news affairs someone who had intimate knowledge of police operations, feelings, policies, etc., and who also had knowledge and appreciation of the media's job. I wonder how many other administrators would have the foresight to see that their P.I.O. had the benefit of education and training before assigning him/her to a most delicate task?

A Different Fear

There is still a reluctance on the part of many police officials to deal with the news media and I believe it stems in great part from their "fear" of the unknown. Police officials who would not hesitate to face down an armed criminal actively avoid confronting a reporter and refuse to be involved in any sort of electronic broadcast program—live or taped. These same officials view the function of a P.I.O. as a necessary evil and they immediately place the P.I.O. at a distinct disadvantage.

To be effective the P.I.O. must be a sort of alter ego of the chief executive. The P.I.O. has to know what the chief executive's views are on almost every facet of police work, has to be in on almost all of the planning and be privy to the most sensitive information that the chief executive possesses and has to "know" the chief executive as well as anyone can know another person. This is a big task and the good P.I.O. takes the task very seriously and approaches it with humility.

The reason the P.I.O. must be and know these things is that the P.I.O. must deal with the media on those occasions when the chief himself or herself were doing it. The P.I.O. must know what is and what is not sensitive material and why it is or is not sensitive, what things are "off-limits" and what things he/she can deal with the media on.

There have been many occasions in my career and in careers of other P.I.O.s when, because we did not know something was sensitive, we inadvertently said something that led the media to the sensitive issue or allowed them to interview others who said or did the "wrong" thing.

Identity Confusion

Because a great responsibility is placed on the P.I.O., there is a tendency on the part of some P.I.O.s to begin to think they "are" the chief executive. P.I.O.s are thrust into a position of some prominence and the "I am a star" syndrome can creep into their minds. P.I.O.s must constantly fight this syndrome and be content to be a true staff person—doing their behind the scenes work, taking the blame for failures and letting others take the credit for successes. This is a difficult task for many, but the intrinsic rewards can be great for those who can do it. P.I.O.s can learn more about the inner working of their police department than can almost anyone else; they can also increase the public support for their departments and help to improve internal morale through their interrelations with professional media people.

The Ideal Traits

These things and more make it imperative that the chief administrator select his/her P.I.O. with great care, select someone he/she can truly work with for a long time and someone he/she can trust implicitly. The selected person should have an extroverted personality but not be an egotist. He/she should have the ability to persuade people to do things and must not use his/her relationship with the "boss" to intimidate them so that they do them. The P.I.O. should also have a good working knowledge of both the agency and the media before he/she is given the assignment. If knowledge of either is missing, the P.I.O. should be given the opportunity to acquire the missing knowledge. The time spent beforehand will be rewarded many times over by the confidence and expertise of the P.I.O.

A Positive Trend

I am very happy to say that over the years I have noticed an increasing tendency on the part of police agency executives to appoint and use P.I.O.s. These executives have come to the realization that they need good public relations and community support to do their job as effectively and efficiently as possible. More executives are taking seminars and special courses in media relations and are giving their P.I.O.s an opportunity to go to seminars relating to their job.

In searching for schools and courses to which to send fledgling P.I.O.s for their education, the agency executive should consider the practical experience as well as the technical knowledge of the faculty. The ability of the faculty to give hands-on sessions in things the average P.I.O. will be involved in is vital: "shotgun" and "gang bang" interviews, setting up media conferences, emergency situations, etc.

At the Institute of Police Technology and Management we believe in giving the P.I.O. the basic "whys" of the trade and connecting these with some skills development in a short, hard working course. We would like to increase the time the students have with us, but we have found reluctance on the part of many administrators to pay the tuition or allow the days necessary for a longer course. We know that we could give more practical knowledge by increasing the number of situations we put the students through and the number of group projects we have them do, but until we can convince administrators to pay as much attention to the P.I.O. function of their department as they do to their most sensitive staff position, we will continue to offer the very best educational training in the limited time available.

Police Press Interplay

Lastly, every good course should have some interaction between the working media and the students. The students, by the very fact that they are attending a media course, can be expected to have some appreciation of the task they face with the media but it is still necessary for them to try to better understand the point of view of the media and that can only come with direct face-to-face communication with a professional from the media who is as dedicated to his/her career as the P.I.O. is to his/hers.

If a newly-appointed P.I.O. is unable to attend a formal course, a concerned administrator should at the very least allow him/her the time to seek out other P.I.O.s in the vicinity who have been doing the job for some months or years and ask questions about what to expect and how to handle sensitive issues. There are also a few geographic areas where working P.I.O.s have formed organizations to help each other learn their trade and to offer mutual support. It would be beneficial to any new P.I.O. to locate these organizations and become active in them.

Media Reaction

As a former media affairs director and as a teacher of media relations, I have found the media personnel generally receptive to a professional P.I.O., that is, a P.I.O. who gives the information the media are entitled to receive without unnecessary delay, who does not try to manage the news or the newspeople, who is available to respond to their legitimate questions, who will assist in obtaining as much factual information as can be released during an emergency or "fast-breaking" situation, and who helps them get interviews with the most authoritative person on the scene as soon as practical. This may sound like a lot to the lay person, but it really isn't. Once we consider that the general public is vitally interested in what is happening and that the mass media provide the public with a way of "being there," then we must also realize that what the media ask for is generally what our interested and supportive public would ask for.

I have found that the media do not want to bother the police unnecessarily when the latter are engaged in the handling of an emergency situation, but they do want to know what is taking place. This means that the P.I.O. must be the link between the busy police officials and the inquisitive media. The police officials must give the P.I.O. full information and then, together, make a decision on what portion of the information should be withheld for legitimate police purposes. Police officials can not treat the P.I.O. as the "enemy" or "an outsider" if they expect anything close to fair reporting.

Media Want Best Source

These officials must remember that most media people are also good investigators and are charged with the responsibility of getting the news. They prefer to get it from the most authoritative and reliable source possible so that it will be as accurate as possible, but they will take lesser sources if others are not available or are hiding. This means that the more newsworthy the episode, the more valuable the informed and educated P.I.O. becomes. I have a very positive image of the media in general, just as I have of the police in general.

The Exceptions

I have been involved with some media people who should not be trusted to leave home without a keeper, but, fortunately, they are the exceptions to the rule. I have met some media people who are very dishonest and some who believe that they are the only hope this country has to avoid chaos. Again, they are, fortunately, a minority. I have also met police who fit this same mold.

What is boils down to is that both media and police come from our general society and they have the strengths and the weaknesses of that society—neither group are superhumans. I think both groups perform their jobs in a credible fashion, I also think there is a lot of room for improvement.

The "Instant" Medium

We are rapidly becoming more and more an "instant" information society and, therefore, the electronic media—especially television—will have a more awesome obligation to the public. There are many indications that some of the electronic media recognize this fact and are doing things to make the discharge of their responsibilities to provide timely information more credible.

Balance seems to be the main issue. It is almost impossible to air all of the views on even the most simple issue, but a way must be found to give the public at least some of the more prevalent ones. Image and opinion makers, in my opinion, must be very careful not to let their own biases creep into their reporting or to lean too far to one side or the other because they think the public wants to hear that particular view.

There is no doubt in my mind that many of the changes in society we have experienced in recent years would never have taken place had it not been for television and its capability of instantly placing the viewer at the scene of a news event as it was taking place. The video that is shown to the public has a lot to do with the opinions that are formed by the public. If the only video shown is, for example, that of a policeman hitting someone with a baton, and no explanation for his action is given and no other viewpoint is presented, then the public may never know that the "victim" was a murderer attempting to escape and that the baton was an alternative to the gun.

Bad Reporting a Bane

Unbalanced reporting can do more harm to a dedicated police department than almost anything else. If I have one objection to the average media outlet, it is that they give far more space and time to the "bad cop" story than to the "good cop" story. I think that the public also has a right to know what their government officials are doing that is good and beneficial as well as what is bad and productive.

I have heard both print and broadcast journalists say that the public would rather be entertained than informed, but I can't believe that is entirely true. I believe that if informative programs were hyped as much as some of the fluff pieces, more people would watch them. I have seen some great informational presentations and have been thrilled by the balance that was given. I am also sorry to say I have not seen many of them offered for viewing.

Print/Broadcast Needs Differ

I have found over the years a difference in the approach to a story between the print journalist and the broadcast journalist. I always attempted to provide television with good visual possibilities that fit the story along with an authoritative "talking head." I also tried to give them the story in the least time possible so they could go on to their other assignments. I tried to give radio an authority voice to take their sound bites from. I also tried to tape-record any speech or statement made at the scene so I could play it over the phone for any radio or print media who did not have an opportunity to come out to the scene. This technique was especially valuable when we had news events that attracted national or international interest.

The P.I.O. has to remember that some media do not have the staff to send to all events, but that they are vitally interested in having the news and will normally reward his/her efforts by giving greater balance to the story.

Print media seem to have more time to ask questions and probe than do broadcast journalists. They also seem to have more time to develop a good investigative story. I always felt more comfortable with print journalists than with broadcast journalists even though they could be potentially more damaging to a police department. If there was nothing wrong, I was able to give them the facts that proved it. If there was something wrong, they seemed to be more understanding if the error was innocent and the department made an effort to correct it rather than cover it up. In general, the print media seemed to me less prone than radio or television (there are some notable exceptions) to take the shotgun approach to an incident; they seemed more methodical.

The print media have the time and ability to do more in-depth reporting than broadcast media, although I can't help but wonder how many people read only the headline and first paragraph and do not take the time to read the full article. Be that as it may, the P.I.O. should try to determine the needs of his/her own local media and try to satisfy those needs to the extent possible.

List of Responsibilities

In conclusion I would like to leave you with a list of just a few of the things I believe a P.I.O. should be responsible for:

- Acting as liaison between the agency and the media.
- Coordinating media conferences and media involvement at emergency scenes.
- Seeking items of special interest to the media from within the agency.
- Maintaining contact and rapport with working members of the media and other key media personnel.
- Promoting a positive image of the agency in the media.
- Mediating minor disputes between members of the working media and agency personnel.
- Issuing the official media releases of the agency.

- Keeping the chief executive officer and other key agency personnel informed about trends in the media regarding police agency coverage.
- Helping to train and educate key agency personnel in how to give effective media interviews.
- Maintaining a log book and/or history of agency news event coverage and coverage of other agencies in the area.
- Establishing contact with P.I.O.s of other agencies in the area and helping to create a mutual aid pact for assistance during extensive media events.
- Maintaining skills through continuing education.

A P.I.O. who makes a conscientious effort to discharge the above responsibilities will be well on the way to rendering creditable service to his/her agency and will soon discover how best to take care of the many other tasks that inevitably arise. I hope that in some measure I have given the P.I.O., both experienced and inexperienced, something of value. I also hope that the administrator who reads this article will gain fresh insight into the duties and responsibilities of his/her P.I.O. and what obligations he/she owes to the P.I.O. Finally, I hope that members of the working media will try to understand the difficulties of the P.I.O.s job and try to work with the P.I.O. in gathering the news the public has a right to have.